Ethno-Pedagogy

AF663337

Ethno-Pedagogy

Education of Tribes, Teachers' Training and Juxtaposition of Status

Rajarshi Roy

SHIPRA

All rights reserved. No part of this work may be reproduced, stored in a retrieval system or transmitted in any form or by any means, electronic, mechanical, photocopying, recording or otherwise without the prior written permission of the copyright owner and the publishers.

SP Rs. 295 SHIPRA

ISBN: 978-81-7541-319-1

2009 Impression
First Published in 2007

Ethno-Pedagogy: Education of Tribes and Teachers' Training and Juxtaposition of Status

© Author

Published by:
SHIPRA PUBLICATIONS
115-A, Vikas Marg, Shakarpur, Delhi – 110092 (India)
Ph.: 91-11-65277210, 22500954 Fax: 22458662;

Branch Office: 115, Munish Plaza, 20, Ansari Road, Daryaganj, Delhi 110002; Ph. 91-11-65946453, 9810522367

Email: info@shiprapublications.com
Website: www.shiprapublications.com

Tribute

A tribute to mother India and my mother who nurtured me

Existence of Human Species is Completely Impossible Ignoring the Concept of Tribe

—Elwin, V.

Foreword

Education is undoubtedly the most visible index of development of a society and the most effective instrument of social change. In India, education was supposed to play a multiple role in achieving equity and social justice since the dawn of the Republic. Such emphasis was considered justified in the context of the composite and complex nature of the Indian society in which different groups were at different levels of social and economic development and certain communities and tribes deserved protective discrimination to be gradually at par with the others. In those cases, education was to fight ignorance, exclusion, obscurantist ideas and superstitions and to improve economic status by empowerment to earn. In this scenario, role of teachers became most challenging, for they had to respond to the special needs, deficiencies and aspirations of the taught. The history of our Republic of about sixty years since Independence is witness to the fact that in the march of the nation to progress education has played a significant role. The teachers and educators experimented with various innovative methods to make teaching appropriate to ground realities in specific conditions that exist in different parts of the country. The success story is more manifest in the tribal areas, particularly in the Northeast, where only two generations have been found to be enough to achieve not only mass literacy but also quality higher and technical education and to improve quality of life of the entire tribe to a visible degree. The literacy rate in Mizoram is close to the highest in the country (next to Kerala), while Mizoram, Meghalaya and Nagaland are among the best-represented states in all-India services.

Rajarshi Roy's *Ethno-Pedagogy: Education of Tribes, Teachers' Training and Juxtaposition of Status* is an interesting and a serious study of the problem of tribal education in India in the context of Bengal and Assam, in which the role of tribal teachers, or the teachers coming from respective tribes that the students do belong, has been meticulously examined and it is boldly asserted that such teachers can highlight and analyse the problems of teaching exclusively from the insider's point of view and suggest the most effective ways to eliminate those problems. In doing so, the author has made a thorough survey of the tribal education scenario in the country, analysed the problems rigorously, critically reviewed the recommendations of the various commissions and committees on the subject, and finally, enumerated the results of his own survey in Bengal and Assam. I am sure, the book will well serve the purpose for which it has been written.

Shillong.

Professor J.B. Bhattacharjee
Ex-Vice Chancellor
Assam University, Silchar &
North-Eastern Hill University, Shillong

Preface

The basic educative agent, irrespective of age and society is the very community within which individual human atom lives and grows up. India, being a multi-cultural and multi-classed society includes a large sizable proportion of indigenous and ethnic population, commonly termed as tribe. A section of those, incorporated under sixth schedule of Indian constitution during the dawn of Independence, on the basis of their socio-economic and educational oppression, came to known as Scheduled Tribes. Irrespective of 'best' efforts of the governments with different political colour and shades, these sections of population are even today remained backward.

As a matter of fact, a nation is developed so much, so as its human resources are developed to utilize natural resources creatively and effectively for the sake of pursuing socio-economic and socio-cultural cultivation. Obviously to uplift them from various umbilical cords and to integrate them in the so-called mainstream as responsible members, special attention need to be zoomed over their education, having tangible impact over their economic and social status. Way back to 1971, Professor N.K. Ambhast in his study explored the need to educate them by the members of the community of their own. Though marginal, however, a part of the teaching community at the present day ascribe the denomination of some Indian tribes. In the present book a humble attempt has been made to explore the status profile of this marginal section of teachers in terms of some specific dimensions of status. The study hinges over the possible components of status of tribe teachers from Assam and West Bengal following juxtaposition.

No study, especially in the arena of social sciences can be completed with individual effort. The present one is not an exception. Since the inception of the study, cooperation was solicited from varied range of people and professionals, including respondent tribe teachers and community people, officials who helped in the process of tracing respondents – viz., block, sub-divisional and district education officers, inspectors of schools and school authorities, resource persons and also the NGOs. The author is grateful to all of them. Acknowledgement is also due to the students, who helped the author during data-collection. Worth noting among them is Debasish Paul and

Dr. Swapan Kumar Dutta, presently lecturers of education in Kamalanagar Govt. College, Mizoram and Assam University, Silchar, respectively.

The author gratefully acknowledges the scholars—Professor Nrishingha Prashad Banerjee, Professor Nikunja Behari Biswas, Sri Sushil Kumar Biswas, Professor N. Sudhakar Rao, Professor Debi Prashannya Mukherjee, Professor Nittyananda Pandey, Professor Ranju Rani Dhamala and many more, who helped him in various phases of the study.

Acknowledgement is also due to Professor Jayanta Bhushan Bhattacharjee, former Vice-Chancellor of Assam University and NEHU, Shillong, who inspired the author during the initial phase of the study and also contributed a 'Foreword' for this volume.

The author gratefully acknowledges the help and cooperation of Mr. D. Kumar, Shipra Publications, New Delhi for his constant support and encouragement for bringing up this volume in its present form.

The author likes to express his heartful thanks to his better half, Anjana and daughters, Apala and Abrizina for their patience and bearing with him for neglecting his family responsibilities during the work.

Lastly he wants to mention the silent and omnipresent inspiration of his deceased mother who nurtured him. Her blessings is the cosmic force, compelled the author to complete the work.

The author will be pleased to communicate (dr-r-roy@yahoo.com) for further clarification of any issue relating the volume.

Rajarshi Roy

Contents

PART III

Psychography of Tribe Teachers

PART IV

Introduction

The emerging area of educational research has started recognizing 'ethnopedagogic research' as one of its major directions in which educationists have started initiating research. Up till the inset of 20th century this domain of research was absolutely dominated by the sociologists in general and social anthropologists in particular, who just touched a very limited components, having (indirect) bearing with education [*Burgess, 1981*]. Realizing the need of Universalization of education for national development, especially at elementary level, education, even among the ethnic communities spread over the universe. The nations, irrespective of their polarized camps, started delving existing system and structure of education (which is mostly non-formal in Indian context) of ethnic population with an intention to accommodate them in the formal educational system. Ethnopedagogic research keeps its focus over the scientific description of education of races and cultures of humankind. For this purpose the method of socio-educational analysis is still in the process of development to examine how ethnic community members construct and maintain orderly activities in socio-educational setup. It is obvious that such research methodology should be used to study the ethnic groups—the social groups having common cultural tradition, denoting origin of birth or descent, rather then nationality.

The ethnopedagogic methods are considered to be particularly appropriate for empirical research on the relatively bounded socio-educational system and also have their place in studying the role of humans involved in the educational setup, holding ascribed status of the very ethnic community [*Burgess, & Adams, 1980*]. Ethnopedagogic research consists essentially description of events that occur within the life of a group or a number of groups with almost equal denomination, (with special regard to the existing social set-up and behaviour as peculiarities prevailing in those groups and group members) and an interpretation, which is expected to be non-ethnocentric, of the meaning of those for the cultural pattern of the ethnic group(s). Ethnopedagogic research, to have more non-ethnocentric interpretation, claims participatory observation to minimize the stranger's or outsider's generalization over some certain educational practice or culture [*Woods, 1977*]. Participation in a group provides investigator with an understanding of the educo-culture, and the interaction between the members, that is different from that which can be obtained from mere observing or administering a scale, or conducting survey or an analysis of documents. The rational approach in this context may be suggested to carryout status questionnaire for the sake of exploring status profile, which should be developed for the specific purpose, after having adequate familiarity and interaction with the groups, apart from adopting the 'observation technique', which should be participatory in nature [*Zigrami & Zigrami, 1980*]. Partial acculturation is a basic requirement on the part of investigator to acquire and to reflect the *insider's knowledge* and *view* for the purpose of such educational research. *'Interviews in a naturalistic setup'* and *documentation* may be adopted as the supplementary technique in this context to retain the qualitative data obtained through *tools* and *techniques.* This documentation process may either be steel photography or may be movies (i.e. video recordings of various activities, performed by the members of the ethnic communities in actual pedagogic setup i.e., real-life situation).

It was probably the British scholar and sociologist *Malinowski* who first emphasized the need of ethnographic research in the scientific point of view at the early 20th century. He laid down the norm to tabulate data and conclusion on verbatim statement and concrete statistical documentation. He stressed the need for the investigator to establish "trustworthiness" in respect of the study. *Malinowski* described the goal of ethnographic study *to reach the native's point of view, his relation to life, to realize his view of his world.* For these purpose, his suggestion to the investigators was to be a member of such ethnic community, though not as it's literal sense, but through building a strong rapport. He also stressed on participatory observation as well as informed interviews. This contact enables the researcher not only to obtain an intimate and broad knowledge of the group, but also helps to test and refine hypotheses and findings about the phenomenon under study.

In consonance with the perception of *Malinowski*, ethnopedagogic research may be viewed as a restricted sphere of ethnographic research, which thrives to explore the pedagogic issues in the very direction.

Ethnopedagogiests up till now mostly and typically use *case study approach* in education for examining and reporting educational affairs. However the author feels that scope remains open to follow other methods of collecting data for the purpose, even ignoring the restrictions. Data within case study are usually gathered by participatory observation—the technique derived from social anthropology. Participatory observation require extended period of 'on the spot (actual setup) observation' by an observer, who is supposed to be respectful of, and sensitive to the special or unique features of particular group or situation or individual, under observation. While observing, the observer should act as a group member, interested enough to discuss any issue openly with the other members of the group (may be students as well as teachers). In addition to participatory observation, educo-ethnographer should use such other related techniques as textual analysis, or conversational analysis, which are expected to be supplemented by unstructured interview, and if possible, through documentation. Therefore it can be easily understood that ethnopedagogic research is difficult to carryout, compared to the other methods of research in the arena of educational research. It just not only requires large investments of time and money, but also a mind-set of the researcher, which should be extremely free from any sort of ethnocentric viewpoint.

While carrying out intrinsic study of this kind by the author in almost all the eastern and northeastern states of India in recent past, it has been realized that the task can be made easy, if the researcher can be a member of the very ethnic group, under study. However it is mere a utopia. Various reports of such kind of research, as it appear through survey, reveals that, unconsciously researchers failed to avoid such biasness. In an average the studies so far carried out in the arenas of ethnopedagogic research, are nothing but status survey, sometimes, which aim to determine or to establish some fact[s] or phenomenon through such research. In the context of prevailing tradition of educational research, ethnopedagogic studies have attracted their share of critical comments—even in Indian scenario. Unfortunately, in various circles of academia, ethnographic approach in Education remain highly suspected, and young academics are often discouraged by the 'so called' academic circles within the discipline (which is obviously a covered expression of their ethnocentric attitude towards the very domain of education, resulting from a high degree of cultural hegemony). In consequence, the entrances of the group members from such groups are restricted in the sphere of education. As a result, the discipline suffers from the actual understanding of the true and alive educational systems of such ethnic groups. To maintain and to assure the national integration among such social groups, it is expected that the academic arena should incorporate the representatives of such groups. Hardly ethnographic researchers in general, admit that their account may be subjective, even after adapting precautionary measures. This trend may results to raise questions, in most cases, about the reliability and validity of such researches. So long the trend will go on, it will be hardly possible to study *"perfectly"* such groups, and research will remain as a *life less report* in the domain. But how long should it be continued? The answer remains with the scholars of education.

PART I: TRIBE, TEACHER AND EDUCATION

1

Education of the Tribes
A Glimpse

"...Education probably the most important medium of all because of its influential aspects. Education changes behaviour. People and nations are as they are because of their educative process." (Hans, 1964)

The Scenario

India is one of the oldest civilizations with a kaleidoscopic variety and rich cultural heritage. The charming geographical variations, long and gripping history, delightful festivals, enchanting arts, variety of languages and people are all contributing in it's variety and shaping the heritage of our motherland. In the words of Monier Williams, "... In all aspects, India is a complete world in itself." In fact, India is an experience, an idea and an ideal. It is distinctive for its antiquity and continuity. Apart from it's own vitality, the continuity of India is largely due to it's ability to adapt to alien ideas without loosing it's own identity. Every country has its uniqueness and individuality, which is mirrored in its academic, social and cultural life and pursuits. This can be termed, as it's 'mind' or 'collective consciousness', which determines the affective domain, including attitudes and directs the gesture of its people. Indian civilization is essentially religious. It is engaged in a continuous and sincere pursuit of the sacredness. People of India has a strong sense of individuality and at the same time a sense of society at large which enables them to think in terms of the common interests of groups and classes. The 'caste' and 'guild' system, the nightmare of all governments for their clannishness and economic power, stem for this ability to congregate. Spread over a huge geographical area, 'Indianism' that is the essence of a polymorphous culture, is difficult to define. It acquires different postures and modes according to taste, attitudes and mental sets of different groups and people united by a typical acceptance of certain constant social and cultural factors, such as—castes, tribes, beliefs, norms and mores and obviously with a sense of nationhood.

The variety of Indian heritage includes the variety of her people, their social structure, sub-cultural variation, symbols and so many other intervening factors. Being a welfare state, India is committed to the welfare and development of its people in general and vulnerable sections in particular. The preamble, directive principles of state policy, fundamental rights and specific sections of the Indian constitution stand testimony to the commitment of the state to its people.

The country has achieved multifaceted socioeconomic progress since independence however the task is yet to be completed. Development of the vulnerable sections should be the necessary utopia at present juncture and for the purpose proper and homogenous development of all sections of its population is essential. It is possible by the way of paying special attention to 'education' which can further help to retain and also to enrich existing cultural heritage of the country. In fact, education provides the necessary tools, skill, knowledge, values and attitude required for realization of four cordial values applicable for all humans, like survival, security, prosperity and progress. Basic learning needs and the way they are to be met will not be same for all peoples and for all ages. *They vary with time and space*. However, education has always been considered as an instrument of social change. In recent days, societies consider education as a sound economic investment because of which all the developing and developed societies are paying greater attention to education. Education has a fundamental role to play in personal and social development. It is one of the principal means available to foster a deeper and more harmonious form of human development and thereby to reduce poverty, exclusion, ignorance and oppression. Education emancipates social atoms from hangover of time old unreasonable and nonrealistic social taboos, superstition and prejudices.

Education promotes all-round and harmonious development of a nation. It nurtures the potentialities of its members and channelizes into appropriate avenues to develop them as effective, productive, efficient and responsible participants in different social roles-instrumental and also expressive. It makes the man rational and enables them to perceive and examine things in proper perspective.

Education for All: A Social Imperative

Education is one of the most important symbols of status and prestige in the society for an individual. It is also considered as an index of all-round development. It is a major basis of socioeconomic progress of a society and of an individual too. It may be seen as a part of the economic foundation of the society in one hand. On the other hand it is a major instrument for social change and modernization. It is considered to be 'the key that unlocks the door to modernization, as well (*Harbinson & Mayers, 1964*). Whatever may be the substantive content of the concept of modernization, in context of under developed economies and traditional societies like India, modernization involves a process of change-social, economical and political. Actually the change goes even deeper and encompasses cultural values and personality orientation as well (*Gore, 1971*).

The economic and social development of a country supposed to be hindered if proper and effective attention is not paid to the education for all. Development of a nation depends on the development of all sections of the society and development of a section, in its turn, depends on the progress of education among its members. According to the latest census report, approximately one-fourth of the countrymen in India are backward. Their estimated population is around twenty seven crore. We will not get the cooperation of these brethren in our cultural, social, political and economic programmes so long as we fail to carry the 'Education' within their reach. This backward section includes the people belong to scheduled caste, scheduled tribes and some other backward classes. Among them the situation of the scheduled tribes is comparatively most pathetic. Tribes, the pioneer backwards suffers most from social backwardness, oppression and economic deprivation, which are all co-existed with their educational backwardness (*Prashad, 1988*). In fact, the massive rate of illiteracy among the tribes is the root-cause of their backwardness (*Rathnaiah, 1974*). Though the government with different political colour had taken many plans and projects for the development of scheduled tribes since independence but till now they are the most deprived section of the population. Though the Scheduled Caste community has lightened a little in the light of education but the tribes are almost in dark.

Who are Tribes?

Verrier Elwin, the ever-recalled scholar, in his book entitled, *Tribal world of Verrier Elwin* once remarked that *existence of human species is completely impossible ignoring the concept of tribe*, which implies that any human species is supposed to be associated with a specific tribe. What he wants to establish that human being belong to certain specific umbilical cord, to be termed as tribe. Obviously this very point of view reflects a gestalt perception. However, anthropologically, tribe is a social group, a number of which live in a community, possesses a common dialect for verbal (and often supplemented by symbolic) communication among the group members, belongs to an uniform social organization and cultural homogeneity with common ancestor, possess political organization and religious pattern.

In Indian subcontinent, some specific groups are termed either as tribes or as ethnic people.

The specification of tribes and tribal communities as *'scheduled tribes'* arose only after the constitution came into force. In the Government of India Act, 1935, a reference has been made to the 'backward tribes' as per the thirteenth schedule of 1, 1936. Certain tribes were specified as backward in the then provinces of Assam, Bihar, Bombay, Bengal, Central provinces, Madras and Orissa.

The first serious attempt to list 'primitive tribes' was made as the case of deprived classes in the census of 1931. The term 'scheduled tribe' was standardized in article 342 of the Constitution of India. In the list of scheduled tribe, prepared in 1950, primitiveness and backwardness were the criteria judged through applying tests for specifying a scheduled tribe.

The most common features of tribes indicated in their lifestyles. They usually live away from so called civilized world, in the remote parts of the forests and hills. Usually tribals belong to one of the three major 'tribe stocks' such as Kegriots, Australoids and Mongoloids. They speak in their own tribal dialect; majorities of them follow specific primitive occupations and way of life. They are largely carnivorous and have 'nomadic' habits, an intrinsic love for drink and (peculiar type of) dance.

Mr. L.M. Srikant, the then commissioner of scheduled castes and tribes during 1950s classified the tribal communities in India into four broad categories. These are:

(*i*) Tribals, (*ii*) Semi tribals, (*iii*) Acculturated tribals and (*iv*) Assimilated tribals.

To him, '…. The groups which are outside the Hindu-fold, suffer most from economic, social and educational backwardness and are isolated in the hills and forested tracts are considered as scheduled tribes'

Tribes in India differ in racial stock, dialects, lifestyles and show considerable variation in their basic economy. More or less, the tribal culture in India are primarily oral, possessing rich oral history of their past society. Out of almost four hundred tribal languages in India, only a very few hand-counted languages have scripts of their own. Due to an ethnocentric bent of mind of the so-called mainstream, their oral culture is often branded as primitive, savage and they are perceived as illiterate and uneducated, as if literacy is the only indicator of education.

Population Profile of Indian Tribes

According to the latest census report available, tribals, who are accorded in the sixth schedule of Indian constitution, inhabit in most of the states except Haryana, Punjab, Chandigarh, Delhi and Pondichery. The distribution of tribal population across the states is not uniform.

Mizoram, one of the seven-sister-states possess highest proportion of tribal population (94.8%), followed by Nagaland (87.7%), Meghalaya (85.5%) and Arunachal Pradesh (63.7%). In the united territories of Lakshadweep, tribal population is as high as 93.2 per cent, which is followed by Dadra and Nagar Haveli (79.0%). Apart from these states and United Territories, high concentration of tribal population is also found in the states like Madhya Pradesh (23.3%), Orissa (22.2%), Gujarat (14.9%), Assam (12.9%), Rajasthan (12.4%) Maharashtra (9.3%), Bihar (7.7%), Andhra Pradesh (6.3%) and in Andaman & Nicobar Island (5.5%).

Education: What Constitution Assures?

Recognizing the special needs of the tribals, the constitution of India made certain special safeguards to protect these communities from various possible sorts of exploitation and thereby tried to ensure social justice. Article 14 confers equal rights and opportunities to all. Article 15 prohibits discrimination against any citizen on the grounds of sex, religion, race, caste and so on. Article 15(4) enjoins upon the state to make special provisions for the advancement of any socially and educationally backward classes. Article 16(4) empowers the state to make provisions for reservation in appointments or posts in favour of any backward class of citizens, which in the opinion of the state is not adequately represented in the service under the state. Article 46 enjoins upon the state to promote with special care the educational and economic interest of the weaker sections of the people, and in particular, the tribals, and promises to protect them from social injustice and all forms of exploitation. Further, while Article 275(1) promises grant-in-aid for promoting the welfare of tribals and for raising the level of administration of the scheduled areas, Article 330, 332, and 335 stipulate reservation of seats for Parliament and Legislative Assemblies and in services. Finally the constitution also empowers the state to appoint a commission to investigate the situations and conditions of the socially and educationally backward classes (*Article 340*) and to specify those tribes or tribal communities deemed to be scheduled tribes (*Article 342*).

The fifth schedule to the constitution lays down certain prescriptions about the scheduled areas as also the tribes in states except Assam, Meghalaya, Tripura and Mizoram by ensuring submission of Annual reports by the governors to the President of India regarding Administration of the Scheduled Areas and setting up of Tribal Advisory Councils to advice on matters pertaining to the welfare and advancement of the tribals [*Article 244(1)*]. Similarly the Sixth schedule to the constitution also utters about the administration of the tribal areas in the states of Assam, Meghalaya, Tripura and Mizoram by designating certain tribal Areas as autonomous districts and Autonomous Regions and also by constituting respective District Councils [*Article 224 (2)*]. To ensure effective participation of the tribals in the process of decision making, the 73rd and 74th amendments of the Indian constitution were made and being extended to the Scheduled Areas through the Panchayats (Extension of the Scheduled Areas) Act, 1996.

More than five decades have already passed and we are approaching to the sixth decade since the constitution was drawn. The progress achieved so far in terms of tribal-development cast serious doubts whether the constitutional objectives are at all attainable even in distant future. A grand majority of the tribal population in India is still shrouded in the darkness of illiteracy. A brief perusal of the literacy-table will give support to the above fact.

Table 1.1: Literacy Rates Among General, Scheduled Caste and Scheduled Tribe Men, Women and Total Population in India

Year	General		Scheduled Caste		Scheduled Tribe	
	Male	Female	Male	Female	Male	Female
1961	34.37	12.90	16.95	3.28	13.04	2.89
1971	39.52	18.70	22.36	6.44	17.09	4.58
1981	46.89	24.82	31.12	10.93	24.52	8.09
1991	64.13	39.29	40.24	19.03	32.50	14.50
2001	75.85	54.16	49.63	27.04	40.00	24.80

Source: Primary Census abstract for General Population, Scheduled Caste and Scheduled Tribes-1961-2001.

Table 1.2: Literacy Rates among General, Scheduled Caste and Scheduled Tribe Population in India

Year	General Caste	Scheduled Caste	Scheduled Tribe
	Total	Total	Total
1961	23.95	10.27	7.99
1971	29.48	14.67	10.89
1981	36.23	21.38	16.35
1991	52.21	30.06	23.63
2001	65.38	38.34	32.40

The tribal population in India was 67.6 million during the end of last century (Chitlangia, 1997) (*i.e.* 8.08 per cent of the total population) which is larger than the ethnic population of any other country throughout the world. Under different articles and schedules of the Indian Constitution [*viz. Article 15(4), 16(4), 19(5), 23, 29, 46, 164, 330, 334, 335, 338, 339(i), 342, 371(b), 371(c), fifth and sixth schedules*], the tribal population has been given protection. Yet they remained the most backward ethnic group, which is clearly evident from their low rate of literacy (*i.e.* the major indicator of educational development).

The Table 1.1 and 1.2 show that the tribes in the context of literacy are more backward, not only in comparison to the general population but also in comparison to the scheduled caste population. Even fifty-eight years of intervention has not made any significant impact for improving the condition of the tribes.

Tribal Education

The reporting of the brochure form Friends of Tribal Society may give a glance view of their existing situation. The Brochure form 'Friends of Tribal Society' reads, "... *Tribes in India, numbering around seven crores live in complete darkness, ignored by progress made over since independence. Eighty four percent of male and ninety five percent of the female tribes are illiterate.*

Ninety five percent of the tribal population have no access to medical facilities and ninety percent have never known what electric light is...." However, their condition may in fact be far worse.

Obviously to uplift them a lot and to integrate them in the mainstream as responsible members, special attention should be focused on 'Tribal Education' along with the other socioeconomic safeguards and privileges. Proper upliftment of Indian society is in far distance until and unless their overall development is taken care of. The tribal communities need a massive persuasion to be educated, not just to be literate, to walk together with the rest of the population of the country. Education is the only and only way to overcome all other barriers of their backwardness.

The tribal education in India presents a dismal sense. It is characterized by low enrolment, high dropout, drift, wastage, limited number of high achievers and little credibility (Dube, 1988) and it is so for a variety of reasons.

Tribal Education: Delving the Scenario

First census after independence in 1951 did not collect data on the literacy rates of the tribes. The literacy rate among the tribes has increased in the post independence period. Literacy rate among the tribes has increased four times from 1961 when it was just 7.99 per cent to 32.40 per cent during 2001. Despite the increase in literacy rates, the tribes have a lower rate of literacy than that of the general population and even that of the scheduled caste, as it reveals from the primary census abstract since 1961 to 2001. As in the other social groups, the rural tribes have lower literacy rate than their urban counterparts. In 1991, the rural tribes have had a literacy rate of 21.8 per cent compared to 46.35 per cent in the urban tribes. However, the rural literacy demands more importance for the tribal population as because 93 per cent of the Indian tribes inhabit in the rural setup (*Census Report, 2001*).

Table 1.3: Gross Enrolment Ratio

Class Grade	*Year Span*	*General*		*Scheduled Caste*		*Scheduled Tribe*	
		Boys	*Girls*	*Boys*	*Girls*	*Boys*	*Girls*
I – V	1980-'81	95.8	64.1	105.4	57.8	94.2	45.9
I – V	1985-'86	111.3	79.8	116.6	73.2	113.2	68.2
I – V	1990-'91	115.3	86.0	121.4	83.6	125.6	82.6
I – V	1995-'96	97.1	79.4	109.9	83.2	115.0	80.2
I – V	2000-'01	104.9	85.9	107.3	85.8	116.9	85.5
VI – VIII	1980-'81	54.3	28.6	41.4	16.2	28.2	10.8
VI – VIII	1985-'86	61.0	34.7	57.8	26.2	41.3	19.2
VI – VIII	1990-'91	73.4	46.1	68.9	36.0	54.1	27.3
VI – VIII	1995-'96	67.8	49.8	71.4	44.5	57.3	35.0
VI – VIII	2000-'01	66.7	49.9	76.2	53.3	72.5	47.7

Source: G.O.I: Selected Educational Statistics, 1980-2001, Ministry of Human Resource Development, Department of Education, New Delhi.

Gross enrolment ratio of the tribal boys and girls are approximately similar to those of Scheduled caste boys and girls in 1990-1991 for class I-IV. However, they are lower to those for the general population. In the case of boys the tribal figure is higher (125.6) than that of the scheduled Caste (121.4) and even the general population (115.3).

But the situation changes in grade VI-VIII. The gross enrolment ratio of tribal boys and girls are low compared to the scheduled castes and general population. In 1990-91, the gross enrolment ratio for the tribal was 27.3 as compared to 36 for the Scheduled Castes and 46 for the general population. In case of the tribal boys, it was 54.1 as compared with 68.9 for scheduled caste and 73.4 for the general population. The relative enrolment ratio of the girls for per 100 boys for the tribal is less than that for the non-tribes (*Selected Educational Statistics, 2001*). We can have a brief perusal of the scenario in Table 1.4.

Table 1.4: Relative Enrolment Ratios of Girls per 100 boys for Tribes and Non-tribes

Year	*Class I–V*		*Class VI–VII*	
	Scheduled Tribe	*Non-Tribes*	*Scheduled Tribe*	*Non-Tribes*
1965-'66	38.6	57.9	27.3	37.3
1970-'71	41.2	60.7	31.5	41.6
1975-'76	45.9	62.5	37.2	46.2
1980-'81	48.7	64.2	38.2	49.9
1987-'88	56.9	70.2	44.3	55.7
1991-'92	62.3	72.4	47.8	61.4
1995-'96	68.7	76.0	46.5	65.0
2000-'01	72.2	77.0	58.0	68.0

Source: Govt. of India: Selected Educational Statistics, 1967-2002, Ministry of Human Resource Development, Department of Education.

There is a much higher rate of dropouts from school for the tribes in class I-V and also in class VI-VIII compared to other non-tribal communities which aggravates the problem of tribal education. The Table 1.5, shows the comparative dropout among the tribes and non-tribes up to middle level grade during schooling.

Table 1.5: Dropout Rates of the Students from Tribal and Other Communities

Year	*Classes I-V*			*Classes VI-VIII*		
	ST	*SC*	*General*	*ST*	*SC*	*General*
1980-'81	57.7	60.2	58.7	86.7	76.8	72.7
1984-'85	69.4	55.4	47.9	82.9	72.2	65.4
1988-'89	64.5	49.6	47.9	78.1	67.8	65.4
2000-2001	60.9	43.2	40.8	58.0	62.6	54.5

Source: GOI: Education for All: the Indian Scene, MHRD, Dept. of Education, New Delhi.

In the successive stages of education dropout in a geometric ratio become a natural phenomenon for the tribals. A large number of tribal students who continue their education, remain confined to the same class beyond the prescribed age due to their inability to grasp the subject matter and their failure to keep pace with the class (*Singh & Jabbi, 1995*).

"Tribal Education" is a very popular field among the Researchers who have identified a large number of factors responsible for the dropout and stagnation of the tribal students. Some of these are: lack of educability due to socio-economic and cultural background; lack of educational facilities in schools; non suitable curriculum, pedagogy and the medium of instruction and so on. All of these problems conglomerates and hinder the education among the tribes. To remove these sequels of problems, several committees, commissions, study-teams, and working groups were formed by the government in due course of time, and recommendations came from those corners to overcome the problems of Tribal Education.

Tribal Education: What Committees, Commissions, Study Teams and Working Groups Recomends?

Roy, Renuka Committee (1959) suggested regarding the pattern of tribal education. The committee emphasis over the problem of alienation of the tribes in educational set-up and suggested not to alienate the tribes from their own indigenous background. It further recommended for imparting education to the primary students in their mother tongue and to appoint at least one female teacher in every tribal school. These recommendations are in tune with the perspectives of Pundit Nehru's *Philosophy of Tribal World* (*Nehru, 1948*), where he suggested to preserve the tribal culture which demands to examine the status of tribes in the filed of education and to be specified on teacher education.

Report of the *Elwin Committee (1960)* on special Multipurpose Tribal blocks has given emphasis on construction of school building in local style and the simplicity in equipment, avoiding unnecessary weightage on enrolment of schools, that is giving emphasis on a qualitative aspect rather than the quantitative aspects of tribal education. The Elwin Committee further suggested appointing sufficient number of experienced and qualified teachers, completely familiar with local language for lower classes. Besides, declaration of school holidays according to local festivals, use of local indigenous institutions as schools, preparation of text books based on the tribal background. Introduction of agriculture and forestry based education at primary level and vocational education at secondary stage were the other important recommendations made by Elwin Committee, which were hardly followed during the implementation of the educational plans on different tribal blocks in the latter phase.

The scheduled areas and Scheduled Tribe Commission under the chairmanship of Dr. U.N. Dhebar agreed to the proposal of the representatives of Ministry of Education in providing social amenities and employment opportunities to the villagers in their own surroundings instead of encouraging continuous drain of vitality and intellects from the village to the urban areas, establishment of schools and colleges to cater the needs of land based section of the society and imparting basic education beyond the secondary stage. However, these recommendations mostly kept in paper and pencil and hardly any of these recommendations were really followed in the later period.

Apart from the 'education' in general, Kothari Commission dealt with the tribal education of the country. The commission recommended to provide 'a five year effective education for all tribal children' by 1975-76 including intensive programme of parental education and education of girls. The commission also recommended various items that have been dealt with by the committee under the chairmanship of Veriar Elwin in respect of teacher's medium of education, textbooks and establishment of Ashram type of schools. The commission gave emphasis to pick up tribal youths, give them training through specially organized courses and use them as workers for tribal upliftment. The commission was of the opinion that 'no expenditure is too great for the purpose of tribal education as it is a major programme of equalization and social and national integration.'

In connection with the teacher's status (for tribal areas) (ref. p. 113) the committee strongly recommended to encourage tribal young man and woman to become teachers in the schools of those areas. The report reads that ... "it is essential to develop cadres of persons who will devote themselves to the service of tribal people ... promising young persons from the tribes should be selected and specially trained to work in tribal areas. The usual prescriptions regarding recruitment or minimum qualifications will often have to be set aside in this programme."

The working group on Tribal Development during sixth five year plan (1980) opined that education is key to tribal development-it has to be tackled on both non-formal and formal levels. The working group suggested regarding non-formal education that the course-content should include instructions as how to deal with problems connected with land, credit, currency, weight and measures, hygiene, local geography, liquor vending and so on. In connection with formal education, the working group suggested that steps should be taken to workout syllabi for education taking into account their culture, indigenous technology, ethos and assimilative power. The working group also gave emphasis on vocational training on agriculture, industry, trades, sports, etc. to provide job-opportunity. Apart from these, special coaching in science and other subjects outside the school hours should be arranged. For better enrolment of the tribal, school uniforms, mid-day meal for students and compensation need to be paid to the tribal parents. The scholarships and stipends should be disbursed well in advance in order to meet the contingencies. The teachers should be imparted orientation training; there should be a special drive for identification of educated tribal men and women and attempt should be made to train them in teacher training institution.

The working group on Tribal Development during seventh five-year plan (1985) recommended that education would be given highest priority in the tribal areas. By identifying low-literacy-area and low-literacy-groups among the scheduled tribes, suitable matching programmes should be started. The working group was also with the opinion that administration of education in tribal area should be rationalized by bringing all such institutions under the control of Education Department. There should be promotion of adult education, improvement of inspection quality, extension of hostel-facilities at different levels of schools and infra-structural aspects. The working group recommended for adoption of tribal languages as the medium of instruction at the primary stage and documentation of tribal culture in the form of music, dance, art, painting, sculpture, and the like.

During the Eighth five year plan, the working group on Development and Welfare of Scheduled Tribes (1998) suggested to take programme for integrating general education with the art and culture of tribal community in order to make education socially and culturally more acceptable, meaningful and interesting to the tribes. The working group suggested for documentation of different aspects of tribal culture and recommended to prepare text-books and reading materials in various major tribal languages with the assistance of Central Institute of Indian Language (CIIL) & SCERTs in order to accelerate and to promote the tribal languages and literature.

The Ninth Plan (1997-2002) on tribal-development aimed to empower the scheduled tribes by creating an enabling environment, conducive for them to exercise their rights freely, enjoy their privileges and lead a life of self confidence and dignity, at per with the rest of the society. This process essentially encompassed three vital components, *viz.* social empowerment, economic empowerment and social justice. To this effect, while the allied departments implemented the general development policies and programmes, Ministry of Tribal Affairs (MoTA), being the nodal ministry, implemented certain innovative programmes for the tribals, emphasizing over their education & literacy, health & family welfare, labor & employment, women & child development and ultimately over the tribal development as a whole.

Report of the Tenth plan (2003-2007), as reported by the planning commission, hinges on the empowerment of the tribes, in actual terms, and opines that those can be realized only when the tribes themselves are bestowed with the right to participate in the process of decision making, besides being equipped to find out the solutions of their own problems. An answer to this was bringing the people-oriented 73rd and 74th constitutional amendments of 1993 into action, besides extending the same to the tribal areas through the Panchayats (Extension to the Scheduled Areas) Act of 1996, (popularly known as PESA Act). With the strength and support of PESA Act, 1996, the traditional *Gram Sabhas* in the tribal areas are being endowed with special functional powers and responsibilities to ensure the effective participation of the tribal societies in their own development and in harmony with their culture so as to conserve and preserve their traditional rights over natural resources. All states in India, except Bihar, have enacted so far, parallel state legislations to give effect to the provisions to the PESA Act, 1996. So in the tenth plan, the PESA Act, 1996 is a landmark legislation, which is legitimizing the involvement of the tribes in their own empowerment process, not only as active participants, but also as effective decision makers, implementers, monitors, supervisors and evaluators.

The National Policy on Education (1986) too recognizes the need of the tribal education. To boost the socioeconomic and educational status of the tribes the committee suggested to accord priority for opening primary schools in tribal areas. The construction of school building will be undertaken in these areas on priority basis under the normal funds for education as well as under the NREP, RLEGP and other tribal-welfare schemes. Strong recommendation was made to establish residential schools including 'Ashram schools' on large scale, apart form establishing sufficient number of non-formal and adult education centers as well as 'Anganwadi centers' especially in the areas predominantly inhabited by the scheduled tribes and other vulnerable sections. In the policy, recommendation was made to formulate incentive schemes for the scheduled tribes keeping in view their special needs and life-styles. For the sake of improving their performance in various courses, suggestion was made to introduce scholarships for higher, technical, paraprofessional and professional courses and to arrange special remedial-courses and allied programmes to remove psychosocial impediments. The National Policy on Education feels that the socio-cultural milieu of the scheduled tribes has its distinctive characteristics. This underlines the need to develop the curricula and devise instructional materials in tribal language at the initial stages, with arrangements for switching over the regional language. It was proposed that the curricula at the stages of education would be designed to create awareness of their rich culture, identity, and also of their enormous creative talent. The National Policy on Education (1986) makes one of the most comprehensive, precise and bold statements – "the status of the teacher reflects the socio-cultural ethos of the society. It is said that no people can rise above the level of it's teachers" ... Educated and promising tribal youths will be encourages and trained to take up teaching in tribal areas.

In consonence with the recomendations made by the NPE (1986), Chopra, Ravi Ranta (1990) came out with the recommendations on his report on the status of the teachers in India highlighting over several aspects of status indicators. However, his main recommendations centered over the issues like improvement of academic and professional qualification, removal of disparities of salary and establishment of national directives by setting minimum qualifications for teachers apart from establishment of a statutory body to look after the welfare benefits for the teachers working at different levels and types of institutions.

Tribal Education: Exploring the Problem

A brief perusal of the recommendations made by various committees, commissions and study teams claim another thought towards tribal education. Irrespective of sufficient budget allotment, expansion of education among the Indian tribes did not reach up to the level of expectation. It is not just due to the lower level of cognitive ability of the tribes rather the present approach of education is bringing 'a cultural shock' which makes the process of educating tribes a tough task as because the present system of education is not at all relevant to their life and future conditions (*NEP, 1986*). Two consequences are commonly visible – where, either they are remaining illiterate and are alienated from education, or among them, those who are educated even ignoring the post-traumatic stress, are alienated from their own traditional community life. In this way, education itself is becoming a problem to them, which is breaking their family and community structure. Inferiority complex of the educated tribes sometimes caused by the cultural hegemony of the non-tribes and to get-rid – of this problem often they find an easier alternative to dilute themselves in greater society, which can be termed as 'detribalization' (*Roy, 1996*).

To deal with 'Tribal Education' and its problems, one has to consider three basic factors of education namely the student, the teacher and the educational institution. It is 'these components' and their application-that matter a lot when one is called upon to tackle the problem of tribal education. Among these components the most important is the teacher whose selection and training should be such as to so as to suit them the tribal needs and requirements, as because the entire system of education depends upon the quality of teachers without which the system cannot run properly. The institutional climate and the students' behaviour can be changed towards the desired direction if the teacher is the right one and effective. But the entire system will be damaged, in spite of the other factors up to the mark, if the teacher has lacking in his performance. Teacher can be considered as an independent and intervening variable where as the student and the institutional situation are the dependent variables, depend upon the teacher (*Dube, 1988*). Teaching as a white collar job is too some extent different from the other professions and the teacher's contribution in shaping the future society cannot be minimized. It was found that the different committees and commissions proposed to involve the community people to minimize the inferiority complex and lack of we-feeling, which occur among the tribal students and hinder the education of the tribes. In fact proper upliftment of the tribal community is best possible if the tribal students are taught by the teachers from their own tribe (*Ambasht, 1971*). A tribal teacher is liked mostly because of his helping attitude and understanding the student's difficulties and problems. To extend the proper education among the tribes, the tribal teachers are the best choice to educate the community students because of their linguistic affinity, loving nature and equal denomination as the students. In fact, the teacher is the sole agent of knowledge who bridge between the education and the students. That is why it is often said that the teachers are the social engineers having a vast scope to reconstruct the society.

Tribal Education and the 'Teacher'

In the pre-independence days, tribal research were mostly done by the administrators and during those days the primary objectives of the tribal studies was to assist the top-brass in determining the strategies of administration in the difficult areas inhabited by the tribes. It was felt that without the basic knowledge of the life and culture of the tribes, subjugation of those ethnic communities was quite impossible (*NEP, 1986*). Thus tribal research in those days was administration oriented and naturally welfare got only peripheral attention. Even then it must be admitted that the colonial administrators were the forerunners of the ethnographic research. The ethnographic studies of post-independence era were, by and large, carried out on that superstructure centering round the socio-cultural bases of tribal life.

After independence entire approach to tribal and welfare development had undergone metamorphic changes. There were long deliberations among the national leaders regarding the ideal approach to tribal development. Nehru approved the anthropological approach of tribal development, but not at the cost of their traditional cultural traits and ethos.

In the pre-independence as well as in the post independence period, it is completely the non-tribes, who studied the tribal-set ups, carried out studies and recommended suggestions for the tribal development (*Sharma Thakur, 1997*).

The tribal people know their problems well and simultaneously the researchers working in this specific 'field' are competent enough to identify those problems. But it is hardly possible for the 'community-people' who are affected by various socioeconomic constraints, to articulate their problem properly. It seems to author that the problems of the school going children form tribal denomination is most crucial as because they are facing the common problems of the tribal-society and the formal school environment (mostly deviated from their familiar cultural set up and there by can be considered as 'exotic environment') is also causing an opposite psycho-social pressure among them. To overcome those massive pressure in this situation truancy become the only way for them.

The teacher from the tribal communities faced lot of problems during their school-days. The situation continues with the present tribal students too. The author observed that the tribal teachers can analyze and can highlight such problems exclusively from their point of view and can suggest the best effective ways to eliminate those problems.

It is often argued today there is no justification to invite suggestions from the researchers from non-tribal denomination for the development of the tribes in connection with their education. Suggestions will be most effective if it can come from the teachers from their own denomination. However, a person cannot perform well in his profession if he is not having any positive attitude and interest in it. Society has a demand for the innovators and inventors who can create a unique. The goal to create a unique can only be achieved when we are in a position to select the right person for the right job (*Sarkar, 1986*). The old says are quite true that the education is the backbone of the nation. It is a process too. School is the workshop to produce the future citizen *i.e.*, the students, and the entire responsibility depends upon the teacher. Teacher is the most important factor contributing to the national development. He is the pivot around which all the educational programmes rotate. Even the best system of education may fail to achieve the desired ends if this very 'factor' is ignored. The teacher not only implements an educational programme by commensurate methods but he is its originator too. It is he, who interacts with pupils of different school stages and ensures that wide ranging educational objectives, which are to be achieved. As an intellectual, he is a social critic, but, with special sense of responsibility to lead in a constructive direction. He is also his own teacher since he continuously works at frontiers of knowledge and often faces problems and situations, which are unprecedented and where past experience is of limited value. As an agent of change he himself has to be flexible and ready to accept the change.

About teachers, the Education Commission (1966) in their report mentions, "*... of all the different factors which influence the quality of education and it's contribution to national development, the competence and character of teachers are undoubtedly the most significant. Nothing is more important than securing a sufficient supply of high quality recruits to the teaching profession, providing them with the best possible professional preparation and creating satisfactory conditions of work in which they can fully effective.*"

The National Policy of Education (NEP) 1986 (op. cit.) rightly points out: "*The status of teacher reflects the socio-cultural ethos of a society; it is said that no people can rise above the level of its teacher.*"

Programme of Action (POA), 1986 states "....*The status of teachers has had a direct bearing on the quality of education and many of the ills of the later can be ascribed to the indifferent manner in which society have looked upon the teacher and the manner in which many teachers have performed their functions.*"

Not only in our country India, but also throughout the world, the importance of teacher in pedagogical activities and advancement of education has been very well recognized. The UNESCO-ILO document on status of teachers (1967) states: *"It should be recognized that the advance in education depends largely on the qualification and ability of the teaching staff in general and on the human, pedagogical and technical qualities of the individual teachers"*.

The joint ILO-UNESCO Committee of experts on the Application of the Recommendation concerning the status of teachers reported in 1988 "... *the status of teachers and status of education are so intertwined that what ever produces changes in the one will normally produce changes in the same direction in the other. If education does not command the respect and support of the entire community, teachers will not command that respect and support.*" The joint recommendation concerns not only the status of teachers; it is concerned with the status and performance of education. It defines goal, progress which will yield benefits in the status of teachers as a profession.

The report to UNESCO of the International Commission on Education for the twenty first century (1996) reads, "... *ways can be found for improving the performance and motivation of teachers in the relationship they establish with local authorities*".

When teachers themselves are the part of the community where they are teaching, their involvement is more clearly defined. They are more sensitive and responsive to the needs of their community and better able to work towards community goals (*Rao, 1996*).

In view of the immediate need to raise the standard of education for the tribal communities, and to keep the teachers from the tribal communities improving their skill, continuous efforts are required to promote the over all status of the teachers. And in order to do so, it is necessary to study the existing status of the teachers from the tribal denomination.

Questions Need Answers

In view of forgoing discussion, it is essential to delve into the deep to get the reply of the following questions:

- What is the present status of the tribe teachers?
- Are they playing their expected role to uplift their society?
- What is the exact figure of educated tribes involved in teaching?
- Are they really interested in teaching?

- What is their attitude towards their profession, students, colleagues, government, society and working environment?
- What role are they performing for the cultural exchange among their students?
- Are they applying their indigenous knowledge during their teaching or not?
- What are the problems they are facing in their profession?

Objectives

The present book is designed to exaggerate the status-profile of the tribal teachers from the two states of Indian Republic-Assam and West Bengal following juxtaposition. For this purpose, the underlying objectives of the present investigation are specified as follow:

1. To study the socioeconomic and academic status of the tribal teachers
2. To ascertain the aspiration for professional education and constraints faced by the tribe teachers in pursuing education during their studenthood.
3. To explore the professional relationship of the tribe teachers with their colleagues.
4. To analyze the role of Government of Assam and Government of West Bengal for improvement of status of the tribe teachers.
5. To study attitude of the tribe teachers towards their profession, students, colleagues, government, society and working environment.
6. To explore the psycho-graphic status of the tribe teachers as reflected by their level of creativity (a composite ability of originality, flexibility and fluency).
7. To explore the status of the tribe teachers within their own indigenous community.
8. To identify the problems faced by the tribe teachers in their professional environment.

The present study deals with the status of the teachers working in the schools (having any of the class grades, ranging within standard VIII to XII) situated within the geographical limit of the states Assam and West Bengal and belonging to any of the scheduled tribe communities.

Note: Though the semantic determination of the word 'tribal' is not beyond doubt, however the word is well accepted in Indian academic.

2

Educational Research
An Anthropological Approach

"A society gets the kind of education system that it deserves, and change will come only if society at large is not just willing to, but actively wants to make that change. The impulses that guide the conduct of school and colleges emerge not that what government decrees but from what society wants. People, who are simultaneously products of the education system and it's users, must want changes and want it badly enough to actively participate in that change. Unless this realization goes home, all policy changes put together will result in little more than superficial, and a new education culture will remain a distant dream."

To meet the demands of the specific objectives considered for the present study and to collect required data, a composite approach has been adopted which can be termed as "Anthropological approach in Educational Research". The approach is, in fact, a combination of educational, ethnographic and psychographic approaches.

Emergence of Anthropological Approach on Educational Research

Education is a continuous process from birth till death – the means and method may differ. It is concerned with the whole life in it's manifestation (*Ambasht, 1971*). The purpose of education is to stimulate and guide the self development (*Whitehead, 1962*). In true sense, Education is an approach for the harmonious development of the individual in the context of the culture of the community to which he belongs. Since education has an intrinsic relation with culture, the need for an anthropological approach for the education of the tribes is essential. Educational sociology and educational anthropology have developed out of this fact. Applied anthropology with respect to education can only operate within very clearly, rather narrowly defined limits, unless the anthropological engineer or the agency for whom she is planning, first operates upon the fundamental ordering of the socio-cultural entity in question – that is, upon the basic technological, economic and social organizations, and second, has the means to enforce the changes recommended and is willing to exercise those means. The definite aims of educational anthropology are:

(*i*) To understand the status and role of human components involved, in general, and in specific, the teacher in community and of the school as an instrument of social progress and social factors affecting schools.

(*ii*) To understand the democratic ideologies, culture, economic and social trends in relation to both formal and informal educational agencies.

(*iii*) To understand the social forces and their effects upon individuals.

(*iv*) To socialize the curriculum and

(*v*) To use the techniques of research and critical thinking to achieve these aims.

In fact the task of an educo-anthropologist is two fold. He can show whether modern educational institutions cause unnecessary dislocation in the lives of the families whose children pass through them; and from what he knows of the life that the adult native will have to lead. He can draw conclusion as to the type of education will be of most real value to him (*Mair, 1961*). Another line of approach would be *study of school and modern teaching* as factors of change in tribal society (*Sachchidananda, 1957*). Mass education and social education cannot, in the true sense of the term, be imparted unless educators know the culture and social values of the tribal societies in which such education is being imparted. On the other hand, the race of teacher is a significant variable in determining the relationship with students (*David, 1964*). The best teacher for the tribal communities can be only those educated people who belong to the very community.

Rational of the Anthropological Approach in Educational Research

Anthropology is the study of humankind and primarily concerned with the species – *Homo sapiens.* In fact, Anthropology is the study of humankind, seeks to produce useful generalizations about people, their status, attitude and their behaviour to arrive at the fullest possible understanding of human diversity in general and the same of a certain human group in particular. However, anthropology is not the only discipline that studies human groups. In this context, it share its objectives with the other social and natural sciences. Like Education (*i.e.* the process through which *Homo sapiens*, gain knowledge), a social science, anthropology do not think of their findings as something quite apart from those of sociologists, psychologist, economists, biologists and social-work professionals, rather share and welcome the contributions of the disciplines to understand and to interpret the findings.

Anthropology is traditionally divided into four branches: Physical/ Biological anthropology and three branches of cultural anthropology, *viz.*,

Archeology, Linguistic anthropology and Ethnology. Ethnology is often termed as socio-cultural anthropology. Ethnography is the systematic study method and description of a culture-group (or ethnic group as a whole or a part of the group) based on first hand observation. Ethnology concentrates on the socio-cultural aspects of the contemporary social groups and study their mind set, their attitude towards various dimensions, their way of thinking, their interest, creative abilities, their flexibility, their problem and so on. In fact, ethnography is a descriptive approach, which cover the broader spectrum of the *status of a group or a part of the ethnic group*. It is only the anthropological approach in education (and to be more specific, ethnographic approach in educational research) which provides the researchers the tool like participatory observation technique for pooling their data from the various ethnic group about their feelings, their consideration and their perception about their group members engaged in teaching profession. The very approach as it is termed as *"Anthropological approach in educational research"* does includes the sequels of factors which simultaneously come under the purview of the status profile of a status group, *viz.*, age, sex, marital status, socio-cultural status as well as the religious, linguistic and psychographic status. The psychographic status is in fact treated as a common sign or symptom of the psychological makeup of a certain status-group and which further helps to study and classify the group members according to their various psychological abilities, *viz.*, attitude towards various dimensions, mental readiness to adopt with certain situation (flexibility), to produce and reproduce unusual ideas (originality) and capacity to accommodate and assimilate with others.

The foregoing discussion of the concept of anthropological approach in educational research justify itself as the best among the available approaches and can be adopted for the educational research which exactly fitting with the objectives and required data for the present investigation. Hence, the very approach is adopted for the present study.

Illustration of the Concepts

The concepts on which the anthropological approach in educational research in connection with the present study hinges on are illustrated as follows:

Status

The concept of status once referred only to inherited status, a fixed, usually hereditary position within the social order (*Park & Burgess, 1921*). Such was the usage of the writers like the distinguished evolutionists, Sir Henry Maine (1822-1888) and two other wide-known American sociologists, Robert E. Park (1964-1944) and Ernest W. Burgess, who in 1921 co-authored the still valuable book "Introduction to the Science of Sociology".

The Ethnopedagogic Approach Model (Roy, 2005)

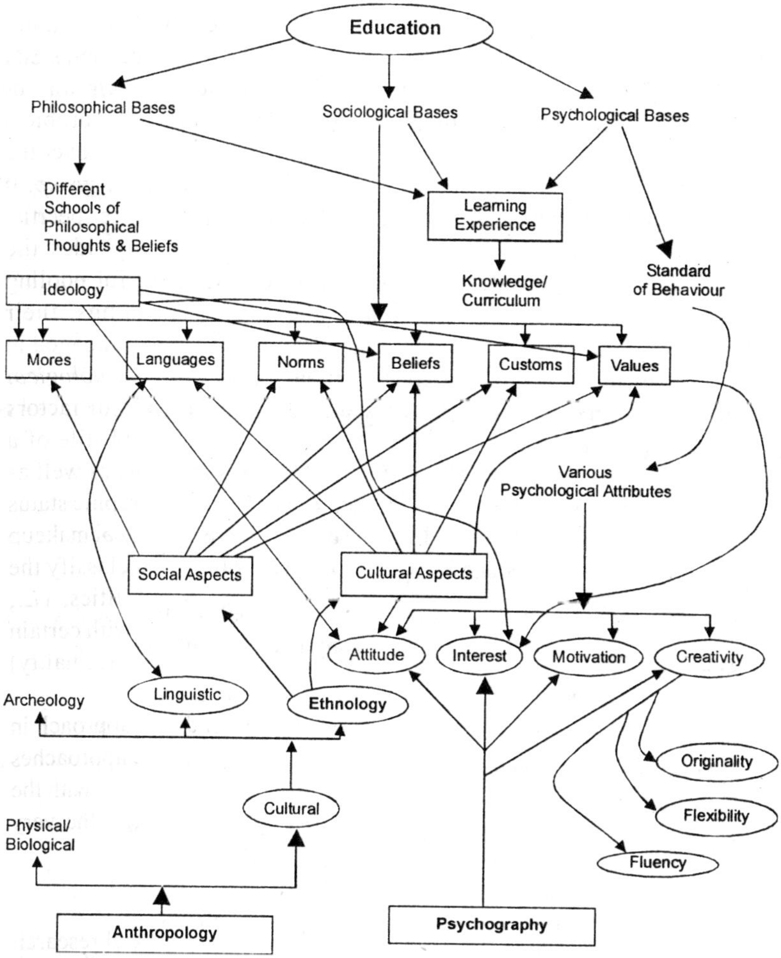

With the development of modern anthropology and sociology, status has been broadened to encompass all culturally prescribed rights and duties inherent in a social position, irrespective of the origin of a social atom. The individual is viewed as having a cumulative or total status, which generally combines large number of subsidiary statuses. The eminent American Anthropologist, Ralph Linton (1893-1953) distinguished between ascribed (or inherited) status – which would have been a redundancy to the earlier theorists like Maine, Park and Burgess, and achieved status – which results from personal attainment of goals set forth by the culture. This distinction has been all but universally accepted in social science (*Park, 1936*). As such there are certain irreducible bases for the determination of status. Among them those mentioned by Linton are: age, sex and occupation. Further more, status, whether the by-product of effort or the result of birth, carries with it the image of exemplary behaviour, a model of collective expectations (*Linton, 1936*). Infact, the role of an individual is a more dynamic aspect of status.

According to the *Encyclopaedia of Social Science*, status is a marked of by the fact that distinctive beliefs about and expectations for social actors as organized around it.

In fact, the term status stands for role and position. It signifies the "*...sum total of various currently ascribed roles*" one has to play and rights and duties inherent in a social position (*Cooley, 1899*).

Oxford dictionary defines the concept of status as a rank or social position in relation to others and person's legal standing which determines his or her right and duties.

Encyclopedia Britannica (Vol. 10, p. 924) reads that the status is the relative rank that an individual holds with attended rights, duties and life style in a social hierarchy, based upon honour or prestige. It accepts the classification of status as done by Ralph Linton as follow:

Status
- **Ascribed** (Assigned to individual at birth without reference to any innate abilities)
- **Achieved** (Requiring special qualities and filled through competition and individual effort).

Status is often ascribed on the basis of sex, age, family relationships and birth, placing one into a particular social group. Achieved statuses normally based on education, occupation, marital status and other factors.

The word status implies social stratification on a vertical scale. The special analogy covers several meanings. A person may be said to occupy a higher position when he is able to control, by order or by influence, other people's conduct; when he or she derives prestige or when somebody's conduct has earned esteem of the fellows. Relative status is a major factor determining the behaviour of people toward one another and competition of status seems to be a prime persuit (*Znaniecki, 1940*).

Status of an individual tends to vary with social context. For example, the position of an individual in his keen-group helps determine his position in the community.

The forgoing discussion is sufficient enough to accept the concept of status as a relative-rank, that an individual or a status-group (here the tribal teachers) holds with attendant rights, duties and life-style in a social hierarchy, based upon honour or prestige – which they achieve (through their individual capability) and ascribe through their birth. In fact, the status is a social phenomenon, which is based upon sex, age, family, class, relationship and also birth – placing one into a particular social group.

An individual or a group can acquire social status basically through education and occupation apart from other previously mentioned factors.

In the present study the concept of 'status' goes in consonance with its illustration to explore the status profile of the tribal teachers which includes various components of status like sex, marital status, cultural status, experience, professional status, linguistic status, religious status, political status, social upbringing, family status, housing status, sociability, social mobility, economic status, educational status, academic status, community status, level of knowledge, aspiration, professional relationship and psychographic status etc. which denotes a holistic perspective or a profile of the tribal teachers. Some of those are illustrated as follow:

Gender: Gender is the basic factor on which the entire living beings are divided. It is a basis of ordering. The social life of human beings consider 'sex' as a component of status and in oriental societies like India, expected role of an individual strictly based on the very component. It is normally the culture, which determine the gender-role and 'role model' guides the individual in a certain way. Sex is the ascribed identity and hence a component of ascribed status (*Nancy, 1971*).

Marital Status: It denotes the status of an individual, based on his sexual relationship with the spouse. Human society considers an individual, more matured, if having sexual experience, which an individual can achieve only through some social-process. Certain maturity can only be achieved with chronology and thus system of role performance differs in terms of this very criterion. It is a bordering status, which can be changed by desire of an individual, and reverse-change is hardly possible.

Cultural Status: Culture consists of the abstract values, beliefs and perceptions of the world that lie behind people's behaviour and that their behaviour reflects. The members of a society share these, and when acted upon, they produce behaviour considered acceptable within the very society. Cultures are learned, largely through the medium of language, rather than inherited biologically and the parts of culture function as an integrated whole. Within a society, different communities may follow sub-cultural variations. Culture is one of the important components of the status profile (*Gamst, 1976*).

Experience: Experience denotes the knowledge or skill resulting from actual or practical acquaintance with facts or events, that determines the role or position of an individual within the society and hence considered as a component of status.

Linguistic Status: Language is a system of communication, using sounds that are put together in meaningful ways according to a set of rules. As a component of culture, it determine the position of an individual by virtue of command to communicate in a certain linguistic-environment (*Woolfson, 1972*).

Religious Status: Religious status may be regarded as the beliefs and patterns of behaviour by which human try to deal with what they view as important and thus the concept incorporates the role of the individual and hence it is to be considered as a component of status (*Walls, 1966*). It serve a number of psychological and social function and control the human-conduct by providing notions of right and wrong – and also used to enhance the learning of oral traditions. Finally, it play an important role to maintain social solidarity (*Malinowski, 1954*).

Political Status: No form of political organization can function in a democratic country without the loyalty and support of those it governs. (*Haviland, 1990*) The present study consider the role of the respondents in terms of participation in various political organization as their political status.

Psychographic Status: Psychographic status deals with the psychological attributes of the individual which determine his role in a certain social setup (*Fowler, 1995*). Psychographic status may also be termed as the distinctive way a person thinks, feels and behaves and in this sense it is the reflection of the psyche of an individual (*Coiln, 1983*). Every sort of psychological traits to a greater extent or less – determine the psychographic status however for the present investigation, the level of creativity, attitude towards some selected dimensions and interest are the factors taken into consideration.

Creativity: Creativity is one of the most highly valued qualities of human beings, which enormously affect all spheres of life may be it individual or social. Those nations, which learn best how to identify, develop and encourage creativity in their people, may find themselves in an advantageous position. Creativity, at it's highest level, has probably been as important as any human quality in changing history and in re-shaping the world (*Roy, 1996*). Creativity essentially relates to potential of an individual for generating new ideas, forms and practices. The degree and quality of creative expression is however relative. It varies from individual to individual and from age to age, as one grows in years, experience and maturity and thus enhances the status of an individual.

Guilford (1950) in his approach defined creativity as a staunch exponent of cognitive functioning. His sole emphasis was on the model of structure of intellect. Morgan (1953) in his approach, emphasized on the uniqueness of the ability, either one or a combination of four aspects – *process*, *person*, *place* and *product* to define creativity. The continuous work of Guilford (1959) help to evolve the structure given as follow which start with a vibration in the brain cell (stimuli) and product occurs following the process.

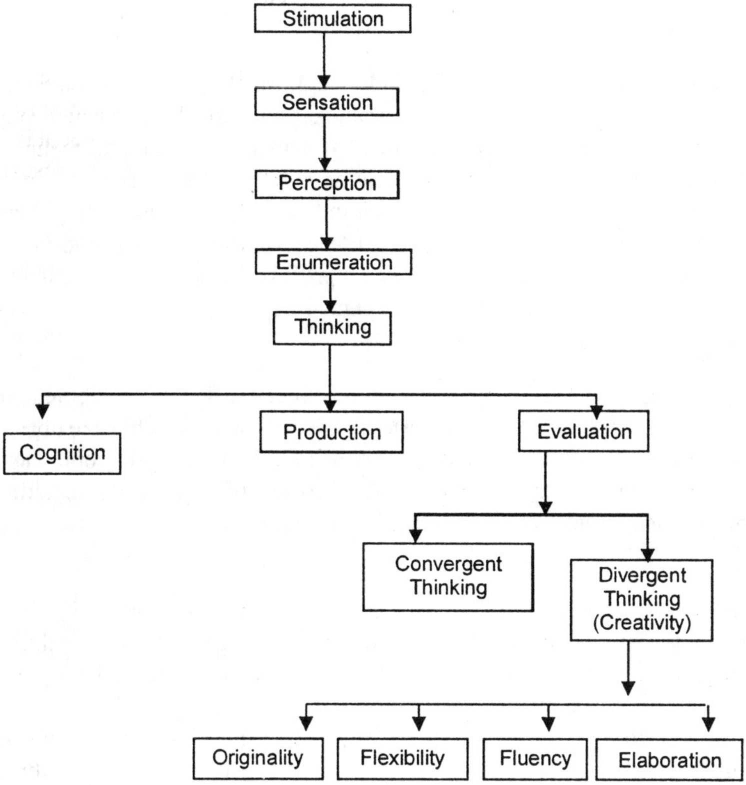

Apart from Guilford, Taylor (1959), Maslow (1962), Mc Kinnon (1961), Wallas (1962), Wertheimar (1945), Cattel (1970) and Eysinck (1972), also defined creativity in various ways encompassing the thought process. Torrance (1965) conceives creativity as a composed of constellation of general abilities, personality variables and problem solving traits, which he considered, can be enhanced through memory, adaptability, self discipline, introversion, divergent thinking ability and supportive climate.

However Indian schools of philosophy, *viz.*, *Jainism*, *Buddhism*, *Nyaya Vaisesikam*, *Yoga* and *Vedanta* agree that creativity is a process of a "superior thought level", which help the individual to eliminate the obstacles in the thought process, *viz.*, passion, instincts, desire, impulses, etc. These schools of thoughts advocates that *Ahimsa* (non-violence), *Sattya* (truth), *Astaya* (honesty) and Brahmacharya (sexual continuance) are the steps to be followed to obtain perfection in knowledge, reasoning and reflection upon environment and upon the person himself, which make him creative.

The present study considers the terms 'creativity' as a composite ability of originality, flexibility and fluency as it was defined by Torrance.

Attitude

Attitude is the way of thinking of an individual, which guides his behaviours (*Fowler & Fowler, 1995*). It is a measurable psychological factor which may be overt or covert. It denotes some total of man's inclination and feelings, prejudices or pre-conceived notions, ideas or convictions about certain things, Individual, object, etc. Here, the term attitude is considered as a component of the psychographic status of the tribal teachers which is measured in six specific dimensions – *viz.*, towards their profession, students, colleagues, government, society and working environment.

Interest

Interest is just a complex as an amalgam of subjective feelings and objective behaviour – the tendencies, which varies in intensity and from object to object. It has close relationship with culture and effort. As an important component of psychographic status, interest is established sets of dispositions, resulting from experience and determines resulting behaviour.

Tribe

Anthropologically, tribe is a social group, a number of which live in a community, have a common dialect, uniform social organization and cultural homogeneity with common ancestor, political organization and religious pattern.

In our country India, here are about four hundred and sixty-one communities including sub-tribes. In the state of Assam twenty-three communities and in the state of West Bengal thirty-eight communities are specified as scheduled tribes.

In the study the term 'tribal' denotes the concept of 'scheduled tribe' accepting the state list of the scheduled tribe communities of the respective states.

Tribal Teachers

The person who belong to the scheduled tribe-community according to the respective state-list of scheduled tribes (see Annexure) and are engaged in teaching profession in the schools of Assam and West Bengal with any of the class-grades VIII to XII are denoted as 'tribal teachers' for the present study.

3

Research Trends in Tribal Education

The existence of the present always rests on the foundation of the past. A view of history always ascertains the firmness of our present situation. Hence, a summary of writings of recognized authorities and of previous research provides evidence what is till unknown and yet to be testified. Since effective research is based upon past knowledge, review helps to eliminate the duplication of what has already been done and provide useful directions and helpful suggestions for significant investigation.

Indeed, review of related literature in general and research based findings in particular, provides academic guide to the investigator and that is why considered as one of the important step of the methodology of educational research. According to Good, C.V. (1959) *Survey of related literature help us to know whether evidence already available to solve problem adequately without future investigation and thus may save duplication. It may contribute to general scholastic ability if the investigator by providing ideas, theories and explanations, help in formulating the problem and may also suggest the approximate method of research.* Van-Dalen's (1973) comment in this regard is also worthnoting; he says, *"The review of educational research gives an excellent overview of the work that has been done in the fields and helps to keep up with recent developments".*

Brief Review of Research Literature related to Tribe, Teacher and Education

The distinctive socio-cultural life of the Indian tribes drew the attention of the researchers from various disciplines and a good number of studies was carried out on the different aspects of the tribals. With the introduction to the socio-economic developmental programmes for the tribals, the scope of research has been widened. The *needs*, *problems* and *response-pattern* of the tribals have become the areas of interest for the researchers. Problems and issues specifically related to spread of formal education among tribals has drawn the attention of the researchers (*Singh and Jabbi, 1996*).

Prior to 1960 hardly any systematic research was carried out exclusively on the education of the tribals; however few articles were published on educational problems by Chattopadhya, K.P. (1953) and Gafoor, K.A. (1952). Some reports were published by – Elwin, V. (1959); Aiyappan, A. (1948); Himendorf, C.V. (1948) and Grigson, W.V. (1947) and they discussed the status and problems of education of different tribal groups and areas. Apart from these, articles were also published by Mazumder, D.N. (1957) on working of schools in specific tribal contexts. All these articles were based on general observations and broad understanding of Tribal situation.

It is NCERT, which took an attempt in 1994 to treat the "*Tribal Education*" as a special filed of concern, establishing a Unit for Tribal-Education. This unit started effort to promote empirical research on tribal education. Micro level studies were also initiated by researchers like Naik, T.B. (1969); Srivastava, L.R.N. (1968) etc. even before the attempt made by NCERT where the researchers adopted qualitative survey and case–study methods.

Good many surveys was initiated by sociologists and were encouraged by ICSSR during seventies to study the sociological aspects of tribal students at secondary and post secondary levels. These studies covered varied aspects like *socio-economic background of students, utilization pattern of various facilities, their interaction pattern with non-tribal teachers and students, their pedagogical problems and so on.*

During eighties, so many studies were carried out on wastage and stagnation of 'Tribal education'. Some of the studies of this kind attempted to compare the *wastage* and *stagnation* between different *types of schools* and *students* with differing *gender*.

Some of the studies conducted in late–seventies and early-eighties were *with a view to examine* the relationship between *educational participation* and *differential socio-economic background of tribal households* mostly depending upon primary data and by applying statistical tools.

Psychological studies were also initiated from early–sixties on the *cognitive* and *non-cognitive domains*, using *experimental tests* on tribal groups. However in depth–studies were initiated by the psychologists like Tripathi, L.B. (1975); Sinha, D. (1980); Rath, R. (1972); Mishra, G. (1977) who developed their psychological tools taking into account the specific tribal–cultural–context.

Evaluative studies were carried out on *Ashram Schools* and *Hostels*. These studies were mostly sponsored by planning commission, Ministry of Welfare, Ministry of Education, NCERT and NIEPA and also by some individual researchers and scholar groups. These studies addressed to issues related to *coverage*, *utilization pattern*, *background*, *beneficiaries* and *administrative problems*, having close relation to macro level policy-implication. However no attempt was made to examine relative effectiveness of individual incentives.

Whatever it may be, these studies covered different states and larger samples. Recent tribal studies under DPEP adopted survey techniques for *evaluation of incentives.* Base line studies on students' achievement conducted under DPEP adopted standardized achievement tests and rigorous statistical analysis. Various statistical techniques were used to analyze the factors contributing to *school effectiveness*–however all these studies were carried out on very small sample.

Anthropologists also carried out a good number of micro level-studies on tribal education. These anthropological studies are of qualitative–cum–holistic in nature. Supported by quantitative data; attempt was made to examine the varied aspects of primary education in context of socio-cultural and economic life of tribals in these studies. Not only the formal schools, but the youth dormitories were also visited by the researchers to delve into the role of dormitories and hostels for the expansion of education. Similarly these studies examined the role of Christian Missionaries in introducing formal education.

Studies carried out by educationists are mostly confined to limited aspects and mostly the tribal students form the unit of sample at institutional level are also taken into consideration. Some of these studies were comparative in nature in which the tribal students were compared with the non-tribal students on different aspects.

On the other hand, studies conducted by sociologists were of mixed type and most of those were macro-level studies and are dependent upon more quantitative data. The studies carried out by psychologists were mostly experimental in nature and those studies tried to compare cognitive as well as non-cognitive abilities of tribals with such abilities of the non-tribal students.

Research on tribal–education was initiated from various angles and the studies carried out in the very filed can be classified into following broad areas:

1. Studies on school aspects.
2. Studies on teacher and related issues.
3. Studies on medium of instruction.
4. Studies on educability, socio-cultural and economic background.
5. Studies on attitude towards formal education.
6. Studies on incentives and infrastructure.
7. Studies on cognitive and non-cognitive abilities.

Studies on School Aspects

Major share of studies on tribal education as reported by Sujatha, K. in this way or the other, centered upon the issue of wastage and stagnation. But till mid-seventies, most of the studies tried to treat 'wastage' as one of the problems. The latter studies focused mostly on wastage and stagnation and examined the extent of wastage at different levels, grades, gender-groups and types of schools. Few hand-counted studies attempted to examine the interrelationship between extent of wastage, attendance and stagnation with those of *family background of children.* The studies sponsored by ICSSR and NCERT (1975) attempted to find out the status of enrolment and extent of wastage among tribals both at secondary and higher secondary education levels. Santra, B. (1985) carried out a national level survey, where she tried segregate the data on wastage for tribals separately. Studies was also carried out on wastage and stagnation of tribal students at different levels by the individual researchers like Bihari, L.R. (1969); Masavi, M.I. (1971); Ambasht, N.K. (1971); Ratnaiah, E.V. (1974); Singh, K. and Ohri, R. (1983);Singh, A.K. (1984); Srivastava, P. (1986); Dhongade U.D. (1986); Sujatha, K. (1987), (1994); Chauhan, S.S. (1989); Kulkarni, P.M. and Krishnamurthy, S. (1992); Dhongade, Pandey, S. (1993) and so on. These studies were mostly exploratory and diagnostic in nature emphasizing on wastage and stagnation. All these studies find that the drop out rate is very high in 1st and 2nd grade and though decreases but in other classes but enhance at 5th standard. The studies reveal that the extent of wastage varies among different schools and in different areas. The road-side villages and villages with hostel facilities have lower rate of dropouts, in comparison with interior and villages without hostel facilities.

Sujatha, K. (1984) carried out their sequential studies on Ashram schools and observed that the extent of wastage and stagnation in these schools was much lower compared to the non–Ashram schools, even when situated in the same geographical area. Even at institutional level, the extent of wastage and stagnation varies among students belonging to different tribal groups. Students from more articulate, exposed and from Christian tribal groups have low-rate of wastage and stagnation and the generation is justified by the common findings of the studies carried out by Toppo, Sita. (1979); Rathnaiah, E.V. (1974); Naik, T.B. (1975) and Sujatha, K. (1994).

Some of the researchers tried to understand the influence of economic condition and social *background of family on dropout pattern.* These studies showed that if the income is higher and the social status of the family is also high, then the drop out rate of the children of such families is low. Bihari, L.R. (1969)'s study indicated higher dropout rate in single-teacher schools in most under-developed areas.

Tribal Research Institutes (TRI) in different states carried out studies on wastage and stagnation. In good number of studies it was found that 70 per cent of the tribal children dropped before reaching fifth grade. These figures vary from state to state. Masavi, M. (1976) carried out his study in the state of Gujarat where he observed that only 9 per cent of the tribal children in grade–I had been able to reach grade–IV. Most of the studies in this direction make it as an axiom that the extent of wastage among the tribal girls was found to be higher than boys.

Besides illiteracy and lack of awareness among the parents most of the studies identified 'poverty' as the major cause for the alarming dropout rate and stagnation. Some of the studies tried to explain cultural reasons like free nature of the tribal children, socialization pattern, early marriages, etc. as responsible for wastage and dropout.

It is not a distant trend in which some of the studies looked into school aspects – like inadequate facilities, problem of medium of instruction, regional language, inadequate training to teachers and their indifferent attitude, lack of teaching and learning materials, absence of proper inspection and supervision of schools and so on. Large number of these studies pointed out that the *present content*, *curriculum* and *pedagogy* are not relevant to tribal context. Lack of convergence correspondence between *cultural experience* and *school curriculum* has been found as one of the reasons of dropouts. *These studies also pointed that non-tribal teachers are ineffective in teaching tribal students*. Some of the researchers strongly argued that tribal dialects need to be introduced in lower-grades as medium of instruction. Though the comments are quite valid but none of these comments are based on empirical evidence.

Studies on Teacher and Related Issues

Teacher was identified as one of the important variables by many studies. Some of the studies carried out by Ambasht, N.K. (1970) Sachchidananda (1971), ICSSR (1975) Panda, S.C. (1983), Joshi, S.D. (1979), Sing, A.K. (1985), Kamilla, B.B. (1985), Sujatha, K (1987, 1993, 1994); Ambasht (1994) and Panda, B (1995) and tried to examine the interaction pattern between teacher, students and community taking into account the teacher's social background.

Many of the non-tribal teachers do not have correct understanding of tribal culture, values and specific needs of the tribal children. *Teacher's truancy* was also reported. These studies pointed out that irregular functioning of schools and frequent absence of teachers contributed to high wastage and stagnation. These studies also recognized that in many a cases teachers are not having appropriate training to teach in tribal cultural–context. Majority of them could not understand tribal dialects resulting in communication–gap between teachers, students and community. Some of the studies revealed that non-tribal teachers have pre-conceived notions, prejudices and indifferent attitude towards tribal children, which in turn affect the teaching-learning process. Some of the researchers like Sachidananda (1975), Singhi, N.K. (1975), Vyas, N.N. and Choudhury, N.D. (1970), Masavi, M. (1970), Rout, P.C. (1985), Kundu, M. (1990), Sujatha, K. (1993 and 1994), etc. agreed over the point that there is a need for special training–courses and programmes for teachers and administrators working in tribal areas. Kundu, M. developed a detailed model for teacher-training. He emphasized that teachers need training to design the school-curriculum based on local resources.

Another study, carried out by Sujatha, K. (1993) in Andhra Pradesh, reveals that the *tribal youths if once become teachers, also behave like other teachers.* The inter-tribal prejudices and social hierarchy are found as problems when *teachers belonging to one tribal community are posted in village of different tribal group.* Due to relaxation of educational qualification, they lack adequate subject and teaching skills, which in turn affects the quality of tribal education. However, the tribal teachers have advantage of having close interaction with community and also can communicate with students with local dialects. Even these teachers tend to 'abstain' form the schools for lack of accommodation and other physical facilities. Sometimes, due to kin-group affiliation, teachers are protected even if they are absent from school for days together. Having exclusively tribal teachers leads to closed and limited interaction between teacher and pupils. However the findings are much case-specific.

Studies on Medium of Instruction

Medium of instruction is one of the important issues that have often been discussed by the researchers. The studies carried out by Srivastava, L.R.N. et. al. (1971) reveals that tribal students are quite unable to understand or speak the regional language till they reach IIIrd standard. The research also pointed that there is wide variation among different tribal groups in learning regional languages. The groups, which have interaction and symbolic relation with the non-tribals, generally understand and speak regional language and they enjoy the advantage in school. It also depends on *geographical location of villages*; sporadic attempts are made to prepare primers in certain dialects. Yet there is no specific empirical evidence – how far they have been successful in imparting knowledge. Evidences from West Bengal show that even if the primers are prepared in tribal dialects, implementing them in classroom teaching is a problem. For instance, in the state of West Bengal, especially for the major tribe 'Santhals' books were prepared in *Alchiki* language but the non-tribal teachers could not transact in tribal dialect and surprisingly even the tribal teachers refused to teach in tribal dialect. As a result the books in tribal dialects were kept unused. However, some of the pilot projects carried out by Central Institute for Languages (CIL) were successful in case of Goa and Karnataka. But these two experiences cannot be taken as 'models' because the small sizes of tribal population and efforts made as an experiment have their own limitations. Recently some NGOs in South and Southeast India are preparing bilingual primers and experimenting at micro level but it is too early to draw any conclusion on their effectiveness.

Study carried out by Sujatha, K. (1993) shows that the parents of the tribal students are having bias towards the regional languages than that of their own indigenous language because the regional languages are more helpful to achieve occupational mobility and also for better educational opportunities. Though it would have been better to have the scope to educate the tribal students in their own dialects but some practical problems cannot be ignored. First of all, the tribals are not homogenous groups. Indigenous groups of tribals are of small size and there are numerous dialects spoken by the tribals. More and more the schools comprise students from different tribal groups. Consequently, no planned effort has been made for preparing teaching–aids in tribal dialects for introducing at institutional level.

Significant finding came out from the study carried out by Gayatonde, N.V. (1977) which refutes the preconceived notion that the tribal students are inferior to the non–tribals in mathematical and linguistic ability. Govind and Varghese observed that the tribal students in residential schools perform better than the non–tribal students, studying in ill-equipped schools. In a different study conducted by Varghese, N.V. (1994) it was observed that difference in performance level between tribal and non-tribal students is not very significant and the tribal students from the schools situated in relatively advanced areas perform better than the non-tribal students studying in the remote areas.

Studies on Educability, Socio-Cultural and Economic Background

A good deal of research work has already been carried out by the researcher to study the socio-economic aspects of the tribal students with emphasis upon their cultural aspects, their exposure to modernity and parental attitude towards their education and expectation from these. Singh, A.K. (1980) and Singh and Jayaswal's (1981) study highlight these aspects. The studies carried out by Madan, T.N. (1952), Naik, T.B. (1975), Ambasht, N.K. (1970), Sachidananda (1974), Srinivastava, L.R.N. (1971), Sharma, B.D. (1978) come to the conclusion that poverty of the parents is having it's effect over the education of the tribal children.

To delve into the reasons of poverty, Ratnaiah, E.V. (1974), Sujatha, K. (1993), Vyas, N.N. (1969), Patel, T. (1983) and Kailash, (1993) observed that tribals are poor at group level but have individual variation at house hold level and the family income and land holdings as well as households has influence on educational participation. However, these two are not the only reason for low rate of participation in education; several other intervening variables are also active in this context. Study of Sujatha, K. (1994) reveals that in some cases economy is having adverse effect over tribal education where income-generating schemes keep the tribal children away from schools though help the families to improve the economy. Some studies reveal that the tribal children whose parents are employed in government service and or in petty business have better educational participation.

Ambasht, N.K. (1970), Ratnaiah, E.V. (1974), Sachhidananda (1967), (1971), Desai, I.P. (1974), Shah, V. and Patel, T. (1977), Heridia, R. (1992), Singh, A.K.(1980, 1983, 1988), Singh, A.K. and Jayaswal, M. (1981) in their study found strong relationship between parental education and educational participation of the children – specially in case of girls. These studies also explored the influence of Christian missionaries on educational participation of the tribals – especially in Bihar. The Christian tribals were found better in utilizing educational facilities than that of their non-Christian counterparts and this difference is even prominent within the same tribe. Some of the above-mentioned researcher comes with the conclusion that the size of family is closely and proportionately associated with the participation rate in the education of the younger members of the family. Again the studies observed strong association between the *geographical location* and *utilization of educational facilities*. Since the tribal education is a recurring phenomenon in tribal areas most of the researchers tried to examine the attitude, awareness, aspirations and expectations from education. While the studies carried out in early seventies observed that lack of awareness about education had negative impact over participation rate and the tribals had fear of formal education for the apprehension that it will detribalize their children and they may be reluctant about their culture. It was further observed by Dasgupta, N.K. (1963), Ambasht, N.K. (1972) and Dhebar Commission (1962) that the tribals are suspicious about formal education. The studies carried out by Pandey, S. (1993), Panda, B.N. (1987) and Masavi (1976) observed a change in attitude of the tribal towards formal education and they started considering formal education as a tool for improving social status and upward occupational mobility.

Studies on Attitude Towards Formal Education

Many researchers examined attitude of the tribals towards schools and teachers. In most of the cases it was observed that the tribals feel that school is the government's institution and not a part of their community and teacher is not a part of their society. Some recent studies, however, show that tribal community has better interaction with the teachers if they belong to their community and reside in the same village. The village leader and those who are having comparatively more exposure to the outer world, found to have better interaction with the teacher. Some of the studies observed a wider gap between the socialization process in the community and school, and such a gap makes the relation between them rather conflicting, which in turn make the students disinterested towards formal education. Nuna, S.C. (1993), Heredia, R.C. (1992) and Sujatha, K. (1987) in their study observed that *distance from school seems to be a disadvantage for tribal school going children due to ecological barriers which hinder their free movement*. So far as utilization of educational facilities is concerned there exists disparities at inter and inter–tribal levels and problems mostly exist in the tribal areas with scattered and sparsely populated habitations without a school in close proximity.

Studies on Planning and Management of Tribal Education

Education is one of the major activities under the welfare department. Besides providing incentives, educational institutions are also run by the welfare department. Planning Commission has sponsored several studies on different aspects of Tribal-development, which includes studies on administration of programmes. However, till recently, very few studies are reported on planning and management of tribal education. Another study was carried out by Sujatha, K. (1994) on the *effectiveness of tribal sub-plan approach on educational development of tribes.* She examined different aspects of planning and management of education at Integrated Tribal Development Project Level. The study shows that the sub–plan approach facilitates micro-level planning with flexibility. This has helped in expanding educational facilities, but the tribal welfare department lacks expertise on educational planning both in establishing and upgrading the schools. One of the important problems of tribal education is that the welfare department and education department administer it dually and there exists lack of coordination between these two departments. A very few studies pointed out the problems related to inspection and supervision of schools in tribal areas. Due to inaccessibility and lack of transport facilities, the schools are not properly monitored.

Studies on Incentives and Infrastructure

In view of equality of tribals, incentives like scholarships, free boarding and lodging, free supply of text-books, writing materials, uniforms, etc. are provided to the tribal students in order to overcome the economic problems. Planning commission, Ministry of Education and Welfare, to examine the coverage and utilization of the incentives, sponsored evaluative studies. The studies financed by NCERT (1971), NIEPA (1980, 1986 and 1990), NCERT (1981) and carried out by Singh (1991), Desai and Patel (1981), Pratap, D.R. et. al. (1971 and 1973), Punalekar, S.P. (1984) are worth-noting in this context.

Several studies carried out at the state level during 1970s reveal that the incentives failed to incorporate the cent percent of the tribal-school-going aged-children population even with the 'saturated-incentive'; and the 'precipitate' is till prevailing. Procedural delay is one of the important causes, noted by those studies. Inadequacies in amount and poor quality of materials are also the auxiliary causes as mentioned by these studies. Individual studies conducted on incentives examined the social class of beneficiaries. The urban and articulate groups have advantage in utilizing the incentives. The allied causes are tied with administrative problems in management of incentives due to cumbersome procedures and apathy of administrators. The findings of those studies also reveal that majority of meaningful incentives are at secondary and higher education levels, and delayed supply are hindering the effects of the incentives.

Although the incentive-schemes are in operation for almost six decades but no studies have been carried out on relevance or relative effectiveness of different incentives. Similarly, no studies have been carried out on the impact of incentives on academic aspects.

Some studies were carried out on special institutional arrangements like hostels, Ashram schools and ITIs. An in-depth study on Ashram school in Central tribal belt, carried out by Shrama and Sujatha, K. (1983) throw partial light on differential utilization of Ashram Schools facilities by different tribal groups. It was observed that the tribal communities with higher literacy levels utilize the provisions of residential facilities in Ashram schools. In this way they get the benefit of higher retention of students. This study observed that though the cost of education in Ashram schools is higher than in non-Ashram schools but the unit effective cost is lower.

Studies on Cognitive and Non-Cognitive Abilities

A good number of experimental studies carried out on cognitive and non-cognitive abilities of tribal children comparing the same with non-tribal students. Studies on intelligence, achievement and motivation carried out by Singh A.K. (1983) Raghava Kumari (1986), Gupta S.P. (1965), Prakash (1972), Chattopadhya (1961), Misra (1987), Kar (1975), Das and Singha (1975), Pandey (1981), Singh (1983), Rath, R. (1974), Mishra, G. and Tripathi, L.B. (1977), Dash (1973), Balakrishna (1986), Chand, J. (1985), Chaudhury, P. and Singha, U.P. (1959), Fatima, S.M.B. (1986), Dutta, M.L. (1983) showed that the tribal students are inferior in terms of their achievement and motivation due to economic, physical and cultural deprivation. Emotional deprivation also prevails among them. The studies reveal that the underlying causes of lower level of cognitive abilities are mostly due to cultural and environmental variation and obviously not due to tribal origin. Beside these, the theoretical and empirical evidence reveal that inter and intra-tribal variation exists in terms of their level of exposure and advancement, which is related to the response towards the developmental schemes.

Studies on Teacher and Related Issues

The *theoretical models* of tribal education are explicable in terms of socio-cultural determinant factors. Such factors further refer to *family background, which* reads that educability of tribal children is restricted due to socio-economic inability of the tribal families. The entire system of education which follows an *institutional model* so far as incentives, medium of instruction, content of transmission to students, pedagogic method etc. which the teacher is constrained to adopt is ultimately not conducive for envisaging a right format for educating the tribal children. The studies related to different aspects of inputs of education system, which incorporates the various incentives, medium of instruction, content, pedagogy and obviously the 'teacher'–adopts the Institutional-Model in the other hand, alleged that the 'System of education' is the responsible factor for the slow progress of education among the Indian tribes. The third dimension on management of schemes and incentives reflects how far the special measures could substitute the socio-cultural problems of the tribals to utilize the educational facilities. Lastly, the studies on psychological aspects provide a broad framework of the cognitive mapping of the tribal education having a direct bearing on pedagogy and inputs for the personality development programmes.

In spite of his best attempt, the author could not able to locate even a single investigation on the status of teachers who belongs to Indian tribe. Although a good deal of research work has already been carried out and presently some research works are in progress, centering round the needs and problems of different Indian tribes. These tribal studies approached form a varied angles. While some of those studies are carried out from economic or educational point of view, bulk of those are either anthropological or sociological studies.

Apart from the 'Tribal-studies', a good number of researches on 'Education' are throwing partial light into tribal study. It is worthwhile to review such literature, which are directly or indirectly connected with the topic related to present problem. The forthcoming presentation is a detail review of related research conducted in developed countries and developing countries, having a bearing with the present problem.

Detailed Review of Related Research Studies Carried out in India

To collect comprehensive information about the schoolteachers at different levels, a survey was carried out by Professor Madhubhai Buch and Singh (1978). The study focused on five aspects of the teachers, viz., the qualification and experience, professional training, participation in professional growth-activities, tenure of appointment and mobility of teachers from teaching profession.

School-information blank and teacher-information blank were used to collect data. They were further analyzed with respect to different categories and also in terms of 'management' of the institutions concerned. The survey was carried out over more than twenty-six lakhs teachers throughout the country, among them 47.38 per cent, 26.02 per cent, 14.40 per cent and 12.20 per cent taught in primary, middle, secondary and higher secondary schools respectively. The study explored the baseline data regarding the gender, categories and level of institutions; in addition, the study reflects the related data regarding the system of management of the schools, part-time and full-time teachers and their professional qualifications in different levels of institutions.

Chopra (1982) carried out a study on the organizational climate of schools in relation to job satisfaction of teachers, though not specifically on the tribal teachers. The first objective of this research was to study the overall job satisfaction of teachers, working in schools having different organizational climates. Sharma's School Organizational Climate description questionnaire and Wali's Teachers job satisfaction inventory was used to collect data from a sample of 272 teachers. The study revealed that among the six types of school-climates, the open-climate schools showed the maximum overall teaching-job satisfaction, followed by the autonomous, familiar, controlled, closed and paternal climate schools respectively. The study further revealed that there is significant difference of job-satisfaction among the schoolteachers coming from open and closed climates.

Goyal (1980) in his study tried to find out the correlation among attitudes, job satisfaction, adjustment and professional interests of teacher-educators, from different strata, based on age, gender, qualification and experience. A sample of 314 teacher-educators was considered sample for the study and data were collected from them through a self constructed attitude-scale, an 'enquiry form' (for collecting information on professional interests), Bell's adjustment inventory and Indiresan's job-satisfaction inventory. The study aimed towards four objectives first of which was to measure all the factors mentioned. The findings of this study reveals that emotional stability among the teacher-educators increased with age, whereas professional interest varies proportionately with experience but majority of them was interested in teaching and was satisfied with the job. The second objective of the study was to find out the difference in attitude, job satisfaction, adjustment and professional interests among groups of the teacher-educators. The study revealed that the attitude and job-satisfaction of different groups did not differ significantly. The study also revealed that, attitude, job satisfaction and occupational adjustment among teacher-educators are associated with one another where as social and emotional adjustment and professional interests are not related with the other variables. While job satisfaction could be predicted by attitude and occupational adjustment but not by the others.

During 1981, a unique study was conducted by Modi in Gujarat University, entitled "Influence of Education on Socio-Economic Status". The socio-economic status was determined by educational qualification, monthly income, administrative authority, residential accommodation, house-rent, possession of vehicles, cost of furniture, cost of electrical appliances and possession of telephone as well as refrigerator. Education was determined by twenty levels, beginning with illiterate and ending with the Ph. D. level. Data where collected from 2100 respondents on both the dimensions, – economic and educational status. Correlation between two sets of characteristics was established. Another sample of 1000 respondents supplied the data on the status enjoyed by two real brothers in the family, caste and habitation.

The study reveals that the status enjoyed by a person depends on his level of education. The literate respondents was with the opinion that their status in the family is determined by the age, but their status within the caste and locality is determined by their economic condition. The educated people opined that education is the determinant factor of one's social status and the age is not at all a factor in this regard.

The study further observed that the level of education does not influence the income of an individual.

Gupta (1978) studied the status of secondary school teachers in Eastern U.P. His objective was to study the educational, vocational, social, economic, political, religious and moral status of the secondary school teachers and to give some suggestions for improvement in the status of the secondary school teachers. The study was a social-survey by nature, carried over 2100 subjects in which teachers, students and guardians were represented equally. Data gathered from the teachers through a self-made secondary school teacher's status questionnaire and through an Opinionnaire from the students and guardians. The study reveals that 48 per cent, 64 per cent, 62 per cent and 32.3 per cent of the teachers had second class certificate in high school, intermediate, graduate and post-graduate levels, respectively. Only15.4 percent, 5.5 percent, 1.1 per cent and 0.7 per cent had first class certificates and degrees in the same order. In addition to this, nearly 86.7 per cent teachers are trained. And only 7.2 per cent were desirous to be obtaining training through summer courses or in leave with pay. Further, 62.1 per cent male and 54.2 per cent female teachers had the habit of reading daily newspapers, weeklies and monthly magazines. Only 9.9 per cent teachers predecided to be teachers. For the rest of the respondents, it was situational. In the opinion of 65.1 per cent of the teachers and 56.5 per cent of the guardians the professional status of the secondary teachers was very low and they did not want to make their wards secondary school teachers. 79 per cent teachers and 68.5 per cent guardians were in favour of framing a code of conduct for teachers. 50.5 per cent teachers and 54.5 per cent guardians favoured nationalization of secondary education for raising the status of teachers.

The teachers in rural areas enjoy more social-respect than those in the urban areas. Majority of the teachers, irrespective of their gender was not satisfied with their low salary and they considered it as the key reason for lowering their status. Only 10.5 per cent and 23 per cent male and 6.2 per cent and 20 per cent female teachers were members of different political parties and/or religious associations. The study was a factual and comprehensive survey of the status undertaken with the purpose to find out whether any special relationship exists between the teacher's role perception and his socio-economic status.

Cl(se and open form of a questionnaire was used to collect data from a group o: 856 teachers selected randomly form the population of 5252 teachers of 336 secondary schools of Poona district. Information in this regard was received from 63 per cent of the sample and it was further analyzed following chi-square text.

Findings of the study reveals that considering education, seven items having a significant bearing on the role perception of the teachers where the goal of secondary education satisfying the factors in the teaching profession, functions of teachers, methods of teaching, personal qualities, teaching ability and method of discipline. A good relationship between teaching-experience and role-perception was observed in the context of handling disciplinary problems, organizing ability and method of discipline. The correlation of socio-economic status of the teachers with their role-perception was highly significant with reference to the goals of secondary education, factors in choosing the teaching profession, satisfaction in the profession, functions of secondary teachers, teaching methods, organizing ability, teaching ability, dealing with classroom discipline, problems, methods of discipline and special attention given to outstanding pupils. Lastly the upbringing environment of the teachers (viz., rural-urban variations) is a significant intervening factor to choose the teaching profession, or pedagogy, pedagogic abilities, organizing abilities, solving pedagogic difficulties and satisfying factors in the teaching profession.

Chilukala (1981) studied an important aspect, i.e., the social attitude of Indian Academic Elites towards education. The study at it's outset assumed that in Indian society, like other societies, there are a few elite groups, having a great influence over the society. These groups provide instructive insight for the structural and functional changes in the society. The study was carried out on a sample of academic elites consisting of 570 college and university teachers engaged in research and academic pursuits. Data were collected through a structured questionnaire incorporating three sets of questions, each covering a broad area like attitude towards food habits, marriage, sex, health, wealth, government and policies, labour unions industrial management, individual income, landed property, etc.

Observation of the study reveals that a majority of the elites having an agricultural background was inspired (and further followed) by the wards of while collar jobholders having an urban background. And showed favourable attitude towards socialistic policies of the governments, welfare of the weaker section, a thorough change in the existing educational policies and religious functions. Overall a negative attitude was reflected by the academic elites towards the caste-system, fixation of daily wages, land ceiling, restriction on the individual income, caste-class-restriction and religious fanaticism.

Sharma (1983) carried out a study of relationship between educational level, social status, attitude and family size of middle-aged parents. A questionnaire and two attitude scale was developed to fulfill the objectives of the study and these tools were administered on 593 parents, having different levels of educational qualifications. Two major objectives of this study were to find out the relationship between social status and family size and to analyze the attitude of the parents with different educational status towards the family size. The findings of the study in context of these two objectives reveal that there is a positive correlation between higher socio-economic status and small family and again, education acted as a contraceptive by itself.

Mishra (1975) carried out a cross cultural study of the status and vocational aspiration among aboriginal tribes of Baster district, covering 258 tribal and non-tribal school students of either sexes from different socio-economic strata. Data were collected through an interview-schedule and was analyzed through 't' and 'F' Tests, product moment correlation-technique, ANOVA, ANCOVA and χ^2 tests. The study revealed that the parent (specially the father)'s economic status is not an influential factor to the offspring for choosing their profession. Significant difference was observed between tribal and non-tribals, tribal males and tribal females, upper caste and tribal, lower caste and tribals – in context of the correlation between vocational status score and vocational aspiration scores. The vocational aspiration of different communities did not differ significantly. The study observed that some tribal communities (viz., Raj Gond and Dhun Gond) were highly accultered and are having socio economically distinct feature from other tribal communities (viz. Muras and Bhatras). Probably the most significant observation of the study was that the accultured tribal communities are comparatively distinct in their aspiration and are ethnocentric even from the lower-cast non-tribals.

Adisai (1978)'s study on creativity and socio-economic status is a worth-noting one. An attempt was made by Adisai to compare the creative thinking potentiality of Indian and the Thai students, 300 from each country, falling within the age group of 13^+ to 16^+ years. Torrance and Passi's tests on creative thinking were used to measure the creativity of the sample. It was observed by Adisai that the Thai students were more creative than that of their Indian counterpart, which, however, appears to the present investigator as a biased finding.

A comparison was made between the respondents of different nationality considering the two variables, creativity and socio-economic status, where it was observed that the students from higher socio-economic status, irrespective of their nationality, were more creative. No effect of socio-economic status was observed upon the creative thinking in this study.

Today it is an axiom that education is the most important medium of all because of its capacity to change the society. Vaikuntham (1980) carried out a study, which was based on this axiom. The time span he considered up to 1920 AD proceeded from 1880. All the primary and secondary sources were considered for collecting data. Apart from a good number of findings, one of the important results of the study was the significant upliftment of Harijan and depressed classes (especially Girijans) due to growth of education. The study delved and established the fact that the depressed classes were being slowly assimilated into the mainstream of Hindu society. They began to receive education and join public services and their status improved considerably during the period 1880-1920 by the efforts of the Missionaries, governments and philanthropists who opened good many new schools and provided scholarships and better opportunities in life. People began to reject the traditional community-profession and join public services, which were based on educational attainments. The study reveals that Education had an impact on the religions, communities and outlook of educated people as well.

Arora (1981) investigated the problems of those who are attending professional courses in education and their personality factors, through a problem checklist and creativity test, including their level of aspiration. He adopted various statistical techniques like 't' test, 'chi-square test', 'product moment correlation technique', etc. He found that high problem – trainees in general, are having less personality, adjustment-capacity, creativity, higher aspiration and self-acceptance.

Jain and Shah (1974) carried out a study in Hyderabad, emphasizing the socio-cultural background and Educational aspirations of rural people. The study aimed to examine the extent to which socio-cultural variables such as family size, age, education, occupation, etc. was related to their educational aspirations.

An interview schedule was administered on a sample of 236 subjects of different age groups to collect data, which was further analyzed by chi-square tests. In this study, the age was found to be a significant factor, influencing the aspiration of an individual and the educational aspiration of the younger age group were relatively less than those of older ones. A marked difference was observed between the literate and the illiterate respondents in this regard. The majority (as many as 59 per cent) of literate respondents found aspired for professional education. There seemed to have a positive relationship between the level of education and educational aspiration. The study observed a difference, quite significant, so far the size of family of the respondents and their aspiration for education is concerned. The subjects belonging to joint families were found to be more aspirants aspired than that of the subjects belonging to nuclear families.

Aswal (1982) in his study tried to investigate student-activism in relation to socio-economic conditions in graduate and post-graduate level. The sample size was 705. Activism scale, socio-economic status scale, personality inventory and adjustment inventory were administered to collect data and were treated through χ^2 and t tests. The study finds that a majority of the students were involved with different national level political parties and a quarter of them admitted that they were arrested for student cause. The study observed that the urban activists were more mal-adjusted with their home-life than that of the rural and semi-urbans, which can be correlated with their status. The study revealed that activism, in general was found to be related to higher socio-economic status.

Chitnis and Altbach (1979) edited a volume which deals with teacher's union, the attitude of teachers from higher learning institution, towards education, politics and related issues, the role of teachers in the process of modernization, the working condition and professionalization of teachers.

The theme of the volume reveals that the academic community functioned in a highly complex and generally unfriendly environment and teachers were affected directly by such environment. Despite these constraints, the teaching community played an important role in Indian society. The contradiction between low status and self-esteem and the actual role played by the teachers was part of the ambivalence, which was a theme of some of the articles edited by the authors.

Farooqui (1975) in his study aimed to investigate the socio-economic background, relationship with the remaining social structure, degree of awareness and participation in various life activities of the academic elites. Data for the study were collected from a representative sample of 300 university teachers, 100 students and 100 community members through different interview schedules. Some case history was supplied to supplement the findings. The study observed that the academic elites were highly exposed to the western culture, though having lower economic status compared to the other community members. The study observed a wide gap among teachers students and community members in respect of ideal role of teachers. Again, the study observed that teaching profession had lost its prestige in the hierarchy of professions and teachers were considered influential not because of their academic skill but because of their political affiliations.

Joshi (1981) in his project aimed to find out the educational facilities available in tribal areas in Trivandrum district and to examine the availability and extent of utilization of educational consciousness, causes of higher rate of dropouts of tribal students and also the teachers' role behind the dropout. Data for the purpose of this study were collected from 400 tribal families through interview and from 54 teachers belonging to non-tribal communities through a questionnaire. The study perused a drastic situation in education of the tribals were 73 per cent tribals were illiterate; 82 per cent of the tribal school-children falling in the school going age do not have the facility to avail school education within one kilometer distance of their residence and 86 per cent are lacking the facility within even three kilometer and there were no transportation facilities at all in those areas.

The heads of the tribal families reported that the teachers do not show favourable attitude towards education of tribal children and educational concession given to the tribal students were extremely inadequate.

Teachers, almost all of them were from non-tribal communities, opined that the tribal students are irregular in attendance, poor in vocabulary and are lacking in learning readiness and scholastics but are advanced in sports, games and art. The study reported that the facilities in the home environment are not adequate from this standpoint. Poverty, lack of learning materials, school facilities, parents consciousness, inaccessibility of schools, language-difficulty, task-master's influence and problem of child-labour plây an important role in hindering the development of the tribal-education.

A study similar to Joshi, N.D.'s one was carried out by Joshi, S.D. (1980) which emphasized on the socio-economic and psycho-pedagogical problems of scheduled tribes and caste students of Baroda district. The study was descriptive-survey in nature and was carried out excluding the Baroda city. Socio-economic status questionnaires, covering psycho-pedagogical aspects, in different sets, were prepared to collect data from students, teachers and parents and the collected data were treated through appropriate statistical techniques.

It was found from the study that majority of the students were first-generation learner, having no facilities to study at home and having low level of educo-vocational aspiration, compared to the average, which was reflected in their lack of clarity about their future. The tribal and outcast students suffer from a feeling of diffidence as they are having a clear image of their strengths and weakness. The 'students' are having a positive and better perception towards schools. The study further observed that majority of the teachers belong to upper caste, did not have any specialized training for working with the scheduled caste and scheduled tribe students in backward areas and had their prejudices towards scheduled caste and scheduled tribe students internalized. As a result of prejudices, the teachers suggested only lower level of occupations for their students and did not provide appropriate educational environment to the scheduled caste and scheduled tribe students.

Bihari, L.R. (1969) aimed to find out the nature and extent of wastage and stagnation at primary education among the tribal students and to explore the causes behind the same. Data were collected from 972 tribal families, following a cohort method. He observed that a good number of tribal-saturated villages had no schools. Several schools are on the record but many of them did not really function. The schools, which are really in existence, are having many students on the roles that never attended classes. The percentage of single teacher school in tribal villages is quite higher; whereas the rate of students attending those schools is very low. The study comments that, lack of proper and adequate consciousness for the need of formal education, parents apathy for education, poor socio-economic condition, house-hold work of children, inadequacy, inefficiency and insecurity apart from teachers, curriculum and teaching methods were some of the major factors responsible for wastage and stagnation.

Mani (1977)'s study encompassed to find out the extent, type, nature and trends of social changes as brought about by education and to trace the generational, social and occupational mobility of teachers with reference to their origin. The study was carried out on a sample group of 100 teachers form different levels of educational institutions in eastern Uttar Pradesh. Interview and observational techniques were adopted to collect data pertinent for the study. The major findings of the study reveals that the social origins of persons as teachers were heterogeneous. Teachers emerged from different classes, castes and strata of the society and most of them had emerged from the agricultural background and middle class families. Social status of a teacher depends upon various factors like community in which he was brought up and taught, social origin, the extent and type of his social interaction and other allied factors. All these factors, in a summated way, influence the capability of social participation of the teachers.

Bastia (1982) in his study tried to identify the problems and needs of the tribals pertaining to their social, economic, political and cultural spheres of life and their perception towards education with addition to it's effect on their achievement and Behavioural changes. Apart from the official records, pertinent data were collected following interview and observational technique. The study reveals that essential physical facilities such as supply-water, road, electricity, educational institutions, banks, co-operative societies, scientific methods of cultivation, etc. were beyond their reach. The socio-economic problems are quite acquit among them due to poor knowledge and consciousness. Training programme, organized by different government agencies was ill planned and inadequate. Dropout rate among the age group of 15^+ to 20 years of the tribal students is substantially high due to poor economic condition. Though inadequate, but the equipment which were supplied by the various organization for the sake of tribal-education were not properly used. Study identified the problem in communication between the subjects and non-tribal trainees due to language of the tribals were not known to the trainees and it was reversibly true. Dearth of qualified trainers, pedagogic instruments, irrelevant curriculum and infrequent supervision were the main bottlenecks in spreading education among the tribals. Lastly, the study observed that the impact of education in relation to the functional development of the tribal people in terms of agricultural improvement was negligible.

Sujata (1980) investigated into the constraints of education of a certain tribal community-Yanadis. She tried to study the background of the land and people and socio-economic, religious and political life with existing facilities and problems in mixed villages and tribal colonies of Nellore district in Andhra. A purposive and stratified sampling technique were adopted for the sake of study and data were collected through field investigation, including various methods like interview, spot studies, questionnaire, observation, informal discussion, case history and also through documentary analysis.

The study observed a huge difference between actual attendance and enrolment of the tribal school children in different schools, covered by the study. Further the study revealed that free nature of Yanadi children and instability of family life due to frequent changes of spouses did not help better enrolment of the community concerned. The reasons for poor enrolment were household and agricultural work and lack of interests on the part of Yanadi children. Distance of the school and poverty were the minor influential factors. The tribal parents were not at all interested for the education of their wards, especially of a girl. The curriculum was not related to the culture, life and needs of the Yanadi community, which turned schooling meaningless, suffocating and unrealistic. And lastly while the tribal welfare hostels are providing a homely atmosphere to the tribal students, the schools failed in this aspect, which brought a problem for tribal-school-education.

Vijayalakshmi, J. (1980) studied the extent to which academic achievement and socio-economic status served as predictor of the creative talent. The hypotheses taken for the study were: firstly, High creative differed significantly from the low creative with regard to academic achievement and, secondly, high-creative differed significantly from low creative with regard to socio-economic status.

The sample was collected from six selected secondary schools of urban and rural Kerala. Sample size was 425. Stratified proportional sampling techniques were adopted for selecting the sample.

Nair's Kerala University Test of Creative thinking and Nair's Socio-economic status scale data-sheet were used for collecting data required for the study, which were further analyzed through t-test.

Major findings of the study reveals that there was significant difference between the high and low creative in academic achievement and socio-economic status; The average academic achievement of the high creative was more than the average academic achievement of the low creative and Socio-economic status had a facilitating effect on the creative ability of the pupils.

Marker, N.S. (1975) carried out a survey on teacher-education in Maharashtra state and tried to trace the development of teacher-education in the communist countries and in USA, UK and Thailand.

The secondary teacher-training colleges were surveyed through an Opinionnaire, a questionnaire and interview, which were further supported by records, reports and documents.

The major findings of the survey reveals that there was substantial increase in the colleges of education since independence and the expenditure on colleges of education also pursued an upward trend in various five-year plans. Increase in the number of trained teachers was more marked than that of untrained teachers. Physical resource development predominated human-resource development in teacher-education programme. Students were dissatisfied with the teaching and evaluation; there was no significant improvement in the quality of teacher-education at the secondary level.

Raina, V.K. (1981) carried out a factorial study on the personalities, attitude towards teaching and level of creativity of 'in-service' and 'student-teachers' belonging to three subject areas. The major objectives of the study was to study personality, attitude to teaching and creative potential of pre-service and in-service teachers.

The sample consisted of 180 in-service teachers and 180 pre-service-teachers specializing in the teaching of science, arts, and commerce subjects. Each group in both the samples consisted of sixty subjects. The in-service teachers belonged to 18 high and higher secondary schools and the preserves teachers belonged to four colleges of education of Ajmer district.

Sixteen personality factors test, standardized by Kapoor and Mehrotra, Minnesota Teacher Attitude Inventory (MTAI), Something About Myself (SAM) and Khatena's Measure of Creative Potential (MCP) were the tools used for the study.

The statistical techniques included analysis of variance, t-test, factor analysis and rank order correlations.

The major findings of the inquiry shows that in-service teachers were highest on factors H (Shy Vs adventurous), C (less stable Vs. more stable), E (submissive Vs dominant), A (reserved Vs outgoing) and F (Sober Vs happy-go-lucky). They were lowest on factors, B (less intelligent Vs more intelligent), L (trusting Vs suspicious), I (tough-minded Vs tender minded), Q2 (group dependent Vs self-sufficient) and O (placid Vs insecure).

There were no significant differences in the attitude to teaching between the in-service science teachers and the in-service arts teachers and the in-service commerce teachers. However, the pre-service arts, science and commerce teachers differed significantly in their attitude to teaching.

The in-service teachers were highest on the factors of intellectuality, self-strength, environmental sensitivity, individuality, initiative and artistry as measured by the test of creative potential.

Sansanwal, D.N. and Jarial, G.S. (1979) in their study aimed to investigate the personality differences among high and low creative teacher-trainees. The sample for the study consisted of seventy-five B.Ed. students studying in the department of Education of the university of Indore during 1978-79. The tools used were creative personality checklist, developed by Passi and Gerge and Hindi version of Cattels's 16 P.F.

The t-test was applied to test the significance of difference between the mean-scores.

The study reveals that highly-creative group's means score on factor-B was significantly higher than the corresponding mean score of the low creative groups which indicated that a student from high creative group was quick to grasp ideas, was a fast-learner and intelligent. On the other hand the low-creative group was slow to learn and grasp and was dull.

The high-creative group tended to be cheerful, active, talkative, frank, expressive, effervescent and carefree, while the low-creative group was sometimes dour, pessimist and unduly deliberates.

On factor L, the low-creative group's mean score was significantly higher compared to high creative group. This indicates that the low creative group tended to be mistrusting and doubtful. They tended to be involved in their own ego, were self opinionated and interested in internal and mental life. On the other hand, the high-creative group tended to be free of jealous tendencies, adaptable, cheerful, uncompetitive and concerned about other people.

The low creative group tended to be tense, excitable, restless, fretful and impatient, where as the high-creative group tended to be sedate, relaxed, composed and satisfied.

Except these four factors, the two groups did not show any significant difference of the other twelve factors.

Kundu, C.L. (1966)'s study was to some extent different, though not irrelevant in the present context. He studied the personality traits of tribal and non-tribal delinquents and non-delinquents, i.e., normal, and evolved a suitable educational programme for tribal and non-tribal delinquents.

The study was carried out on a sample of tribal and non-tribal court convicted delinquents and non-delinquents, 25 from each group, and ten cases of juvenile murderers belonging to de-notified tribes and ten non-delinquent-non-tribes of age range 11+ to 16 years. The court-convicted cases were selected from Udaipur and Tonk jails. The sample size was 120 with a distribution of (25 × 4) + (10 × 2).

Observation, interview, jail records, life history, Bhatia's battery of performance test and Rorschach's Ink-blot test on personality were the different data gathering tools and techniques, used in the study.

Collected data were analyzed through chi-square test, contingency co-efficient, F test, pooled variance and t-test.

The study revealed that, for the tribals, delinquency was related moderately to instability at home, less degree of satisfaction with self, poor health condition and power of observation and the relation was low with poor sleeping condition. Low general intelligence was related significantly to delinquency of both tribal and non-tribal groups. The non-associative factors for delinquency in tribals were – desire to be away from home; parent-child relationship; parents objection to the kind of companion; permanence of residence; position in the family; level of general anxiety; feeling of resentment; depressive trends and originality.

Bhattacharya, S.K. (1984) carried out a study entitled "Social Stratification and the system of Education – A study of social Mobility in three generation in West Bengal". The study aimed to examine:

(*i*) The relationship between the availability of differentially distributed educational opportunities for the individuals and groups in the socio-economic situation during 1984 at West Bengal and their utilization reflected in the differential placements of individuals and groups in the then socio-economic structure,

(*ii*) The way in which the educational opportunities provided by the socio-economic structure of West Bengal were utilized by the individuals belonging to different socio-economic strata,

(*iii*) The nature and degree of social mobility facilitated by differential socio-economic educational structure and

(*iv*) The sub-system-level particularities of the educational structure in relation to the different social-strata in West Bengal.

225 families, 21 educational institutions and 51 working organizations from four regions with different socio-economic set up were taken as sample for the study following a stratified-random sampling method.

Data were collected through interview schedules and questionnaires, developed by the investigator.

Collected data were analyzed by statistical measures like chi-square test, Spearman's rank-corelation, etc.

The study reveals that inequality of educational opportunity has existed in the state for a long run past. The observation on social mobility over three generations revealed that majority of the population having lower social strata remained socially immobile. Social mobility was somewhat evident in the middle class but it was restricted within the overall boundaries, whereas upper class-people could not protect and maintain their status in the society but enhanced their attributes over the years. The study further reveals that inequality of educational opportunities emerged out of the interaction of logistic support and cultural inequalities at home with the organizational climate and effectiveness of the system of education. The system of education stabilized the status and the impact of the system of education acted as reinforcement to social stratification and inequality.

Chakraborty, H. (1984) in his study aimed to observe the various socio-economic and socio-cultural problems hindering educational dynamism in a backward society and to understand the relation between occupation and demand for (elementary) education followed by some other objectives.

Students from 10 primary and 8 secondary schools, teachers, 46 in number from those schools and 26 social workers from eight villages in Purulia district constitutes the sample.

Community information blank (CIB), school-information schedule, checklist and interview schedule were the tools used for the study to collect the needed data from the sample. The design of the study was classificatory in nature considering converted percentages and ranks from frequency-count. The study reveals that the overall rate of educational dynamism for boys was quite higher, compared to their 'girl' counterparts and again it was highest for caste-Hindus and lowest for scheduled tribes within the Hindu fold. Educational opportunities in terms of their utility to the community did not directly restrict educational dynamism, but it was not conducive to the mass-scale programme of primary education. The study observed a wide conflict of opinion among teachers, social workers and guardians regarding non-participation; Teachers considered 'ignorance and illiteracy of guardians' as the major causes for non-participation of both boys and girls whereas social workers considered the prevalent social habit of not sending children to schools' and guardians considered 'inconvenient school hours' (for boys) and 'prevalent social habits' (for girls) as major causes of the low participation of the school – going – aged boys and girls in education.

Joshi, N.D. (1985) carried out a survey on the socio-economic and educational conditions of the tribals in Kerala. 242 teachers, 50 welfare officers, 50 social workers and local leaders from 30 tribal communities of Kerala constituted the sample. The study was descriptive as well as analytical survey in nature. Questionnaire, rating scale, interviews, socio-economic status scale, participatory and non-participatory observation were the tools and techniques, adopted for the study. Secondary sources like, records in government offices and in schools were also analyzed to collect the data, required for the study.

The studies observed that majority of the tribes were extremely backward in their socio-economic and educational context. The tribal groups were not fully conscious of their backwardness, exploitation, sanitary needs, economic improvement, opportunities, civic-rights and responsibilities.

The attitude of the tribals towards government officers was on the whole positive; they had adjusted somewhat to the new job-opportunities, but still maintained some of their traditional cultural activities; the tribal students, who attended the ordinary schools were below average in studies and above average in sports and cultural activities; lack of accommodation, lack of traveling facilities, unsuitable location of schools, inconvenient school buildings, shortage of materials and the like where the major difficulties faced by the teachers in tribal areas; the traditional dwellings of the tribals were very poor and did not have facilities for children's study at home. Many of the houses allotted to tribals by the government were not properly built and some of the tribals were not willing to live in tiled and white washed houses.

Adiseshiah, M.S. and Ranathan, S. (1974) took up a project to collect reliable and relevant information to assess the types and extent of educational problems of schools and college students belonging to scheduled caste and scheduled tribe communities and simultaneously to make an objective evaluation of the government policies for those students and further planned to suggest measures, if to achieve better and quicker results with their implications to the present policy and method of implication.

The study was conducted on a sample of 1027 respondents, selected from forty institutions, taking two schools and two colleges each from the five scheduled caste districts and five scheduled tribes districts of Tamilnadu. The four fold break-up of the sample was (i) 232 scheduled caste and 59 non-scheduled caste school students and 50 teachers, including head-teachers; (ii) 187 scheduled caste colleges students, 51 non- scheduled caste college students and 70 college teachers, including principals; (iii) 174 scheduled tribe school students, 51 non scheduled tribe school students and 48 teachers including head-teachers and (iv) 47 scheduled tribe college students, 16 non-scheduled tribe college students and 30 college teachers including principals. The multi-staged-random sampling technique was adopted for the study.

Questionnaires, interview-schedules, census publications, government records and reports were used to collect data, pertinent to the study. Data were quantified and statistical mapping of the education conditions of scheduled castes and tribes were tried.

The study revealed that rate of school attendance seemed to vary inversely with the size of the tribe; the tribal students did not participate in extra-curricular activities; the tribal girl-students had clear educational and professional aspirations and unlike the boys did not find teaching as difficult. Smaller tribes had proportionately higher college youths than the larger tribes, although majority of the tribal students reported of financial difficulties, only 6.4 per cent were totally dependent upon state-scholarship. A higher percentage of scheduled tribe students opted for arts courses; those who opted for science had reportedly a comfortable financial position; in spite of their financial difficulties, majority of the tribal students planned to continue up to the post-graduate level. The unique finding of this study is the girl-students from tribal communities, interviewed, had never failed; aimed at post-graduation, expect one and they wanted to become teacher.

Bose, S. (1963) in his investigation attempted to study the socio-psychological background of adolescent tribal children from Himalayan region of West Bengal for the purpose of national integration in relation to co-curricular participation.

The sample consisted of 1000 adolescent school going tribal children from Nepali, Lepcha and Bhutia tribes, residing in the hill towns of Darjeeling district.

Data for the study collected through a multiphasic inventory, consisting of168 items prepared in Likert's method (the language of the inventory was Nepali) and through Darley and McNemar's Minnesota Personality scale.

The study revealed that the children of middle socio-economic status were educationally backward having religious communal feelings and were not rigid about inter-tribal group relations. The respondents also spoke in favour of regular participation and making efforts towards forming a cohesive and cooperative group.

Chitnis, Suma (1974) took up a project to assess the status of the scheduled caste and scheduled tribe students in the institutions of learning and also to identify the kinds of discrimination and types of difficulties and obstacles that they face.

It was observed from the study that among Scheduled tribe students, very few women went for higher education. Majority of the tribal students were first-generation learner and are from disadvantaged home in rural areas where their father involved in rural occupations. It was observed that scheduled tribes are more disadvantaged than the students belonging to scheduled caste communities and by and large they were in the arts faculty and not at all akin to co-curricular activities due to their appreciably high educational and occupational aspiration. The majority of the tribal students had a very poor opinion of the educational facilities provided to them and they seemed to be quite aware about the job-facilities for them. The study revealed that majority of the students had exposure to mass media but level of politicization was very poor. Mostly they made a choice of a career entirely on their own. One of the unique findings of this study was the tribal females and girls are better-integrated with other communities than the males. According to the teachers, the scheduled students were as good as or slightly poorer than other students and younger teachers were least sympathetic to these students in respect of their academic calibration and the facilities provided to them.

An investigation aimed at developing a profile of education among the scheduled tribes of Gujarat was carried out by Desai, I.P. (1970) in terms of state literacy, change in literacy between 1961 and 1971 decadal period, changes in enrolment at the primary, secondary and higher stages of education, the distribution of primary and secondary schools, and the utilization of hostel and scholarship facilities.

For the purpose of collecting data a profile was developed on the basis of information available in the census reports and other official record of the Department of Education and Social Welfare of the Gujrat Government.

The major findings of the study revealed that during the decade of 1961-1971 when the enrolment in primary school raised up to 73 per cent, the literacy among scheduled tribes rose up to only of 2.43 per cent. Only 6 per cent of the students in primary school went to the secondary schools and only 11.8 per cent of the tribal students went to the higher education. An important observable trend in enrolment was the increase in the number of women students at the primary and secondary education level. The pathetic observation of the study was, that out of 8732 villages in the tribal-districts, there was not a single school in 1736 villages and these villages were unevenly distributed over different taluks.

The researchers conducted a survey over 235 scheduled tribes students and pertinent data were collected through questionnaire, interview and census literature. For the partial fulfillment of the study, 108 non- scheduled tribes, 193 scheduled caste students and 156 teachers were also requested to provide information.

The study revealed that, in large number of cases the scheduled tribe students were first-generation learner and the percentage of primary educated parents being large among non-scheduled tribes. Adult education seemed to have made very little impact on the spread of literacy. Ideationally the tribal students were more nationalistic as indicated by their choice of ideal persons than the scheduled caste students who gave the first place to the leaders of their caste and community and the second place to the national leaders. The tribal students participated largely in the co-curricular activities and without any inhibition. In their general interactions with other students and teachers, the tribal students did not feel discriminated and they were found to cherish the values and norms of their surrounding non scheduled tribe society. A good percentage of tribal students believed that their condition had improved, but their status still remain lower than that of their non-tribal friends. By and large, the tribal students felt that governmental policies were helpful to them and should be continued. But there were some, who believe that governmental help is creating a sense of dependency in them.

Dubey, S.M. (1974) undertook a study to investigate the socio-economic background of the SC and ST college students of Assam and to see how their education affected their aspirations and performance, their way of life, their participation in other activities and their feeling and opinion about their status. The study was conducted on a sample of 246 scheduled caste, 223 scheduled tribe students and 129 teachers from 20 colleges. Random sampling technique was adopted for the study. Questionnaires and interview guide were the research tools used for collecting data from the sample.

The study observed that majority of the tribal students were the first-generation learners. The tribal students had high educational and occupational aspiration. The study revealed that degree of relationship between teachers and tribal students was very low. A small percentage of tribal students, participating in political activities. Tribal students felt that their socio-economic conditions had improved. Most of the tribal students received their education as being a hostler and a significant percentage of them were exposed to mass media. Participation of tribal girls, in higher education was extremely low.

George, E.I. (1975) in a study similar to those of Dube, S.M. (1974), Desai, I.P. (1974) and others, finds that the number of scholarships offered to the tribal students was inadequate and the system of disbursement was complicated. The study suggested that the tribal parents need to be educated about the governmental programmes in order to ensure proper utilization of resources. The study finds it irrelevant to allot separate hostels for tribal students and commented the practice as 'Socially unhealthy" as it widened the gap between tribal and other non-tribal students. It was observed that a considerable number of scheduled tribe students suffered from certain feeling of inferiority and they needs to be protected through proper guidance and if possible, through vocational training in order to be self-dependent. Good number of the teachers were found to be always with a helping attitude, which encouraged the tribal students.

Education has its tremendous impact on any social setting. Lakra, S. (1976)'s study in this respect is worth-noting. He kept forward the objective to investigate into the damages that had occurred due to education in the tribal people, especially in their socio-economic and political spheres. The sample included the representative tribes, viz., the Mundas, the Oraons and the Kharias.

Data were collected with the help of mailed questionnaire from the educated tribals in the urban and rural areas of Ranchi district. Personal-interview, observation and case study were the other methods for collecting required data.

Progress of education of these tribes before and after independence and its impact on their social, cultural, political and economic development have been presented historically.

Before the advent of the missionaries, the tribal *gowned* under the *grinding* heels of poverty and debt. The Christian missionaries, having *proselyfication* as their objective, did some laudable efforts to spread education among the tribals and protected them from the clutches of moneylenders. Education brought three fold benefits to them, viz., they got their lands back, got emancipation from forced labour and had their self respect reinforced. During the year 1857 the work of the missionaries was disturbed due to *Sepoy Mutiny*, but as soon as the peace was restored, it was taken up with double vigor. During the year 1863, more impetus were given to girl's education. Though Roman Catholic Church began its work late, it spread a network of schools, hospitals and churches in the tribal belt of Ranchi district. Conversation reached its peak in 1885. As tribal language was not the medium of instruction, tribals started liking English and forgot their own dialect. In the same vein, they began to develop a test for western music and dance and neglected their own heritage of music and dance. Standard of living rose with the level of education, but the economic status did not rise proportionately. Education made them free from poverty, ignorance, social taboos and superstitions. Even though the tribals went up to high school only, there was a change in their outlook towards life. They picked up clean habits about food, shelter, dress and gave-up the habits of discipline, thrift, hard work, etc. Gradually the tribals became education-conscious and sent their children to schools.

Girl's education made headway in the first-quarter of twentieth century and they were admitted to co-educational institutions. The tribals gradually became politically conscious and fused their several associations into *Adibasi Maha-Sabha*.

With the dawn of independence, educated tribals were at an advantageous position but they were in need of training for specific job-skills and more education. Gradually, the social distance between Christians and others began to disappear. The intelligentsia among the tribals is highly qualified in the fields of arts, science, medicine, technology, agriculture, law, etc. Less educated tribal-youths were gradually becoming delinquents because of various unwanted situations. Primarily agriculturist tribals were gradually migrating to cities, neglecting agriculture, tribal-handcraft and traditional mode of living. Recently there has been a re-awakening among more educated and brighter section for the preservation of all the good in the culture of the tribals.

Vyas, N.N. and Chaudhary, N.D. (1970) carried out a study on the drop-outs in a tribal situation. The major objectives of the study were (i) to assertion the extent and magnitude of wastage and stagnation amongst students belonging to scheduled tribes, scheduled castes and other castes and (ii) to analyse the factors responsible for wastage and stagnation in education among the students. The study was conducted extensively and intensively. The extensive study covered primary stage of education in Kotra and Jhadol Panchayat Samitis. The intensive study covered primary, middle, secondary and higher secondary stages of education in a sample of schools in the same panchayat samities. Questionnaire was used for the extensive study, whereas interview technique was used for the intensive study. Wastage was measured by calculating total number of dropouts, whereas stagnation was measured by the percentage ratio of students who failed in a class to the total number of students who took the examination in the same class.

The study revealed that incidence of dropouts and stagnation occurred among students belonging to scheduled tribes, scheduled castes and other castes and there was no evidence to show that it occurred more amongst a particular group of boys and girls. At times the percentage of dropouts and stagnation was found more among students of other castes than among the students of scheduled tribes. The parents of the tribal students were engaged only in agriculture whereas the parents of scheduled caste students were engaged in agriculture and also in their traditional occupations.

Om Prakash, S. (1986) carried out an in-depth survey, underlining the causes of educational, psychological and social problems of the student of Indian Institute of Technology, Kanpur.

The sample consisted of 160 socially advantaged and 80 socially disadvantaged B.Tech students of I.I.T., Kanpur.

Tools used for the purpose of collecting data were students profile, under-privileged Students Interaction Scale, family-information questionnaire, Bell's adjustment inventory. Students Personal Problems index (by Wig & Nagpal, 1980) and a self devised interview schedule.

Collected data were treated by descriptive statistical techniques, t-test, product-moment-co-relation, chi-square and factor-analysis.

The study revealed that those who were socially advantaged (SA), were better adjusted than that of their socially disadvantaged (SDA) counterparts with regard to academic, social, financial and psychological dimensions. SDA's had problem in all these four dimensions of adjustment. The socially advantaged did not perceive any difficulty that the socially disadvantaged ones faced during academic interaction. The socially advantaged group did not have healthy social interaction with the socially disadvantaged group. The socially disadvantaged students did not enjoy much happiness as compared to their socially advantaged counterparts. The academic measures indicated that disadvantaged students were trailing behind the socially advantaged students in all the four academic years. Socially advantaged students had conducive family-size, better interaction of father with child, better financial position, higher educational background of family and progressive ideas and composite childhood experiences. Study revealed that socially disadvantaged students had maximum problems in academic area, which led to frustration. Social distance being imposed on the backward community students forced them to withdraw into solitary and isolated shells enhancing a feeling of insecurity and to add more, counseling did not help them, due to it's poor administration.

Shah, K. (1982) in his investigation studied the socio-economic conditions of primary-school-teachers to ascertain their status of education to enquire about their attitude towards job, to find out the problems they faced in their profession and to enquire into their job-satisfaction.

475 teachers from 78 primary schools, situated within the Varanasi Corporation area formed the sample for the study. A stratified-random sampling technique was followed for selecting sample.

Data for the study were collected through interview and were analyzed with the help of simple percentage.

Major findings of the study revealed that majority of the teachers in primary level were female and were Brahmin by caste and were from lower-middle class.

Neither the educational level of the subjects, nor of their family was remarkable. Majority of the subjects belonged to joint family and were religious-minded. The study further revealed that almost all the teachers were satisfied with their job but dissatisfied with the low pay scale; till they wished to stay in the profession. Teachers reported that there were very few opportunities for professional growth and other facilities, i.e., pension, residence and medical benefits. Despite low scale of pay, the subjects preferred 'teaching' because it traditionally commanded high esteem. The teachers discussed the problems related to their job. Prominent among those were low salary, lack of different kinds of physical facilities, poor buildings and poor teaching-materials.

Chopra, R.K. (1993) in her study aimed at investigating the status of teachers in India with three specific objectives, viz., (i) to investigate into the status of teaching manpower in terms of quality and quantity at different levels, (ii) to assess academic, economic, professional and social status of teachers in India and (iii) to found out the areas of improvement and deficiencies in order to suggest future programmes for action to accelerate teacher development.

Data were collected through a detailed questionnaire covering three major aspects of status, viz., professional education, economic status and professional status from different administrative agencies and reports were analyzed keeping the objectives specified for the study in view.

The study explored national scenario in terms of teacher's status with special reference to the components of status, viz., progress achieved in school education, teachers and their qualification, professional participation of teachers, recruitment procedure of teachers, service condition of teachers, working condition and economic status, social status, professional status and draw a comparison of those.

Review of Few Research Programmes Carried out Abroad

Foster, M. (1994)'s research based article, entitled 'Teaching diverse population: Formulating a knowledge base' published from New York Press, was basically a review of DATABASE on African American teachers after 1980. It comes with suggestion stressing the need to increase the number of African-American (an ethnic community) teachers. The justification advanced here is very often a role-model argument rather than an analysis of any unique characteristics. In this context, pedagogy or philosophy of education is believed to be presented by African-American teachers who work primarily with African-American students.

Goodson, I. (1988) in the study 'Teachers, life histories and studies of curriculum and school' did not consider the influence of racial identity on their belief system. This is despite the fact that the previous life experience of teachers, their backgrounds, identities, culture and the critical incidents in their life-helped them to shape their view of teaching.

Provenzo, E. (1988) in his study 'Black and White teachers : Patterns of similarity and difference over twenty years' observed that both the black and white group of teachers differs in various dimensions. Provenzo observed that majority of the black and white group of teachers differ so far as their job satisfaction patterns is concerned and also with regard to their perception of status of their profession and school-environment and both the groups believe that changes are required in order to educated African-American students effectively.

Murrell, P. (1991) in his article entitled 'Cultural Politics in Teacher Education: what missing in the preparation of minority teachers?' Comes with the conclusion that significant difference exists in the belief system between the Anglo teachers and the African Black teachers.

Sterling, P. (1972) in his survey over the ethnic group of teachers, reported under the title 'The real teachers' 30 inner – city school teachers talk honestly about who they are, how they teach and why ?' says that positive portrayals of teachers from ethnic groups are infrequent especially when compared with those of white teachers. As a result, researchers have perhaps unwilling through omission, draw excessively negative portrayals and conveyed the idea that African American teachers are indifferent uncaring and un-sympathetic.

Foster, M. (1990) in another study entitled 'The Politics of Race: Through African American teacher's Eyes examined the beliefs and practices of effective African-American teachers have found that such teachers from ethnic communities have strong attachments to the black community and considered themselves as part of their own indigenous community.

Foster, M. (1991) in her other case-based study entitled 'Just got to find a way" Case studies of the lives and practice of exemplary Black high School teachers' noticed that, unprompted-irrespective of gender and grade level, more than 50 per cent of her sample used kin terms of metaphors to describe their relationship with students through which they use to solve different socio-personal problem of the students from their own community. With a broader illustration, the subjects opined that the Black teachers have to convince Black students of how important education is, and how they are all part of the Black umbilical cord, because a lot of black teachers-though not consciously, but are forgetting about their own roots, about how they are connected to the cord and about everyone they are left behind.

Ladson-Billings, G. (1991) in his study-paper on 'Returning to the source: Implications for educating teachers of Black students' observed that the attachments between the black teachers and black students were further strengthened by intergenerational employment and extended community-residence patterns of Afro-American Teachers. The case-evidence of the study further suggests that in many cases, these interactions extended beyond school into larger community.

Casey, K. (1990) in her case-based article, entitled 'Teachers as mother: Curriculum theorizing in the life-histories of contemporary woman teachers' published from Cambridge Journal of Education, observed that interrelationship is a prominent feature of contemporary African-American family life – with particular to those who are occupying institutional-roles (say teachers). Non the less, almost without exception, connectedness to black communities seem to be a recurring theme which is being practiced widely and becoming a feature of the teachers from ethnic-communities.

Siddle-Walker (1993) in her research based article entitled 'Relationship between Community and School' emphasized the salience and pervasiveness of caring relationships within the different components of educational environment. With live example, she shows how caring was expressed in the daily interaction between teachers and students from the ethnic communities and how students responded to an atmosphere of inter-personal setup. She also analyzed the implications of those findings for current school reforms.

Conclusion

A detail perusal of the 'review' clearly shows that the studies carried out in India on 'tribal education' at the outset of sixtieth decade, specially emphasized on the various school aspects – such as school curriculum, medium of instruction, massive drop out and stagnation of the students from tribal communities, etc. These studies are by nature, mostly exploratory and diagnostic and in some cases, influence of economy and effect of habitation was also taken into consideration by the respective researchers. The findings of these studies have a restricted significance for the present research.

Further, a large number of research works reviewed in the latter phase were conducted by the institutions like NIEPA, ICSSR, NCERT, etc. long time ago, and in the mean time, they perhaps has lost their validity even in the specific areas where those studies were conducted. These studies were basically on socio-economic background of the students, pedagogical problems of the tribal students and the general teachers, facilities availed by the tribal students, their cognitive and non-cognitive aspects, attitude towards education, socio-cultural background, poverty and also on the planning process of tribal education as well as the incentives in terms of hostel facilities and rarely on teachers from Indian tribes.

Therefore, a gap in respect of data and the variables can easily be perceived from the review of the researches. The present study is expected to fill the gaps, at least partially, with regard to the tribal teachers status. The author has also come across about thirty studies carried out abroad on various indigenous communities out of which ten studies has a direct bearing with the teacher education of those communities. Such studies were conducted in very recent past, emphasizing on curriculum, language, classroom problems, teaching constraints on academic life, race–politics, gender issues on education, teacher education and its loop-holes and school community-relationship of the indigenous people.

After reviewing all these studies in specific, conducted in India and thirty studies from abroad on the tribal education and education of the indigenous people respectively, it was observed that hardly any study has yet been carried out in India encompassing the status of tribal teacher so far. The research studies reviewed in the foregoing sections of this chapter has enlightened the another to single out the appropriate and necessary aspects of the status of the tribal teacher which should be thoroughly investigated into. Again the review of research has provided an idea to the another about the methodology to be adopted in terms of sources of data, procedure to be followed for collecting data and to analyze and interpret those. Keeping these points in view, methodology and the approach for the present investigation has been deduced, which has been discussed in the next chapter.

4

Method to Study the Teachers from Tribal Denomination

In the absence of study in the area of the status profile of the tribal teachers the author has adopted a compound approach to study the teachers from tribal denomination. The present chapter provides details regarding the method that has been adopted for carrying out the work with respect to each objective.

Data: Nature and Sources

The present study adopted the existing approach in educational research along with the ethnographic, as well as psycho-graphic approaches. The approach adopted in context of collecting required data is a composite approach which can be treated as an "Anthropological approach in educational research", and has already been illustrated in the theoretical framework of the study. However, a methodological diagram is presented in Table 4.1 to have a familiarity with the methodology of the present study at a glance.

The required data for the study were obtained from the sources classified as follows:

Exploration of the Field

The field of the study was explored through inter-communication with the District Education Officers (DEO's), District Inspectors of Schools (DIS's) as well as the other allied educational officials of different districts, visits to district headquarters. During the field survey it was observed that data supplied by the government educational officials, in many a cases, were quite obsolate and author was explored the base-line data with the help of the local and Regional Teacher's Associations and the non-government agencies and organizations, active in those remote parts of the field.

Exploration of Documents

To drive the study in its proper direction and thereby to reach the objectives, the number of documents had been explored in addition to the research literatures, to acquire data.

Table 4.1: Methodological Diagram of the Study

Objectives →	*Data-gathering, Tools/Techniques* →	*Nature of the Tools/Techniques* →	*Sources of Data and Their Number* →	*Nature of the Data*
1. To study socio-economic and academic status of the tribal teachers	Status questionnaire	Self-developed and Standardized	Tribal Teachers N = (150 × 2)	Qualitative as well as quantitative
2. To ascertain the aspiration for professional education and constraints faced by the tribal teachers in pursuing education during their student-hood.	Status questionnaire	Self-developed and Standardized	Tribal Teachers N = (150 × 2)	Qualitative as well as quantitative
3. To explore the professional relationship of the tribal teachers with their colleagues	Status questionnaire Attitude Scale Problem checklist & Follow up Observation	Self-developed and Standardized	Tribal Teachers N = (150 × 2)	Qualitative as well as quantitative Quantitative Quantitative Qualitative
4. To analyze the role of Government of Assam and Government of West Bengal for the improvement of status of the tribal teachers	Documentary Survey Interview Attitude Scale	Self-developed Self-organized Self developed & Standardized	Documents & Resource Persons, (N = 40); Tribal teachers N = (150 × 2) Do	Qualitative Qualitative Qualitative Quantitative
5. To study the attitude of the tribal teachers towards their profession, students, colleagues, government, society and working environment	Attitude Scale	Self-developed & Standardized	Tribal Teachers (N = 150 × 2)	Quantitative
6. To explore psychographic status of the tribal teachers as reflected by their level of Creativity (as a composite ability of Originality, flexibility and fluency)	Torrance Test of Creative Thinking (TTCT)	Adopted and Translated	Tribal Teachers (N = 150 × 2)	Quantitative
7. To explore the status of the tribal teachers within their own indigenous community	Participatory observation cum discussion	Self-organized	Indigenous Community groups (4 × 2)	Qualitative
8. To identify the problems faced by the tribal teachers in their professional environment	Problem Checklist	Self-developed and Standardized	Tribal Teachers (N = 150 × 2)	Quantitative

Consultation with the Experts

Essential data as well as information, required to carry out the study was creamed out by the way of formal consultation and asking opinion to a group of experts and scholars – particularly knowledgeable in tribal culture and education. This experts-scholar-group includes forty members, twenty from each state, incorporating eminent educationists, sociologists, and officials from government, non-government and voluntary organizations and are involved in welfare programmes for the tribal-upliftment. The expert-group was formed keeping proportionate weightage on their ascribed status.

Consultation with the Indigenous Community Groups

Participatory discussion was carried out in an informal manner with a few of eight indigenous tribal communities with a view to explore the status of the tribal teachers within their own indigenous community. The groups with which the consultation – sessions were carried out were *Barmans, Karbi, Mizo* and *Rabha* from the state of Assam and the *Santhals, Bhumij, Munda* and *Oraon* from West Bengal.

As the purpose of the technique was to explore the status of the teacher within his/her own indigenous community, so the discussion centered round their relationship with the teacher from their own community.

Sampling Technique

Basic first-hand data were collected from a sample group of educated Tribal people, involved in teaching profession at secondary school level. These group of 'sample' tribal teachers were considered as the major source of data. The estimated size of the population was 37427 tribal secondary school teachers from two states during study.

A stratified – random sampling technique was adopted to draw the sample group of tribal teachers from both the states. The sampling technique ensured proper representation of each and every sub-division within the districts concerned. The sample size was 300, incorporating 150 respondents from each state.

The five districts covered from Assam were Cachar, Hailakandi, Karimganj, North Cachar Hills District and Karbi Anglong. Rest five districts taken from West Bengal were Birbhum, Bankura, Purulia, Undivided Midnapore (during the study) and North 24 Parganas – covering some part of the greater Kolkata. All these ten districts were taken keeping in view the tribal population density as well as the density of the secondary schools therein.

A Brief Classification of Data Sources

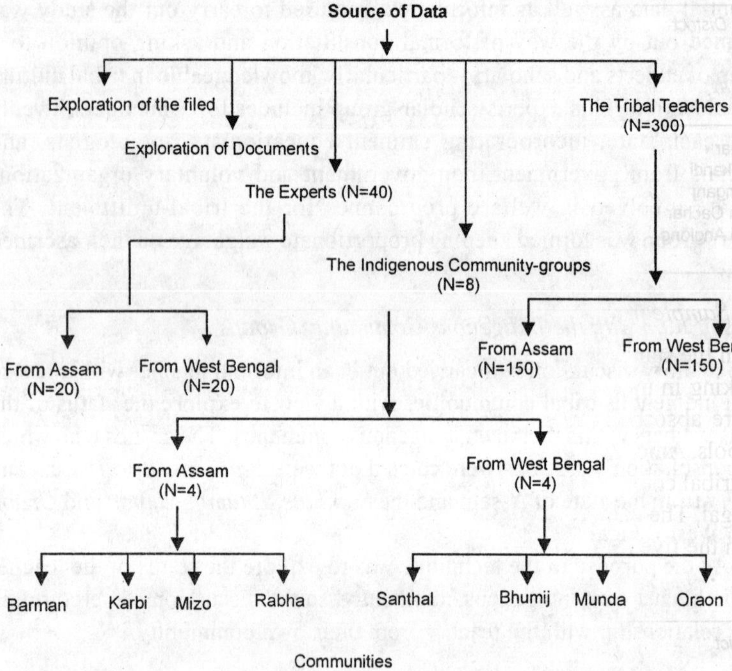

The national scenario reveals that during the study 4258260 teachers are absorbed in various levels of schools throughout the country. Out of them 732187 male and 390249 female teachers, together forming a group of 1122436 teachers are absorbed in 160182 middle school scattered over the country.

On the other hand 955884 male and 489812 female teachers, comprising a total of 1445696 teachers are engaged in 63663 high and higher secondary schools in the country during study.

The estimated numbers of tribal teachers, working in all these types of secondary schools (including the schools having any of the class – grade VIII-XII) throughout the country, numbered around 179769 are constituting the universe of the present study.

The Sample from Assam

In the state of Assam the total number of teachers engaged in teaching at school level (excluding the primary schools) was 166720 and were absorbed in 6944 middle schools and 2906 high and higher secondary schools. Among them 15004 teachers at the secondary level belonged to the tribal communities. The distribution of teachers from the five districts of Assam is presented in Table 4.2.

Table 4.2: The Sample from Assam

District	*Number of Schools*		*Total Number of Teachers at Secondary Level*	*Tribal Teachers*		*Number of Sampled Tribal Teachers at Secondary Level*
	Middle	*High/Higher Secondary*		*Total no. at Secondary Level*	*Per cent*	
Cachar	309	106	2209	26	1.177	26
Hailakandi	264	36	1690	03	0.178	03
Karimganj	266	65	2069	08	0.004	08
North Cachar Hills	79	41	912	117	12.83	49
Karbi Anglong	173	118	1528	192	12.565	64
Total	1091	336	8408	346	4.155	150

The Sample from West Bengal

From the state of West Bengal during the study the total number of teachers working in middle and secondary school level was 280291. These teachers where absorbed in 2856 middle schools and 4513 high/higher secondary schools. Among this group of secondary school teachers those who belong to the tribal communities where numbered around 22423 from the state of West Bengal. The district-wise distribution of the tribal secondary school teachers from the five districts of West Bengal can be perused in Table 4.3.

Table 4.3: The Sample from West Bengal

District	*Number of Schools*		*Total Number of Teachers at Secondary Level*	*Tribal Teachers*		*Number of Sampled Tribal Teachers at Secondary Level*
	Middle	*High/Higher Secondary*		*Total No. at Secondary Level*	*Per cent*	
Cachar	309	106	2209	26	1.177	26
Hailakandi	264	36	1690	03	0.178	03
Karimganj	266	65	2069	08	0.004	08
North Cachar Hills	79	41	912	117	12.83	49
Karbi Anglong	173	118	1528	192	12.565	64
Total	1091	336	8408	346	4.155	150

The above Table reveals that 346 tribal teachers are teaching at the secondary level in the five districts of Assam and 1497 tribal teacher are working at the same level in the rest five sampled districts from West Bengal. In total 1843 tribal teachers are forming the basic population-group from the ten districts from the two states taken for the study. The population group includes the secondary school teachers from any of the tribal communities from the state of Assam and West Bengal.

Factors and Variables

In order to study the status-profile of the tribal teachers, the following factors and variables were considered:

Factors

- Social Status
- Economic Status
- Academic Status
- Political Status
- Religious Status
- Professional Environment
- Role of Government
- Professional Relationship
- Educational Facilities

Variables

The variables considered for the present study can be classified in two phases, so far their nature is concerned. While some variables are quite independent, others are some how depending on the independent variables. These are as follows:

Independent Variables

- Level of Originality
- Level of Flexibility
- Level of Fluency
- Attitude towards Profession
- Attitude towards Students
- Attitude towards Colleagues
- Attitude towards Government
- Attitude towards Society
- Attitude towards Working Environment

Dependent Variables

(*i*) Creativity (as a composite ability)
(*ii*) Composite attitude

Note: The study includes the variable – 'creativity' as a composite ability of originality, flexibility and fluency. One of the important components of creativity is 'elaboration' which is not included as a variable due to the reason that it is difficult to measure the elaboration capacity.

Operational Definitions of the Key Terms

The key terms used in the present investigation on which the entire study hinges on are:

Status Profile

The concept of 'status-profile' can be better defined in continuation with the concept of 'status'. The terminology "status-profile" indicates the 'holistic-view' of status, which is based upon the interaction-effect of 'status', and its 'various components'. In the present study emphasis has been given to the components having direct (or indirect) intervention over the education of the tribals in general and as reflected by the key-agents from the tribal denomination engaged in imparting education (*i.e.* the tribal teachers). Hence, the status profile of the tribal-teachers is explored through the interaction model presented below:

Diagrammatic Sketch of Status Profile

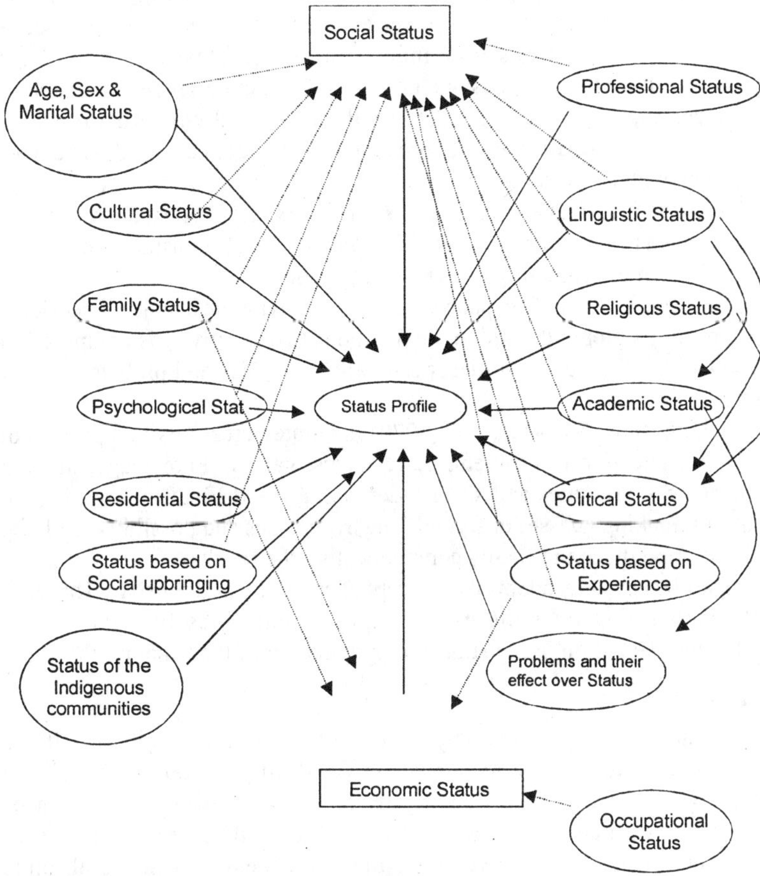

Tribal Teachers

The person who belongs to the scheduled tribe community according to the respective state-list of scheduled-tribes and are engaged in teaching profession in the schools of Assam and West Bengal with any of the class-grades VIII to XII are denoted as 'tribal teachers' for the present study.

Creativity

Creativity involves the ability to discover or produce new solutions to problems, new inventions or unique performance. While directed thinking (*i.e.*, the problem solving ability) has finding the correct solution or answer as it's goal, creative thinking is open-ended as because the solutions are not pre-defined in their scope of appropriateness.

Creativity leads itself to numerous meaning and shades. Creativity essentially relates to the potential of an individual for generating new ideas, forms, practices and so on. The degree and quality of creative expression is however relative. It varies from individual to individual from age to age and from culture to culture as one grows in years, experience and maturity.

According to Eysenck, *et. al.* (1979) the term 'creativity' is defined as an ability to see new relationships to produce unusual ideas and to deviate from traditional patterns of thinking.

According to David Ausubol (1952) a person is creative who can be distinguished from others in respect of his/her action. He considered creativity as a reflection of originality and creative product.

Torrance, E.P. (1965) conceives creative behaviour in a multi-dimensional fashion. In it's global definition, he mentions that creativity is composed of constellation of general abilities, personality variables and problem solving traits.

In latter time, Torrance, E.P. (1970) illustrated creativity as a process of becoming sensitive to problem, deficiencies, gaps in knowledge, missing elements, disharmonies and so on; identifying the difficulty, searching for solutions, making guesses or formulating hypotheses and possibly modifying and re-testing them and finally communicating the results.

The present study adopts the concept of creativity as defined by Torrance, E.P, emphasizing over the psychological capabilities like expression, production, invention, innovation and imagination of the tribal teachers.

Originality

One of the most important components of creativity is originality. It is a factor of divergent thinking, listed by Guilford in 1950. To him, "...a common connotation of originality is 'uniqueness'. But nothing can be considered unique in the prospective of the entire realm of idea of constructs of the nature. Therefore, the uniqueness, not in the absolute form but in the relative sense, can be considered as originality". In this present study the word originality denotes the capacity of the respondent tribal teachers to make unusual and appropriate responses towards common situation or stimuli.

Flexibility

J.P. Guilford first stated the term Flexibility, in his book "Personality", published from London in 1959. It is a new term in the field of psychology even today. It's meaning is similar to 'pliancy' or 'adaptability'. Flexibility is an important quality of a creative person. Antonym will be 'rigidity'. The present study considers the terminology to denote the psychological capacity of the tribal teachers as a base component of creativity.

Fluency

As a psychological term this word was first used in "The nature of human intelligence" written by J.P. Guilford, published from New York in 1967. Fluency is a rapid flow of ideas and tendency to change direction and modify information, measured by test in which a number of answers, which satisfy the same conditions, must be given. According to Guilford, fluency belongs to divergent thinking for which he defined twenty-four factors.

The present study considers the definition of fluency as defined by J.P. Guilford.

Interest

Interest is a tendency to behaviour, oriented towards certain object(s), activities or experience which tendency varies in intensity and generally from individual to individual.

Factor analytical studies of interest have been shown about fifteen independent dimensions. Some of those dimensions are technology, music, art, politics, economics, etc.

Vernon, P.E. (1967) in his book "Personality test and assessment" says that interest is just a complex as an amalgam of subjective feelings and objective behaviour – tendencies, and it is difficult to specify certain fixed number of dimensions of interest.

According to Crow and Crow, interest may be reflected to the motivating force that compels us to attend to a person, a thing or an activity; or it may be the effective experience that has been stimulated by the activity itself, and other word, interest can be the cause of an activity and the result of participation in the activity.

According to the Penguin dictionary of psychology, the term "interest" employed in two senses:

(1) *The functional interest*: It designates a type of feeling, earned by experience, which might be called 'worthwhileness' – and associated with attention to an object or course of action.

(2) *The structural interest*: It indicates an element or item in an individual's makeup, either congenital or acquired, because of which individual tends to have his feeling of 'worthwhileness' in connection with certain objects or matters relating to a particular subject or a particular field of knowledge.

In the investigation the term is used to find out the tendency of tribal teachers towards their profession (*i.e.*, teaching) – that is, whether they feel any urge towards their profession – which may be positive or negative.

Attitude

It is a psychological factor having some similarity with traits and interest. Attitude is a reflection of personality. It may be considered as a manner, mode of response of an individual towards a thing, idea, person, object or a situation. Attitude is chained with stimulus in the following way:

Stimulation → Sensation → Perception → Habit → Traits → Interest
Set of mind → Goal → Motivation
} *Attitude*

Attitude denotes "...... *some total of man's inclination and feelings, prejudices or preconceived notions, ideas, fear, threats or convictions about any specific topic*".

In the present study the terminology "Attitude" indicates the tendency as well as feeling of the tribal teachers towards some dimensions, already stated.

Secondary Schools

Any school from the state of Assam and West Bengal, having a class-grade – falling within VIII to XII grade (including these two grades) are considered as secondary school.

The Techniques

Techniques adopted for the present study are as follow:

Situational Interview Technique (For the Experts)

From the very outset of the study, this very technique was followed to fulfill the purpose mentioned below:

(*i*) To gain feedback from the experts and scholars about the entire design of the study. It is worth noting to mention that this group of scholars are particularly knowledgeable in the tribal life, culture and education, not only in theoretical context but are having field-experience to work on tribal-welfare in either of the states – Assam and West Bengal.
(*ii*) To be introduced with the subjects
(*iii*) To validate the tools
(*iv*) To share their experience
(*v*) To pool their reflective thinking on tribal issues.

Participatory Observation-cum-Discussion Technique (For the Indigenous Community Groups)

The technique, quite essential for ethno-pedagogic research, was adopted with a view to explore the status of the tribal teachers within their own indigenous community. The groups representing at least three tribal teachers, working at secondary schools, were listed out and then after proper sampling, eight groups

– four from each state, were identified. The technique was applied with those specific eight tribal communities in a systematic manner and in their natural settings.

The Tools

Tools used for the present study were as follows:

Status Questionnaire (For the Tribal Teachers)

Status questionnaire is a device – a tool, basically descriptive in nature, which claims to pool data – qualitative and quantitative as well, regarding ascribed and achieved status of a certain group of people or of an individual. A good status questionnaire is capable to collect data related to the status and incorporates almost all the possible factors and variables on which the status depends.

Rationale for Designing a Status Questionnaire

Though there were good number of status scales available in the field (*i.e.*, developed by Singh and Sexena, Alhuwalia, Mishra and Tripathi, Kulshrastha, Srivastava, Bharadwaj, and others). But none of those scales appropriately fitting to the present study and to be more frank, when the study is aimed to explore the status of tribal teachers belong to different ethnic groups, the author felt the need to develop a new status questionnaire.

Construction Procedure

At the outset of construction of the status questionnaire, twenty specific unit dimensions were identified, which can be considered as the component of status and are falling within a continuum with two specific ends – the ascribed status and the achieved status. In some cases it was observed that components within the 'status-continuum' stands with a major domination of either of those two extreme ends. Hence, inspite of classifying the components of status, those are simply listed out.

Identification of the Components

The components of the status questionnaire are identified as follow:

(*i*) Occupation and interest towards occupation
(*ii*) Type of institution, where the respondents are employed
(*iii*) Age and length of experience in profession
(*iv*) Gender and marital status
(*v*) Social upbringing
(*vi*) Education – general and professional – Attitude towards education
(*vii*) Linguistic status
(*viii*) Religious status
(*ix*) Status of the family at present

(*x*) Migration – the intervening factor of status
(*xi*) House and house hold assets
(*xii*) Economic status – of the respondents and their family
(*xiii*) Determinant factors of 'economy' and their perception on the same
(*xiv*) Political status
(*xv*) Status ascribed – as reflected by community and clans
(*xvi*) Status – dependent – on participation in social programmes
(*xvii*) Cultural status
(*xviii*) Status based upon their student's attitude towards their indigenous knowledge
(*xix*) Perceptual rating of their own status and perception about social mobility
(*xx*) Attitude of the community towards certain aspects

Keeping in view, the objectives of the study, the form of questions, as far as possible, was converted into 'multiple-choice type' questions by the help of the experts so that the respondents can easily respond towards the questions. The different choice of response and their extent was determined by the help of the expert – group. The step ensured the objectivity of those questions as well as of the possible responses.

Pilot Study

After construction of the first draft of the status questionnaire incorporating as many as ninety-two (92) questions, a pilot study was carried out. After repetitive administration of the draft questionnaire over a sample group of hundred (100) respondents drawn from both the states [fifty (50) from Assam and fifty (50) from West Bengal] the number of questions reduced from ninety-two (92) to seventy-eight (78), then up to fifty-nine (59) and latter in it's final shape the status questionnaire consists of thirty eight (38) questions.

Reliability and Objectivity of the Status Questionnaire

Data obtained by the draft status questionnaire was quantitative as well as qualitative. The consistency of the responses against the questions (*i.e.*, the data) were checked and verified in the phase of first, second and third tryout of the draft questionnaire. Actually no differences in the responses were noticed in these processes of administrating and re-administrating the draft questionnaires, except some repetitions of the questions in different forms were identified. In fact the similar question in different forms were placed in the draft questionnaire with an intention to eliminate the faking of responses through cross verification. In the final shape of the questionnaire such similar items were amalgamated in a unit question and hence the total number of questions were reduced.

Quantitative data analysis ensured objectivity of the questionnaire where as, both qualitative and quantitative data analysis ensured the reliability of the questionnaire to a great extent. In the process of ensuring the consistency of the responses towards the items of the questionnaire, valuable opinions from the resource-persons from tribal denomination and also from the eminent educationists from the filed of tribal studies, were taken into consideration – which further ensured the reliability of the status questionnaire.

Validity of the Status Questionnaire

After assuming adequate reliability for the status – questionnaire, the validity of the status questionnaire was drawn by the process of analyzing the content. In the successive stage, the interpretation of data collected through the draft questionnaires were presented in front of experts. Experts expressed their satisfaction with the content-validity of the questionnaire.

Pattern of the questionnaire revealed its face-validity by assumption and definition.

In the very phase of analyzing items during repetitive try-out, logical validity of questionnaire was gained by checking items because the unit – questions incorporated in the questionnaire are directly concerned with the 'conceptions' and 'components' of 'status' – which the status questionnaire intended to measure. In substantial number of cases, follow-up observation of respondent's behaviour at a particular time was made. The hidden investigation over some subject's status was also empirically explored, matched and verified with the responses collected by the status questionnaire. All these treatments revealed the predictive validity of the questionnaire.

So it can be concluded that the status questionnaire for the tribal (secondary) teachers, as it was developed, ensures it's face validity, content validity, logical validity and predictive validity. As such the questionnaire is a valid one for the purpose of present study.

Standardization of the Status Questionnaire

The questionnaire was further standardized by re-arranging it's items in systematic way, keeping proper emphasis and parity with each of the components of the status, considered for the study, and also of it's objectives.

Analysis of Data Obtained through Status Questionnaire

Already it has been mentioned that data obtained through the status questionnaire was qualitative as well as quantitative in nature. Data obtained through the objective questions were analyzed, without allotting any numerical score towards them. This way, the data collected through these structured multiple choice type questions were analyzed through percentage and calculating correlations of a certain phase with the other possible aspects. Qualitative analysis was made for the rest of the items of the questionnaire.

Attitude Scale (for the Tribal Teachers)

An attitude scale is a psychological device that claims to measure the attitude, a psychological factor, having some similarities with traits. In fact, attitude scale reflects the attitude.

Here, the terminology 'Attitude' was considered as the tendency of the tribal teachers (from the state of Assam and West Bengal) towards some specific dimensions and to measure these, the scale was essential.

Purpose of the Attitude Scale

To achieve the third, fourth and fifth objectives of the study (*i.e.*, to explore the professional relationship of the tribal teachers with their colleagues and also to analyze their attitude towards their Profession, Students, Government, Society and Working Environment) attitude scale was developed.

Rationale for Designing Attitude Scale

It was a fact that a good number of attitude scales were available in the market and some of those were specifically developed for measuring teacher's attitude. However, none of the available standardized attitude scales was specifically meant for the 'teachers' who are coming from a specific ascribed status-group (*i.e.*, tribal denomination) and are working in the two specific states – Assam and West Bengal. Almost all the available attitude scales were standardized for the teachers from Northern India long back, when participation of tribals in teaching profession at secondary level was a rare phenomenon. Another point is that, none of the available attitude scales covered all the six dimensions, granted for the present study. Therefore, need was felt to develop a new attitude scale for the tribal secondary school teachers, covering all the above-mentioned six dimensions.

Construction Procedure

The attitude scale was developed, following Likert's method. At the outset, one hundred and eighty (180) statements were framed and gathered, referring to relevant readings, keeping equal emphasis over all the six specified dimensions. These are:

(*a*) Attitude towards profession
(*b*) Attitude towards colleagues
(*c*) Attitude towards students
(*d*) Attitude towards government
(*e*) Attitude towards society and
(*f*) Attitude towards working environment.

Help of existing teacher's attitude scales were also taken in this respect and a draft scale of one hundred and eighty (180) items were prepared.

The draft-scale was given to the experts for cross-verification of the items and according to their verification one hundred and fifty (150) statements were retained.

This underwent revision many a time and finally the list contained one hundred and twenty (120) items, both favourable and unfavourable, equal in number and twenty (20) in each of the six (6) dimensions. Thus evolved the draft scale.

The scoring key for the favourable items were decided to be 4-3-2-1-0 for the responses – strongly agree (SA), agree (A), undecided (U), disagree (DA) and strongly disagree (SD) respectively, and for the unfavourable items, the scoring key was reversed (*i.e.* 0-1-2-3-4).

The scoring key is shown in Table 4.4.

Table 4.4: The Scoring Key for Attitude Scales

Degree of Choice	*Score for Items*	
	Favourable	*Unfavourable*
Strongly agree	4	0
Agree	3	1
Undecided	2	2
Disagree	1	3
Strongly disagree	0	4

This five-point attitude scale with one hundred and twenty (120) items were tried out on a group of one-third of the sample, *i.e.*, one hundred (100) tribal teachers taking fifty (50) from each state. For this purpose, all these hundred twenty (120) statements were shuffled and placed randomly in the draft-scale.

After trying out, the scales were collected from hundred (100) respondents, and scoring was made. Then the filled up scales were arranged in the ascending order, basing on total scores obtained by the respondents.

Twenty-seven percent (27%) scales from top and twenty seven percent (27%) from the bottom were taken apart. Thus two groups, *viz.*, higher and lower scoring group were formed. The score obtained by each teacher on each individual item and each dimension was separately found out. The discriminating-power was obtained by calculating the 't' value. The final scale consists the items having 't' values, significant at 0.05-0.01 level. Thus sixty best discriminating items, arranged (more or less) in the descending order of 't' value were selected out of the entire hundred twenty (120) items. Thus emerged the final form of the attitude scale for tribal teachers.

The discrimination power of each item was calculated by applying the formula:

$$ULI = \frac{R_U - R_L}{f}$$

Where ULI stands for upper index in the discriminating power; R_U stands for the number of respondents, giving 'right answer' in upper 27 per cent lot and R_L for the number of teachers responding rightly from the lower 27 per cent lot, towards a certain item.

In this context, let the author make it clear that the 'right answer' means, an attempt to the positive or favourable items as 'strongly agree' and award of four (4) marks were given against such responses. Similarly an attempt to a negative or unfavourable item as 'strongly disagree' was also considered as a 'right answer', and four marks were awarded to such responses.

Thus the award of four (4) marks was given against each right response, irrespective of upper or lower group.

'f' indicates the number of respondents in the group.

The item having discrimination power of less than eight (8) were eliminated. The respondent was required to indicate their choice of responses to each of the items on the five-point scale.

Following the above method, sixty (60) items were retained in the final scale, ten (10) from each dimension. The items in each dimension were then matched. In this step, some items were converted into the negative form from their affirmative form and reverse to keep five (5) positive and five (5) negative statements from each dimension. The structures of the statement remained unchanged in this very process of conversion.

Identification of the Dimensions

The dimension-wise distribution of the items in the final from of the attitude scale is shown in Table 4.5.

Table 4.5: Dimension-wise Distribution of the Items in the Attitude Scale

Dimension	*Direction*	*Serial Number of the Statements*
A. Profession	Positive (+)	1, 13, 25, 37, 49
	Negative (–)	8, 20, 32, 44, 56
B. Student	Positive (+)	7, 19, 31, 43, 55
	Negative (–)	2, 14, 26, 38, 50
C. Colleague	Positive (+)	3, 15, 27, 39, 51
	Negative (–)	10, 22, 34, 46, 58
D. Government	Positive (+)	9, 21, 33, 45, 57
	Negative (–)	4, 16, 28, 40, 52
E. Society	Positive (+)	5, 17, 29, 41, 53
	Negative (–)	12, 24, 36, 48, 60
F. Working Environment	Positive (+)	11, 23, 35, 47, 59
	Negative (–)	6, 18, 30, 42, 54

Arrangement of the Items in the Final Scale

The selected sixty items were mixed up irrespective of their specific dimension and placed in the final scale, following an alternative approach in a systematic way. The final scale reveals that all the odd items were positive where as even items were unfavourable or negative.

Reliability of the Attitude Scale

The reliability of the attitude scale was determined following split-half method. The test was administered on the pilot group, which includes hundred subjects.

Spearman Brown *prophecy formula* was applied for determining the split – half reliability of the scale. Two equal halves of the scale, each having thirty (30) items was arrived at by collecting first and second half of the scale. The score on both the halves were given separately. So, each subject obtained a score on first half and a score on second half.

Statistical analysis of the scale revealed that it possess a reliability coefficient of 0.841. The co-efficient of the reliability of the attitude scale, with its different dimensions were also estimated separately, which was also found satisfactory and which established the reliability of the entire attitude scale as well as its different dimensions once again. For the brief perusal, the dimension wise reliability co-efficient (up to two-decimals) are presented in Table 4.6.

Table 4.6: Reliability Coefficients of the Various Dimensions in the Attitude Scale

Dimensions	*Reliability Co-efficient*
A. Attitude towards Profession	0.86
B. Attitude towards Students	0.79
C. Attitude towards Colleagues	0.85
D. Attitude towards Government	0.81
E. Attitude towards Society	0.87
F. Attitude towards working environment	0.86

Objectivity of the Attitude Scale

The Likert's method following which the attitude scale was developed and also the scoring process ensure the objectivity of the attitude scale.

Validity of the Attitude Scale

In the process of construction of the attitude scale, it was ensured that the face validity and content validity has duly been taken care of while writing and finally selecting the statements by undertaking statistical technique and expert's opinion.

Thus, the attitude scale for the tribal teachers, towards six different dimensions was accepted as a valid tool to measure the attitude of the tribal teachers.

Standardization of the Attitude Scale

The attitude scale was further standardized by re-arranging it's items in a systematic way, keeping proper emphasis on each of the six different dimensions, considered for the study. The nature of the scoring system reflects the objectivity of the scale. And hence, the scale can be considered as a standard scale for measuring attitude of the tribal teachers.

Analysis of Data obtained through the Attitude Scale

Data gathered through the attitude scale was analyzed quantitatively. Standard score for each dimension of attitude were calculated separately for each individual respondent. Different statistical techniques which were applied to analyze and also to interpret those data are simple percentage, correlation, and "t" test.

The Problem Checklist (for the Tribal Teachers)

Problem checklist is a device to check the problems faced by the subjects in a specific field.

The Purpose of the Problem Checklist

To delve into deep of the eight objectives (*i.e.* to identify the problems (as well as the sources of those problems and intensity of occurrence of those problems) a problem checklist was developed to examine the problems faced by the respondent secondary school teachers.

Construction Procedure

At the outset of developing the checklist, frequent visits had been made by the author in different schools, where the tribal teachers are working, to observe the actual set-up, within which the respondents are working. Beside observation, the author consulted the teachers and administrators and obviously the tribal teachers separately to realize the actual situation. Frequent visit was also made to different tribal punjis (*i.e.*, tribal pockets). Available research-literatures over the problems of tribal education and interaction with the 'experts' in the 'field' helped the researchers to specify the problems of the tribal teachers. In this way, lists of seventy-five (75) problems as well as the possible sources of those problems were prepared.

This initial list was placed in front of expert-group and according to their suggestion, some 25 more problems were included. Thus a list of hundred (100) problems was evolved. Apart from collecting and listing up the problems, the author tried to classify the possible sources of those problems (*i.e.*, the responsible factors causing the problems) by the help of experts and a group of tribal teachers.

The list (contained hundred problems) is then edited properly as per the advice of the experts, deleting the 'almost common' problems and keeping such problem only, in a single frequency and thus seventy-two most relevant problems were incorporated in the draft list, keeping sufficient space against each problem.

The draft problem check-list was then administered over the pilot group [a group of hundred (100) tribal teachers, fifty (50) from each state] and are requested to check those problems, which they had already experienced and simultaneously specify the source and factors of those problems.

The data, in this way, obtained from the first try-out revealed that problems, which the tribal teachers are facing, are mostly coming from two broad – spheres, these are:

(*i*) Problem caused by the society, outside the institution
(*ii*) Problem caused by the different factors involved within the institution

The data further revealed that the problems, caused by 'the society – outside the institution', varied with a huge range of factors where as within the institution, the problems were mostly caused by the colleagues, students, non-teaching staffs and school administration.

The scale was then modified with a little extent for the second try-out on the same sample group, where, provision was given against the same list so that the respondents may indicate the frequency of occurrence of each and every problem with three options (*i.e.*, always, often and rarely).

Data obtained from the second tryout of the problem checklist revealed that out of seventy-two (72) problems, the group mostly responds over thirty (30) items. Remaining forty-two (42) items which were, either quite untouched or are accepted by less than five percent of the respondents, with a lowest degree of occurrence (*i.e.*, rare-occurrence) were dropped in the final from of problem checklist.

Basing on the data obtained by the first and second try out, the final form of problem–checklist was devised. Two different columns were provided (*viz.*, column – A and B). The respondents were asked to check the frequency of occurrence of the problems in column A, with three (3) options, *viz.*, always, often and rarely; where as in column B, they were supposed to check the sources of the problem (*i.e.*, whether it is occurring within the institution or outside the institution.

As it was observed from the data pooled during the first try-out, that the problems which they are facing outside the institution is due to varied reasons (in other words, a huge number of factors are responsible), so according to the suggestion of the 'experts', the 'column-B' in its first half, was not sub-divided further (as because that may invite complexity in the checklist and responses might be affected due to the complex nature of the check list) and are placed under a single sub-head "society – out side the institution". However, the second part of the same column (column-B) was sub-divided with four (4) options – and respondents were given free access to opt as much as they think out of four (4) options. These four (4) options were given basing on the frequency of the responses deduced from the pilot-group's response, over the second draft-list.

The Format of the Problem Checklist

The format of the problem – checklist is shown below.

Table 4.7: The Format of the Problem Checklist

Specification/ Nature of the Problem	*A*			*B*				
	Frequency of Occurrence			*Problem Caused by*				
					Inside the Institution			
	Always	Often	Rarely	*Society outside the institution*	Colleagues	Students	Non-teaching Staffs	Administration

Arrangement of the Items in the Problem Checklist

So in final shape of the problem checklist, thirty (30) specific problem were listed out, where as, in search of unique uncommon problems, though not frequently faced by the substantial number of tribal teachers, scope were kept open to the respondents to specify such type of problems, in the blank space provided from item number thirty-one (31) to thirty-five (35) of the checklist.

The items were arranged in a descending order of the responses and frequency, as obtained by the draft-check-lists to place the 'problems' from serial number one to thirty. Five blank-space were provide after that keeping a continuation up to thirty-five (35).

Objectivity of the Problem Checklist

The construction procedure and the nature of this data-gathering tool itself ensure cent percent objectivity of the tool.

Reliability of the Problem Checklist

The data obtained by the draft problem checklist was quantitative in nature. The consistency of the responses of the pilot group was checked and verified in the phase of first and second try-out of the draft-checklist. No differences in the responses were noticed in this process of administering and re-administering the draft checklists. In this process of ensuring the consistency of the responses towards the different individual problems, valuable opinions of the resource persons from tribal denomination and the opinions from the eminent educationists from the field of tribal studies were taken into consideration – which further ensured the reliability of the problem checklist.

In a word, it can be said that the construction procedure of the problem checklist ensured its reliability in terms of its purpose.

Validity of the Problem Checklist

After assuming adequate reliability for the problem checklist, the validity of the problem checklist was drawn by the procedures mentioned below:

(*i*) The interpretations of the data gathered through the draft checklist were compared with its final form. Further, those were presented in front of experts. The experts expressed their satisfaction so far the validity of the content of the final form of the problem checklist is concerned.

(*ii*) In the process of analyzing the individual items of the checklist during repetitive tryout, the logical validity of the checklist was gained.

(*iii*) The pattern of checklist revealed its face validity so far the purpose of the tool is concerned.

(*iv*) The predictive validity of the problem checklist was ensured through the process of comparing the data obtained from some of the respondents and observing their institutional as well as social setup within which they were working. It appeared to the researcher that follow-up observation totally co-exists with the data, supplied by the respective individual respondent tribal teachers.

All the preceeding rationales are sufficient enough to accept the problem checklist as a valid tool for the purpose of the present study.

Standardization of the Problem Checklist

The problem checklist, in its final form as it has already been mentioned, arranges the items in a descending order of the 'frequency' of acceptance of the problems and providing enough scope to the respondents to specify problem in the last phase of the check list, can be taken as a standard one.

Analysis of Data Obtained Through the Problem Checklist

Data obtained by the problem checklist was quantitative in nature. So quantitative analysis was made applying different statistical techniques mostly in simple percentage. However, the quantitative data were supplemented by the qualitative introspection gained through ethnographic study.

Torrance Test of Creativity Thinking (TTCT)

Torrance test of Creative Thinking is a scientifically devised culture fair test on Creativity, which claims to measure Creative ability as a composite form of originality, flexibility and fluency of the individual. This test is applicable to measure the Creative ability of the person from any age group of concrete operational thought level.

Introduction of Torrance Test of Creative Thinking (TTCT)

Torrance Test of Creative Thinking (TTCT) developed by E.P. Torrance and his associates (in 1966) can be administered to individuals at all educational levels starting from kindergarten through post-graduate level. This test consists of four batteries of test-activities – verbal form – A and verbal form – B (an equivalent form to verbal – A) and figural form – A and figural form – B (an equivalent alternate form to figural form – A).

Both these forms (figural and verbal tasks) of activities of *Torrance Test of Creative Thinking* assess the products in terms of Guilford's divergent thinking factors (fluency, flexibility, originality and elaboration).

In order to obtain scores on the three major components of creativity (*viz.*, originality, flexibility and fluency) as well as scores on the composite ability, *i.e.*, creative thinking, it was decided to use TTCT, verbal form A (1974 edition). But before the decision to use TTCT was made many theoretical and statistical considerations were carefully examined. The aim was to measure the creativity of the tribal-teachers working in the secondary schools, by using the best among the available instruments, those are designed to measure creative thinking ability. Finally the same was translated in two regional languages Bengali and Assamese.

Conclusion

Tools and Techniques are quite essential to pool required data in the process of research, however, the application of tools, techniques and method does not bear any meaning until and unless the pooled data are analyzed in a systematic and scientific way. The forthcoming chapters will deal with analysis and interpretation of the data collected by the tools and techniques, following the methodology illustrated in this chapter.

PART II: STATUS OF TRIBE TEACHERS
Empirical Observations

5

Profession, Experience and Job Satisfaction

Present chapter deals with the data related to professional status of the tribal teachers from different perspectives.

It has already been described that *access towards education* for the students, from the tribal communities, is a dependent variable which fully depends on the teachers, and access to education become easy for the tribal students when they are taught by the teachers form the communities of their own (*Ambasht, 1971*). That is why one of the major dimensions of tribal-education is the 'teacher' for the purpose of fulfilling the needs and requirements of tribal students (*Chatopadhyay, 1973*).

Number of Teachers

The teaching profession has the largest number of members compared to any other profession in India. In terms of gender, 71.65 per cent of men and 28.35 per cent of women are engaged in this profession, in different levels of educational institutions, across nation (*Chopra, R.K., 1993*), with a grand absorption of 1493000 teachers at the high and higher secondary schools. Among them 65.77 per cent are male and 34.23 per cent are female (Selected Educational Statistics, MOE & C, 1996-97). However, a trend of deviation can be observed in the same sketch in case of the states of Assam and West Bengal.

In the state of Assam, out of a total number of 17641 teachers at the tertiary level of school education, 72.95 per cent teachers were male and rest 27.05 per cent were female where as, in West Bengal the total number of teachers in the same level was 38,039, of whom 76.49 per cent were male and rest 23.52 per cent were female during the field study.

The present study was carried out over five districts of southern Assam, where the total number of secondary school teachers belonging to tribal denomination was 346, the estimated number of tribal teachers from the five districts of West Bengal was 1497. In total 1843 tribal teachers were found working in the secondary schools, from these ten districts taken for the study during the field survey.

Table 5.1: Number of Teachers: Gender wise Distribution

State→	*Assam*	*West Bengal*	*Total*
Male	102 (68%)	126 (84.00%)	228 (76.00%)
Female	48 (32%)	24 (16%)	72 (24.00%)
Total	150 (100%)	150 (100%)	300 (100%)

Table 5.1 reveals that 68 per cent of the sample respondents from the state of Assam are male and 32 per cent of them are female, which implies that in the state of Assam only one third of the tribal teachers are female.

The picture is almost same in the state of West Bengal where females are even lesser in number (less than even one fifth) than that of their male counterparts to a greater extent. In this state, 84 per cent of the tribal teachers where male while only 16 per cent where female.

The overall picture is also in favour of comparatively more participation of the male-tribal teachers when both the states are taken into consideration. More than one-third of the entire sample group is male (*i.e.*, 76 per cent) and only 24 per cent of them are female. This goes in consonance with the deficiency in the literacy-percentage among the female tribals in the nation, as well as in the states taken for the study. The Census Table on literacy percentage of the tribal population is shown here for brief perusal and comparison:

Table 5.2: Literacy Percentage of Scheduled Tribes

	Total Population	*Male*	*Female*	*Difference*
Assam	49.16%	58.93%	38.98%	19.95%
West Bengal	35.70%	49.95%	19.86%	30.09%
India	29.60%	40.65%	18.19%	22.46%

Table 5.3: Marital Status of Teachers

State →	*Assam*			*West Bengal*			*Grand Total*
Sex → / ↓ *Marital Status*	*Male*	*Female*	*Total*	*Male*	*Female*	*Total*	
Married	97 (95.10%)	41 (85.42%)	138 (92%)	92 (73.02%)	20 (83.33%)	112 (74.67%)	250 (83.34%)
Unmarried	04 (3.92%)	06 (12.50%)	10 (6.67%)	34 (26.98%)	04 (16.67%)	38 (25.33%)	48 (16%)
Widow/ Widower	00 (0%)	01 (2.08%)	01 (0.665%)	00 (00%)	00 (0%)	0 (0%)	01 (0.33%)
Separated	01 (0.98%)	00 (0%)	01 (0.665%)	00 (0%)	00 (0%)	0 (0%)	01 (0.33%)
Total	102 (100%)	48 (100%)	150 (100%)	126 (100%)	24 (100%)	150 (100%)	300 (100%)

Table 5.3 shows that overall 83.34 per cent of the respondents found married while sixteen per cent of them found unmarried. Rest of them were found widow/widower or separated with equal proportion and are negligible in number.

In Assam ninety-two per cent of the respondents are married while only 74.67 per cent of the teachers from West Bengal found married. This difference is basically due to different socio-cultural setting of the tribal communities, where marriage usually takes place in comparatively early age in the northeastern region of India. It can be assumed that the ascribed statuses of the sample groups as well as their life-styles are the intervening variable, which caused this difference.

So far the marital status of the male respondents is concerned, this difference is quite prominent however, this difference is not that much significant in case of females.

Location of School

It is often said that India lives in its villages. It is very much true in case of the tribals. A grand majority of the tribal population are village-dwellers. However not only the higher education, education irrespective of levels reflect biasness towards urban areas, as because most of the educational institutions are concentrated in urban localities. Whatever the situation may be, the fact cannot be ignored that tribal children receive their school-education mostly from the rural institutions. A due care is necessary apart from the teachers, to reduce the rate of dropout of the tribal children and there is no harm if it is expected from the teachers from same denomination. In this context let us zoom our view over the distribution of the tribal teachers in terms of the location of institutions, where they are working. Table 5.4 presents the participation of the respondents in terms of the location of schools where they are employed.

Table 5.4: Participation of the Respondents in Terms of Their Location of Schools

State	*Assam*			*West Bengal*			*Grand Total*
Sex → *↓ Location of School*	*Male*	*Female*	*Total*	*Male*	*Female*	*Total*	
Urban.	41 (40.20%)	33 (68.75%)	74 (49.33%)	7 (5.56%)	2 (8.33%)	9 (6.00%)	83 (27.67%)
Sub-urban	12 (11.76%)	6 (12.50%)	18 (12.00%)	11 (8.73%)	1 (4.17%)	12 (8.00%)	30 (10.00%)
Rural	49 (48.04%)	9 (18.75%)	58 (38.67%)	108 (85.71%)	21 (87.50%)	129 (86.00%)	187 (62.33%)
Total	102 (100%)	48 (100%)	150 (100%)	126 (100%)	24 (100%)	150 (100%)	300 (100%)

It was observed that mostly the tribal teachers are working in the schools situated in the rural areas, which constitute 62.33 per cent of teachers. 27.67 per cent teachers are working in rural areas and only ten per cent of them are working in suburban areas. The picture is little bit different in the two states.

In Assam, almost half of the respondents (49.33%) are engaged in urban schools but in West Bengal huge majority (86 per cent) are teaching in schools, situated in rural areas. This difference reveals that, though in general, tribals are leaving in remote rural areas, but their rate of migration towards urban areas, irrespective of reasons, is quite high in Assam. Only twelve per cent of them from the state of Assam and just eight per cent from West Bengal are working in suburban areas.

Table 5.4 further reveals that while grand majority (86%) of the respondents from West Bengal, including 85.71 per cent of male and 87.5 per cent of female respondents are teaching in the schools situated in rural areas, substantially lesser number of respondents (*i.e.*, 38.67%) in total, including 48.04 per cent of male and 18.75 per cent of female respondents are working in rural areas in the state of Assam.

A juxtaposition of the location of schools of the respondents indicates that substantially higher percentage of respondents from West Bengal are working in rural areas, however the extent is more higher if the female groups are taken into consideration.

The Table shows that majority of the female respondents from Assam while working in the schools situated in urban areas, the females from West Bengal are working mostly in rural institutions.

Table 5.5: Teachers Working in Different Types of Schools

State	*Assam*			*West Bengal*			*Grand Total*
	Male	*Female*	*Total*	*Male*	*Female*	*Total*	
Co-Ed.	91 (89.22%)	27 (56.25%)	118 (78.67%)	73 (57.94%)	17 (70.83%)	90 (60%)	208 (69.33%)
Girls	0 (0%)	19 (39.58%)	19 (12.665%)	18 (14.29%)	7 (29.17%)	25 (16.67%)	44 (14.67%)
Boys	11 (10.78%)	2 (4.17%)	13 (8.665%)	35 (27.77%)	0 (0%)	35 (23.33%)	48 (16%)
Total	102 (100%)	48 (100%)	150 (100%)	126 (100%)	24 (100%)	150 (100%)	300 (100%)

Table 5.5 reveals that majority (69.33 per cent) of the respondents are working in co-educational institutions including 89.22 per cent and 57.94 per cent of male and 56.25 per cent and 70.83 per cent of females from the states Assam and West Bengal respectively. In Assam 78.67 per cent and in West Bengal 60.00 per cent of the tribal teachers are having the opportunity to

teach both the boys as well as the girls – students where as only 14.67 per cent of the entire group is working in Girls' schools which includes 12.665 per cent of the teachers from Assam and 16.67 per cent from West Bengal. This indicates that, comparatively more teachers from West Bengal are engaged in girls' schools.

It may be perused from the Table 5.5 that 39.58 per cent of the female teachers are working in girls' schools, and none of the males are working in girls' schools in the state of Assam. However 14.29 per cent of male tribe teachers and 29.17 per cent of female tribe teachers are working in girls' school in West Bengal. The picture reveals that participation of female tribe teachers in girls' school is more in West Bengal compared to Assam.

On an average 16 per cent teachers are working in boys' schools, which includes 8.665 per cent of the respondents from Assam and 23.33 per cent of the total respondents from West Bengal.

Only 10.78 per cent and 27.77 per cent of the male tribal teachers from Assam and West Bengal are working in boys' school respectively. Participation of female teachers in boys' school is nil in West Bengal however, though less but 4.17 per cent of the female respondents are employed in boys' school in Assam.

It can be further observed that out of the entire sample group, males have no access to teach in girls' schools in Assam and in the other hand females has no access to teach in boys school in West Bengal.

Level of School

In common, teachers' professional status depends on the level of schools in which they are absorbed. In fact this absorption is related to level of education, which is one of the vital indictor of status in most of the societies. A teacher from higher secondary school enjoy higher status compared to others working in secondary school and the secondary school teacher's status is higher than a middle school-teacher.

The most important transitional phase of the structure of education system of any country is its secondary (or school) education phase which bridge the elementary and higher education structure. By definition, the study incorporates the tribal teachers at secondary level, which further denotes the teachers, ascribing the status of any tribe and are working in the schools having any of the class grades falling within a class range VIII-XII, including those class grades too. After identifying the sample group, it was observed that the samples are working basically in three types of schools *viz.* middle (V-VIII), secondary (V-X) and higher secondary schools (V-XII).

Table 5.6: Teachers Working in Different Levels of Schools

Levels of Schools	*Assam*			*West Bengal*			*Grand Total*
	Male	*Female*	*Total*	*Male*	*Female*	*Total*	
Middle	0 (0%)	2 (4.17%)	2 (1.33%)	13 (10.32%)	8 (33.33%)	21 (14%)	23 (7.67%)
Secondary	84 (82.35%)	17 (35.42%)	101 (67.34%)	61 (48.41%)	9 (37.5%)	70 (46.67%)	171 (57%)
Higher Secondary	18 (17.64%)	29 (60.41%)	47 (31.33%)	52 (41.27%)	7 (29.17%)	59 (39.33%)	106 (35.33%)
Total	102 (100%)	48 (100%)	150 (100%)	126 (100%)	24 (100%)	150 (100%)	300 (100%)

Table 5.6 reveals that majority of the teachers (57 per cent) are working in secondary schools followed by those who are working in higher secondary schools (35.33 per cent) and only 7.67 per cent of the respondents are working in middle schools.

State wise distribution indicates that 1.33 per cent and 14 per cent are working in middle schools, 67.34 per cent and 46.67 per cent are working in secondary schools and 31.33 per cent and 39.33 per cent are working in higher secondary schools in Assam and West Bengal respectively.

Among the male respondents, 82.35 per cent and 48.41 per cent are working in Secondary schools where as 17.64 per cent and 41.27 per cent are working in higher secondary schools in the states of Assam and West Bengal respectively. However, only 10.32 per cent are working in the middle schools of West Bengal and none is working in such schools in Assam.

The participation of the female respondents in the middle schools from West Bengal is 33.33 per cent. The scenario in Assam shows that only 4.17 per cent of the female respondents are working in such schools.

Further it is observed that the majority (60.41%) of the female respondents from Assam are working in higher-secondary schools where as it is the secondary schools where majority of the female respondents from West Bengal are absorbed.

Management of Schools

One notable feature of the secondary schools throughout the country is their variation in terms of management, in terms of their control and funding agencies. These classifications incorporate the schools, which are absolutely financed and controlled by the respective state-governments in general, and sometimes by Central government, as well as government aided schools, private schools and schools mostly organized by religious trusts.

Table 5.7: Distribution of the Respondents in Different Types of Schools (Control-wise)

Types of Schools	*Assam*			*West Bengal*			*Grand Total*
	Male	*Female*	*Total*	*Male*	*Female*	*Total*	
Fully Govt.	12 (11.76%)	17 (35.42%)	29 (19.33%)	3 (2.37%)	2 (8.33%)	5 (3.33%)	34 (11.33%)
Govt. Aided	55 (53.92%)	9 (18.75%)	64 (42.67%)	81 (64.29%)	13 (54.17%)	94 (62.67%)	158 (52.67%)
Organized by Religious trust	19 (18.63%)	18 (37.50%)	37 (24.67%)	37 (29.37%)	9 (37.5%)	46 (30.67%)	83 (27.67%)
Private	9 (8.82%)	4 (8.33%)	13 (8.66%)	0 (0%)	0 (0%)	0 (0%)	13 (4.33%)
Others	7 (6.87%)	0 (0%)	7 (4.67%)	5 (3.97%)	0 (0%)	5 (3.33%)	12 (4%)
Total	102 (100%)	48 (100%)	150 (100%)	126 (100%)	24 (100%)	150 (100%)	300 (100%)

During the survey it was observed that 19.33 per cent of the sample group from the state Assam and only 3.33 per cent of the sample group from West Bengal are working in Government Schools from a grand total of 41 and 33 numbers of fully government controlled secondary schools, funded by the respective state governments, incorporating 11.76 per cent and 2.37 per cent of the sampled male teachers and 53.42 per cent and 8.33 per cent of the sampled female teachers from the state – Assam and West Bengal respectively.

In both the states the absorption of female tribal teachers in such kind of schools is as much as four-times, compared to their male counterparts.

However the government schools are absorbing only 11.33 per cent of the entire sample group in the secondary level and cannot be considered as the basic agency in this respect. Secondary education is mostly running as a joint-venture between government and local-educational authorities, generally known as school-managing committees, throughout the country. The states considered for the present study are not the exception and the same picture is reflected by the present study. Apart from the ascribed status of the sample group, it was observed that most of the respondents (52.67 per cent) are working in this specific kind of schools, which further includes different sub-categories. For the convenience, those categorization has not been considered for the present study and such schools are termed as 'government-aided' schools. From the Table 5.7 it can be observed that 42.67 per cent of the respondents from Assam, incorporating 53.92 per cent male and 18.75 per cent of female are working in such schools. However 62.67 per cent of the entire sample group from West Bengal, incorporating 64.29 per cent of male and 62.67 per cent of female teachers from the state of West Bengal are working in these government aided schools.

This juxtaposition indicates that tribal secondary school teachers are mostly absorbed in the job in the 'government aided' schools from both the states, whereas the extent of absorption is quite much in West Bengal, and is a fact even if compared in respect of gender.

The third type of agency in this context is the different religious organizations of different sheds in general and Christian-religious-trusts in particular are contributing their share for educational development – by organizing secondary schools. During survey, it was observed that most of these kind of schools are running in different tribal belt – often in remote areas, where neither the government, nor the local administration is active enough to ensure school-education. These categories of schools are second largest agencies to absorb the tribal teachers, followed by Govt. Aided schools in the ten districts from the two states, taken for the study. From Table 5.7, it can be observed that 27.67 per cent of the entire respondents are working in such type of schools including 24.67 per cent and 30.67 per cent of the sample drawn from Assam and West Bengal. From both the states, 37.50 per cent of the sampled female teachers are working in this type of schools. Whereas 29.37 per cent of male from West Bengal and only 18.63 per cent of the sample male teachers from Assam are working in such schools.

The fourth category of schools imparting secondary education, are neither government controlled or government aided, nor organized by religious trusts. These sorts of schools are negligible in number in West Bengal and none of the respondents from West Bengal are serving in private schools. However, in Assam 8.66 per cent of the sample group (incorporating almost equal percentage of male and female teachers) are working in the private schools in Assam.

These schools which are not falling within any of those three categories mentioned above are classified under "other types of school" considering their salient features in various respect. None of the female respondents from any states are working in such schools. Only 6.87 per cent of the male respondents from Assam and 3.97 per cent of the male respondents from West Bengal are teaching in those schools.

Experience

Being one of the important components of the status, experience of the tribal teachers, as like the other profession, cannot be denied. That is why the experience of the respondents in teaching profession was also considered in the study. Status varies proportionality with the experience of the professionals. The heterogeneous experience of the respondents for the present study varies from less than a year to more than thirty year.

Table 5.8: Distribution of the Respondents in Terms of Their Experience

Experience Range	Assam			West Bengal			Grand Total
	Male	Female	Total	Male	Female	Total	
Less than 5 years	17 (16.67%)	0 (0%)	17 (11.33%)	73 (57.94%)	6 (25%)	79 (52.67%)	96 (32%)
5-10 years	31 (30.39%)	20 (31.67%)	51 (34%)	26 (20.63%)	10 (41.67%)	36 (24%)	87 (29%)
More than 10 yrs. but less than 15 years	13 (12.75%)	11 (22.91%)	24 (16%)	16 (12.70%)	8 (33.33%)	24 (16%)	48 (16%)
15-20 years	25 (24.50%)	6 (12.50%)	31 (20.67%)	8 (6.35%)	0 (0%)	8 (5.33%)	39 (13%)
More than 20 years	16 (15.69%)	11 (22.92%)	27 (18%)	3 (2.38%)	0 (0%)	3 (2%)	30 (10%)
Total	102 (100%)	48 (100%)	150 (100%)	126 (100%)	24 (100%)	150 (100%)	300 (100%)

Table 5.8 reflects in total, 32 per cent of the sample group joined in their profession less than five years earlier. Considering the length of their experience, the entire group has been classified in five categories, ranging from 'less than five years' to 'more than twenty years'. It was observed that their actual experience ranged from 3 months to 31 years.

One notable difference was observed among the tribal youths form the two states where in one hand, from West Bengal 52.67 per cent of respondents including 57.94 per cent of male and 25 per cent of female respondents are having their experience less than five years, where as on the other hand, in Assam this percentage is only 11.33 per cent, which further includes only 16.67 per cent of male and not even a single female teacher was found in the state. This trend reveals that the educated tribal youths from Assam are not that much interested to join in teaching profession compared to their counter respondent group from West Bengal. This may be due to lack of physical facilities in teaching-job, compared to other official or administrative jobs. However the tribal youths of West Bengal has been taken teaching as their profession to uplift their social status (by removing the social stigma). This is probably due to much more materialistic outlook of the societies in north eastern region of the country compared to eastern India.

The next group on the basis of their teaching experience, (which ranged from five years to ten years) incorporates 29 per cent of the entire sample, further incorporating 34 per cent and 24 per cent of the respondent groups drawn from Assam and West Bengal, which further incorporates 30.39 per cent and 41.67 per cent of male and 41.67 per cent and 41.67 per cent of female respondents from the respective states.

The third group formed by those teachers having experience in the profession ranging from 'more than ten years but less than fifteen years.' This group includes only 16 per cent of the entire respondents. The figure remains intact even when the sample from the separate states are taken into consideration.

While 22.91 per cent and 33.33 per cent of the female teachers are falling in this experience-category, from the state of Assam and West Bengal respectively, only 12.75 per cent and 12.70 per cent of male respondents were found falling in the same category. That is why it is obvious that participation of tribal male falling in this experience category is significantly less than that of their female counterparts from both the states.

Only 13 per cent of the total sample, including, 20.67 per cent and 5.33 per cent from the states of Assam and West Bengal respectively, were found falling in the experience category ranging from 'fifteen years to twenty years' having 24.50 per cent and 6.35 per cent of male participation from the states under consideration with an addition of 12.50 per cent of female teachers from Assam. Not even a single female teacher from West Bengal was found falling in this category.

A juxtaposition of the number of participants of both the states in this experience category implies that, participation of the sample group from the state of West Bengal is substantially less, as compared to their counter respondent group from Assam.

In case of the respondents having more than even twenty years of experience, it was observed that they aggregately comprise only 10 per cent of the entire sample group. 15.69 per cent of male, 22.92 per cent of female and 18 per cent of the total sample group from the state of Assam is having more than 20 years of teaching experience while in West Bengal these figures are only 2.33 per cent; 0 per cent and 2 per cent accordingly.

While considering the teaching experience, a common feature was observed among the tribal-teachers from both the states that their participation in different (experience) categories except the first one, is increasing which should definitely increase the student-taught ratio in the secondary level – if not, at least keep hold the existing ratio. However it is also observed that in the state of Assam the scenario among the less experienced teachers is somehow giving reverse indication. The number of teachers, both male and female has been decreased among those falling within the experience range 0-5 years. This trend indicates that the educated tribal youths in the state of Assam are less interested to join in teaching profession, whereas a proliferation is observed in the enrollment of tribal students in B.Ed. courses, organized by different universities in Assam.

The low participation of the tribal youths from the state of Assam during last eight years requires a through flash where some other intervening variables should not be neglected. Among those, the drastic economic situation of the state government is the prime one, due to which the government failed to provide salary regularly to the teachers and the state treasury is allied to over-draw the capital allotment. This affects the economic circumstances of the secondary school teachers, who are supposed to be paid by the state government. In continuation the teachers have perused an adverse effect when their economic esteem is taken under consideration.

On the other hand the economic condition of the state government of West Bengal is though not absolutely stable, however special effort has been made for last two and half decade to enhance the social status of the teachers in general.

Teaching Interest

Teaching interest is a tendency of behaviour of the teachers, oriented towards their profession. A person can't perform better in his profession without having positive interest to it. Teachers are not the exception. Teaching interest is the reflection of the psycho-professional status of the teachers. Indirect question helps to study the interest and for the purpose questions where designed.

Table 5.9: Choice of the Respondents Towards Other Profession Before Joining Teaching

State →	*Assam*			*West Bengal*			*Grand Total*
Gender → / *↓Response*	*Male*	*Female*	*Total*	*Male*	*Female*	*Total*	
Yes	23 (22.55%)	11 (22.92%)	34 (22.67%)	40 (31.74%)	9 (37.5%)	49 (32.67%)	83 (27.67%)
No	48 (47.06%)	32 (66.67%)	80 (53.33%)	54 (42.86%)	10 (41.67%)	64 (42.67%)	144 (48%)
No Such Specific Choice	12 (11.76%)	1 (02.08%)	13 (8.67%)	22 (17.46%)	3 (12.5%)	25 (16.66%)	38 (12.665%)
Cannot Say	19 (18.63%)	4 (8.33%)	23 (15.33%)	10 (7.94%)	2 (8.33%)	12 (8%)	35 (11.665%)
Total	102 (100%)	48 (100%)	150 (100%)	126 (100%)	24 (100%)	150 (100%)	300 (100%)

In response to a certain question, *i.e.*, "Before you took to teaching as a carrier, did you wish to choose any other occupation?", it was observed that the positive response came from 27.67 per cent of the respondents in total. Further analysis show that 22.67 per cent of the respondents from Assam and 32.67 per cent from West Bengal gave positive responses. It was also observed that 22.55 per cent and 31.47 per cent of male and 22,92 per cent and 37.50 per cent of female respondents from the states of Assam and West Bengal, respectively, gave a positive responses. This reveals that they had preference towards other professions except teaching which indicates their lack of interest towards teaching profession at the time of taking up this very profession.

A juxtaposition of the percentage of the respondents from two states who responded positively towards this very question indicates that comparatively more respondents from West Bengal entered in teaching profession, failing to join into the profession of their choice.

However, in total, 48 per cent of the respondents negate the view, including 47.06 per cent and 42.86 per cent of male, 66.67 and 41.67 per cent of female and 53.33 per cent and 42.67 per cent of the total respondents from the state of Assam and West Bengal respectively, saying that they were intended to be a teacher.

The picture indicates that this bulk group of respondents who respond negatively towards this very question, had their pre determined choice to join teaching profession; while juxtaposing the response of this groups of respondent, it was observed that the female respondents from Assam show maximum interest to take up teaching as their profession, even prior to join in the profession.

Only 11.665 per cent of the respondents from the entire sample, including 15.33 per cent and 8 per cent of the total respondents from the states – Assam and West Bengal respectively, avoid this question. 12.665 per cent of the entire respondents, including 8.67 per cent and 16.66 per cent of the samples from Assam and West Bengal replied that they did not had any such specific choice towards teaching and for them, opting this very profession is quite incidental.

From Table 5.9, with a more specification, it can be said that, 11.76 per cent and 17.46 per cent male and 2.08 per cent and 12.5 per cent of female respondents from the states of Assam and West Bengal respectively, joined teaching incidentally.

The response of the sample from the state Assam denotes that majority (53.33 per cent) of them had their interest to be teachers, while in case of the respondents from West Bengal, comparatively less (42.67 per cent) respondents were indented to be teacher.

Table 5.10: Persuasion of Any other Occupation, Apart from Teaching

State →	*Assam*			*West Bengal*			*Grand Total*
Sex → / *↓ Response*	*Male*	*Female*	*Total*	*Male*	*Female*	*Total*	
Yes, before taking into teaching	30 (29.41%)	3 (6.25%)	33 (22%)	37 (29.37%)	11 (45.84%)	48 (32%)	81 (27%)
Yes, in past, simultaneously with teaching	19 (18.63%)	2 (4.17%)	21 (14%)	5 (3.97%)	2 (8.33%)	7 (4.67%)	28 (9.33%)
Yes, at present, simultaneously with teaching	0 (0%)	4 (8.33%)	4 (2.67%)	9 (7.14%)	3 (12.5%)	12 (8%)	16 (5.33%)
No	53 (51.96%)	39 (81.25%)	92 (61.33%)	75 (59.52%)	8 (33.33%)	83 (55.33%)	175 (58.34%)
Total	102 (100%)	48 (100%)	150 (100%)	126 (100%)	24 (100%)	150 (100%)	300 (100%)

Table 5.10 represents the respondents' persuasion of any other occupation, other than teaching, in their carrier.

When the sample were asked of whether at any stage of their career they pursued or is currently pursuing any other occupation apart from teaching, 27 per cent of the entire respondents incorporating 29.41 per cent and 29.30 per cent of the male, 6.25 per cent and 45.84 per cent of female and again 22 per cent and 32 per cent of the respondents in total from the states of Assam and West Bengal, respectively, replied that they pursued some other kinds of profession before they took to teaching – which implies that, to them teaching is not the first profession and they joined 'teaching' after serving in some other profession.

Replying to the same question, only 9.33 per cent of the entire respondent group, incorporating 14 per cent and 4.67 per cent of the sample groups from Assam and West Bengal, respectively, answered that they took up some other profession(s), in addition to teaching job in past, but during the survey they are continuing only with teaching profession. 18.63 per cent and 3.97 per cent of male and 4.17 per cent and 4.67 per cent of female respondents from the states of Assam and West Bengal respectively are falling in this response category.

Though a very marginal percentage of teachers, only 5.33 per cent of the entire respondents, including 2.67 per cent and 8 per cent respondents from the states of Assam and West Bengal respectively, replied that teaching is not the only profession to them and they are performing some other occupation(s) simultaneously with their teaching job; virtually it is difficult to this group of respondents to concentrate absolutely in the teaching job and they are supposed to deviate from their professional commitment to teaching.

However, majority of the respondents (58.34 per cent) was found engaged only in teaching to whom, teaching is the only and only job in their entire carrier. If we consider this response as a real commitment towards teaching profession, it needs to be noted here that irrespective of the intervening environmental variables respondents – from Assam is having commitment towards the profession to a greater extent, compared to their counterparts from West Bengal.

Job Satisfaction

Job satisfaction requires more than a decent salary. Greater recognition of teachers and of excellence in teaching is one means frequently suggested for raising the perceived status of teachers. Because recruitment of better quality teachers is important. Unfortunately a good number of teachers are engaged in the profession failing to join in their desired profession. It definitely asserts the status of the teachers.

Table 5.11: Respondent's Agreement to Shift to Some other Profession Having Same Emoluments

State →	Assam			West Bengal			Grand Total
Gender → / ↓ Response	Male	Female	Total	Male	Female	Total	
Yes	10 (9.80%)	6 (12.50%)	16 (10.67%)	15 (11.90%)	0 (0%)	15 (10%)	31 (10.33%)
Yes, it would have been good to have; but it is too late	25 (24.51%)	1 (2.08%)	26 (17.33%)	13 (10.32%)	0 (0%)	13 (8.67%)	39 (13%)
No	67 (65.69%)	41 (85.42%)	108 (72%)	98 (77.78%)	24 (100%)	122 (81.33%)	230 (76.67%)
Total	102 (100%)	48 (100%)	150 (100%)	126 (100%)	24 (100%)	150 (100%)	300 (100%)

To a question related to the respondent's willingness to change their profession with some other, having same emoluments, majority (76.67 per cent) of the respondents negates the choice. The group includes 65.69 per cent and 77.78 per cent of male, 85.42 per cent and 100 per cent of female teachers and 72 per cent and 81.33 per cent in total from the states of Assam and West Bengal, respectively. It can be observed that female respondents from both the states are more in numbers who are willing to continue with their present profession, *i.e.*, teaching, even if they are given equal facilities and emoluments with some other profession. This sort of response can be taken as a sign of occupational 'rest-ness', definitely which is predominantly a 'female characteristic' among the respondents.

Where as on the other hand, in an average 10.33 per cent of the entire sample group are quite in favour of changing their present occupation. Definitely, these groups of teachers are exhausted with their existing profession.

13 per cent of the entire respondents opined that it would have been better to have some other profession, however they are not ready to take the risk to change their existing profession. This group shows lack of interest towards their profession and courage to switch-over other profession; and incorporates 24.51 per cent and 10.32 per cent of male respondents from the states of Assam and West Bengal respectively.

6

Education, Training and Constraints

As observed from decadal literacy rates, spread of education among the ethnic communities in India is yet to rich desired level. It is the axiom of the day that educating tribes in formal system is best possible if students from ethnic communities be taught by teachers from same denomination. Unfortunately present status of tribe teachers in Indian social fabric, with especial focus towards education, training and educational constraints are till unknown. The chapter attempts to explore the status of tribe teachers, especially their educational status and constraints of education as well, in relation to specific parameters in two specific states from two regions following juxtaposition.

Education has always been considered as a tool for social change, having its blizzard effect on the society. It further reflects the society, which is a by-product of prevailing instructional strategies. On other hand, social fabric of India is not at all homogeneous. As such, a common instructional strategy can never lead to the stratocircus of the same. It is fact that earlier silent status-groups among specific sections of Indian tribes are becoming vocal today and are rightly demanding their share of congealed labour as their legitimate claim. Neo-status groups are emerging among the indigenous societies due to consciousness by virtue of education. Infact education for them is *status-quo-ante*, which is enhancing the process of social mobility, further feeded by supportive power of creativity.

Success of an educational system largely depends upon the quality of teachers available to it and the status they are assigned by the society within which the system functions. Keeping in view the need to raise the standard of education, it is essential that adequate attention be paid to study the existing status of the teachers, especially those engaged at school level in India, considering voluminous participation at the very level, and their implication in the light of follow-up actions (*PoA, 1996*). It is to be noted here that formal system of Indian education, as like of other developing and developed countries include several segments among which secondary education possess grand major share. It is the secondary school teachers who comprise more than two-third of the total manpower, engaged as teachers in educational sector of India (*Selected Educational Statistics, 2001*).

Today status of teacher and status of education are so intertwined that whatever produces changes in one, will normally produce changes in the same direction in the other (*Chopra, 1993*). If education doesn't command respect and support of the entire community, teacher will not command respect and support (*UNESCO, 1996*). Ways needs to be found out to improve the performance, effectiveness, efficiency and level of motivation of teachers and the relationship they establish with society (*Roy, 2005*). When teachers themselves are the part of the unitary community where they teach, their involvement is more clearly defined. They are more sensitive and responsive towards the need of their community and better able to work towards community goals (*Rao, 1996*).

In Indian social setup, the scenario of tribal education cuts a dismal sense till date. Low enrolment, high dropout, drift and wastage, limited number of high achievers and little credibility characterizes it (*Dube, 1988*). For proper development of tribal communities, special attentions need to be zoomed over the status of the teachers, belonging to Indian tribes (*Roy, 2005*). Unfortunately, studies in the very direction are too meager and hence the sphere demands special attention of the researchers. A very few studies, which hinge on the educational status of tribes, observed that the tribal students use to prefer tribe teachers due to linguistic affinity, loving nature and of their same denomination (*Ambasht, 1970; Roy, et. al. 2006*). However the status of tribe teachers in India is still less-known[1]. Common feature of Indian tribes sketches a group or community-cohesiveness, which often keeps them different from mainstream. Irrespective of sufficient budget allocation, expansion of formal education among tribes didn't reach up to the level of expectation[2]. Recent studies establishes that it is not due to the level of cognitive ability, rather the present approach of education is becoming somewhat a cultural shock to the tribes and thereby making the process of formally educating tribes a tough task. Present approach of formal education is not at all relevant to their life and future conditions (*Roy, 2005; Roy, et. al. 2006*). As a result, two consequences are commonly visible, where either they are remaining illiterate and are alienated from education, or among them, those who did able to be formally educated even ignoring the post-traumatic stresses, are alienated from their own traditional indigenous community-life[3]. In this way, education itself is becoming a 'problem' to them, which is breaking their family and community structure. Inferiority complex of the educated tribes sometimes aggravated by cultural hegemony of the non-tribe counterparts and to get-rid-of these problems often they find an easier alternative to dilute them in greater society, which may be termed as 'detribalization' (*Roy, 2006*).

Present chapter explores educational status profile of the tribe teachers from the states of Assam and West Bengal and to juxtapose the same. The basic aim of the present chapter is to delve into the educational status profile of the teachers belonging to various tribes from Assam and West Bengal. Notable here is, while from eastern India, majority of the tribes inhibits in plain lands, grand majority of the tribes from northeast India are highlanders.

Educational Constraints and Aspiration for Education

To meet, the specific objective, the study encompassed its vision to the educational constraints and the aspiration of the respondents for education – which is having an indirect bearing with their status.

Table 6.1: Where from the Respondents Mostly Pursued Education

State →	*Assam*			*West Bengal*			*Grand Total*
Sex → / *↓ Place*	*Male*	*Female*	*Total*	*Male*	*Female*	*Total*	
Own house and Family	59 (57.84%)	32 (66.67%)	91 (60.67%)	34 (26.99%)	7 (29.17%)	41 (27.33%)	132 (44%)
Relative's house	7 (6.87%)	0 (0%)	7 (4.66%)	9 (7.14%)	0 (0%)	9 (6%)	16 (5.33%)
Rented house/Mess	5 (4.90%)	2 (4.17%)	7 (4.665%)	25 (19.84%)	0 (0%)	25 (16.67%)	32 (10.67%)
Hostel	30 (29.41%)	14 (29.16%)	44 (29.33%)	49 (38.89%)	17 (70.83%)	66 (44%)	110 (36.67%)
In Some Other Place	1 (0.98%)	0 (0%)	1 (0.67%)	9 (7.14%)	0 (0%)	9 (6%)	10 (3.33%)
Total	102 (100%)	48 (100%)	150 (100%)	126 (100%)	24 (100%)	150 (100%)	300 (100%)

Table 6.1 represents the distribution of the respondents in terms of places, from where they pursued their education.

It is observed from the Table that 44 per cent of the entire respondents pursued education from their own house. However, a major variation can be observed so far as the percentage of the teachers from the two states are concerned. While majority (60.67 per cent) of the respondents, incorporating 57.84 per cent of the male and 66.67 per cent of the female pursued education from their own house in Assam, only 27.33 per cent of the respondents from the state of West Bengal, incorporating 26.29 per cent of the male and 29.17 per cent of the female, had the opportunity to avail education, staying with their family.

The juxtapositional sketch from two states reveal that in West Bengal education is comparatively beyond the reach of the respondent group and scopes are limited to avail education from their own house when compared to their counter sample group from Assam. It is not just that in West Bengal the educational facilities are centralized towards the urban areas; the same scenario can be observed in Assam too. The basic reason lies behind is the rate of migration of the tribal communities from their natural "punjis" to the urban areas is substantially higher, as compared to West Bengal.

Only 5.33 per cent of the respondents, out of which 4.665 per cent from Assam and 6 per cent form West Bengal, reported that they availed education, mostly staying in some relative's house.

The study observed that a total of 10.67 per cent of the entire respondent group carried out their studies, mostly staying either in some rented house or in mess and individually 4.665 per cent of the respondents from Assam and 16.67 per cent from West Bengal comprised this group. In search of causes, it was noted that this group, though marginal, felt it better to pursue education, staying in mess or in some rented house as it would have been impossible to pursue education if they stayed in their own house; on the other hand they were not provided with hostel facilities by the educational institutions. The situation makes it clear that in their school (or college) days, hostel facilities were not adequate for the tribal students.

In West Bengal, male students mostly faced this problem; however in Assam the problem stands proportionately both for males as well as for females.

A handful of 36.67 per cent of the respondents, including 29.33 per cent form Assam and 44 per cent from West Bengal responded that they pursued their education, mostly staying in hostels attached to institutions. This group incorporates 29.41 per cent and 38.83 per cent of males and 29.16 per cent and 70.83 per cent of females from the states of Assam and West Bengal, respectively.

It can be assumed that a good proportion of the respondents were benefited by the hostel facilities; and most of them are of the opinion that it would have been impossible for them to carryout their education, if they would not have been provided with such facility.

While juxtaposing the respondents of the two states, from this response category, one can find that the respondents from West Bengal were benefited much, compared to that of Assam so far extension of hostel facilities are concerned.

A total of 3.33 per cent of the entire sample opined that they pursued education neither staying with their families or relatives houses nor staying in hostel, messes or rented houses. Anecdotes reveals that this groups of respondents, in order to carry out their studies were forced to opt for some household jobs against the shelter provided by their employer. The days were more stringent to this group of respondents.

Training

The central role of teachers in the delivery of learning opportunities implies that they must be key actors in the education for all initiatives. The status of the teachers depends upon their performance, which can be improved through pre service and in-service training.

Table 6.2: Distribution of Respondents in Terms of their Persuasion of Training

State →	*Assam*			*West Bengal*			*Grand Total*
Sex → / *↓ Type*	*Male*	*Female*	*Total*	*Male*	*Female*	*Total*	
Trained	31 (30.39%)	15 (31.25%)	46 (30.67%)	79 (62.70%)	16 (66.67%)	95 (63.33%)	141 (47.00%)
Non-Trained	71 (69.61%)	33 (68.75%)	104 (69.33%)	47 (37.30%)	8 (33.33%)	55 (36.67%)	1590 53.00%)
Total	102 (100%)	48 (100%)	150 (100%)	126 (100%)	24 (100%)	150 (100%)	300 (100%)

Table 6.2 represents the number and percentage of trained as well as non-trained tribal teachers who comprised the sample. It was observed that only 47 per cent of the sample group were trained, while considering the national scenario, almost 91 per cent of the entire secondary school teachers are trained.

However, the picture is to some extent satisfactory in case of the state of Assam where 30.67 per cent of our sample group is trained. Although, in an average, only 30 per cent of the secondary school teachers in general, are trained in this state (Source: Selected Educational Statistics, MHRD. GOI, Department of Planning Monitoring and Statistics Division). From this state, 30.39 per cent of male and 31.25 per cent of the female tribal secondary school teachers are found trained and a bulk of 69.61 per cent of male and 68.75 per cent of female teachers were found non-trained.

The scenario is quite drastic in the state of West Bengal compared to the teachers in general, where only 62.70 per cent of the male and 66.33 per cent of the female sample group was found trained in contrast to 73 per cent of the total trained teachers in the secondary level. So, it is not only the literacy rate but also the rate of trained tribal teachers is not sufficient if compared to the general masses from this state, irrespective of existence of a good number of training colleges in this state.

Table 6.3: Trained Respondents' Response Towards Certain Issues Related to Training

State	Assam			West Bengal			Grand Total
Sex → ↓ Response	Male	Female	Total	Male	Female	Total	
No. of Trained Teachers	31 (30.39%)	15 (31.25%)	46 (30.67%)	79 (62.70%)	16 (66.67%)	95 (63.33%)	141 (47.00%)
As deputed Teacher	24 (77.42%)	12 (80.00%)	36 (78.26%)	49 (62.03%)	13 (81.25%)	62 (65.26%)	98 (69.50%)
As Fresher	5 (16.13%)	3 (20.00%)	8 (17.39%)	30 (37.97%)	3 (18.75%)	33 (34.74%)	41 (29.08%)
Received Spontaneously	19 (61.29%)	6 (40.00%)	25 (54.35%)	58 (73.42%)	14 (87.50%)	72 (75.79%)	97 (68.79%)
Received under Compulsion	12 (38.71%)	9 (60.00%)	21 (45.65%)	21 (26.58%)	2 (12.50%)	23 (24.21%)	44 (31.21%)
Faced Test/Interview during Admission	23 (74.19%)	8 (53.33%)	31 (67.39%)	70 (88.61%)	14 (87.50%)	84 (88.42%)	115 (81.56%)
Did not Faced Test/Interview during Admission	8 (25.18%)	7 (46.67%)	15 (32.61%)	9 (11.39%)	2 (12.5%)	11 (11.58%)	26 (18.44%)
Feels that those training are worthwhile for developing professional skills	31 (100%)	15 (100%)	46 (100%)	61 (77.22%)	15 (93.75%)	76 (80.00%)	122 (86.52%)
Eager to receive more training	31 (100%)	15 (100%)	46 (100%)	58 (73.42%)	13 (81.25%)	71 (74.74%)	117 (82.98%)
Not eager to Receive any training	0 (0%)	0 (0%)	0 (0%)	21 (26.58%)	03 (18.75%)	24 (25.26%)	24 (17.02%)

Table 6.3 may be considered as an illustration of the previous Table, indicating the status of respondents and their responses on nine specific dimensions.

Out of a total number of 300 teachers with tribal ethnicity, it was observed that only 47 per cent are trained and among them 69.50 per cent received training or other professional courses as a 'deputed teacher'.

The state-wise percentage of trained teachers, received training as a deputed teacher is 78.26 per cent from the state of Assam, incorporating 77.42 per cent of the trained male and 80 per cent of the trained females. However comparatively less percentage (62.03 per cent) of male trained and marginally higher percentage (65.26 per cent) of female trained teachers and a total of 65.26 per cent of the trained teachers from the state of West Bengal received training as 'deputed teachers'.

On the other hand, 16.13 per cent and 37.97 per cent of male, 20 per cent and 18.75 per cent of female and 17.39 and 34.74 per cent of total respondents from Assam and West Bengal, respectively pursued training as fresher condidates and were well equiped with professional training even before joining the profession.

Therefore, it can be mentioned in the present study that the male trained teachers from the state of West Bengal and female trained teachers from the state of Assam and over all, the teachers from West Bengal are quite advanced from their respective counter groups so far possession of professional training is concerned.

To an other question, 61.29 per cent and 73.42 per cent male, 40 per cent and 87.5 per cent of female and in total 54.35 per cent and 75.79 per cent of the trained teachers from the states of Assam and West Bengal, cumulatively forming a group of 68.79 per cent of the entire trained-group of respondents said that they received the training spontaneously. The juxtaposition of the respondent's response from the states reveals that both the male and female group, as well as the entire sample group from the state West Bengal shows comparatively a better degree of interest and professional preparation towards teaching profession.

However, 38.71 per cent and 26.58 per cent of the male, 60 per cent and 12.5 per cent of the female and in total, 45.65 per cent and 24.21 per cent of the sample groups, who pursued some kind of training, from the states of Assam and West Bengal, respectively, forming 31.21 per cent of entire trained group, responded that they received training, related to teaching, under compulsion. Definitely this group of respondents shows some sort of negative attitude/interest towards professional education and further, if the percentage of trained respondents could bc juxtaposed, it will be observed that the trained group from Assam shows a greater degree of disinterest towards the professional education.

To an other question, it was observed that 74.19 per cent and 88.61 per cent of trained male, 53.33 per cent and 87.57 per cent of trained female and 67.39 per cent and 88.42 per cent of the entire trained sample groups from the states of Assam and West Bengal respectively, did face either some sort of written test or interview or both the test and interview, during admission to the professional training courses, where as 25.18 per cent and 11.39 per cent of trained male, 46.67 per cent and 12.5 per cent of trained female and 32.61 per cent and 11.58 per cent of the entire trained group of sample from the two states respectively, cumulatively forming a total group of 18.44 per cent of the trained respondent did not face neither any test, nor any kind of interview and were directly admitted by virtue of a entry point examination certificate or of a deputation certificate, and joined the professional training programmes.

While expressing their feeling towards a question regarding the worthwhileness of the professional training(s), that the respondent group has pursued, cent per cent of the respondents, both trained male and female teachers from Assam and 80 per cent of the trained respondents from West Bengal, incorporating 7.22 per cent of trained male and 93.75 per cent of trained female replied that they feel that the training(s) they pursued are quite worthwhile for developing their professional skill for teaching.

Expressing their eagerness, while all the trained respondents from Assam said that they are eager to receive more such professional training programmes, 74.74 per cent of such respondents from the state of West Bengal, including 73.42 per cent of trained male and 81.25 per cent of trained female expressed agreement towards the reply and only a quarter of the trained respondent group from West Bengal, including 26.58 per cent of trained male and 18.75 per cent of trained female said that they are not at all eager to receive any more professional training.

While 47 per cent of the entire sample group was found trained, the majority (53 per cent) of the respondent groups are continuing the teaching profession, without having any professional training corresponding towards the national scenario, where only 9 per cent of the teachers at secondary level are not having any professional training. The responses extracted from this group of non-trained respondents regarding some specific dimensions of their professional training are presented in the following Table.

Table 6.4: Non-trained Respondent's Response Towards Certain Issues Related to Training

State →	*Assam*			*West Bengal*			*Grand Total*
Sex → ↓ *Response*	*Male*	*Female*	*Total*	*Male*	*Female*	*Total*	
Non Trained	71 (69.6%)	33 (68.75%)	104 (69.33%)	47 (37.30%)	8 (33.33%)	55 (36.66%)	159 (53.00%)
Eager to receive training	62 (87.32%)	21 (63.64%)	83 (79.81%)	47 (100%)	8 (100%)	55 (100%)	138 (86.79%)
Not eager to receive training	9 (12.68%)	12 (36.36%)	21 (20.19%)	0 (0%)	0 (0%)	0 (0%)	21 (13.21%)
Feels that training has their value for developing professional Skills	64 (90.14%)	21 (63.64%)	85 (81.73%)	47 (100%)	8 (100%)	55 (100%)	130 (81.76%)
Do not think that training has their value for developing professional skills	7 (9.86%)	12 (36.36%)	19 (18.27%)	0 (0%)	0 (0%)	0 (0%)	19 (11.95%)
Total	71 (100%)	33 (100%)	104 (100%)	47 (100%)	8 (100%)	55 (100%)	159 (100%)

In the state of Assam 69.33 per cent of the sample group was found non-trained including 69.61 per cent of the male and 68.75 per cent of the female tribal teachers; however in the state of West Bengal where only 27 per cent of the entire secondary school teachers are yet to receive professional training courses, 36.66 per cent of the sample group, incorporating 37.30 per cent of the male and 33.33 per cent of female respondents found untrained. The sketch reveals that the tribal secondary school teachers are, too a greater extent, are remaining untrained. While responding towards certain questions, cent per cent of the untrained respondent from the state of West Bengal expressed their eagerness to receive training.

On the other hand, 9.86 per cent of male and 36.36 per cent of non-trained tribal teachers negates this view. Some minimum educational and professional qualifications have been prescribed as necessary qualification for school teachers at different levels by various committees however these qualification varies to a little extent from state to state.

Level of Education

Innovation and quality of education require growth, improvement and mobilization of all human resources. The knowledge, efficiency and initiatives of teachers are increasingly scarce resources at a time when the expectations and tasks of education are increasingly complex. A basic requirement for proper education, besides quality, is to recognize the need for teachers to be highly qualified and well trained intellectual workers. However the respondent groups of tribal teachers are holding, to some extent a heterogeneous status, due to their heterogeneous level of education. In this context, it was observed that our respondent group is divided in four categories. Table 6.5 presents the detail picture about the level of education of the tribal teachers.

The present study covered the teachers working in three types of schools: *viz.*, middle, secondary and higher secondary schools, where the minimum educational qualification, required, is not same. Apart from the recommendations made by Kothari Commission (1964–66), a secondary school teacher is supposed to be a graduate, however, the person from deprived section will be given some relaxation in this context. The Table 6.5 presents the distribution of the respondents in consonance with their educational qualification.

Table 6.5: Distribution of the Respondents According to their Level of Education

State →	*Assam*			*West Bengal*			*Grand Total*
Sex →	*Male*	*Female*	*Total*	*Male*	*Female*	*Total*	
↓ *Level of education*							
Matriculation	24 (23.53%)	1 (2.08%)	25 (16.67%)	0 (0%)	0 (0%)	0 (0%)	25 (8.33%)
Higher Secondary	15 (14.71%)	5 (10.42%)	20 (13.33%)	5 (39.68%)	2 (8.33%)	7 (4.67%)	27 (9.00%)
Graduation	38 (37.25%)	27 (56.25%)	65 (43.33%)	68 (53.97%)	15 (62.50%)	83 (55.33%)	148 (49.34%)
Post Graduation	25 (24.51%)	15 (31.25%)	40 (26.67%)	53 (42.06%)	7 (29.17%)	60 (40.00%)	100 (33.33%)
Total	102 (100%)	48 (100%)	150 (100%)	126 (100%)	24 (100%)	150 (100%)	300 (100%)

From the entire respondent group, it was observed that in terms of their level of education 49.34 per cent are graduate, followed by 33.33 per cent of Post Graduate, 9 per cent intermediate (*i.e.*, below the level of graduation but above the level of Matriculation) and only 8.33 per cent of them were only matriculate.

At this stage, while 6.31 per cent of the teachers at the national level are matriculate, 8.38 per cent of the entire sample group was found possessing education at that level. From the Table it can be further observed that while there is none from the West Bengal, 16.67 per cent of the sample group from Assam, incorporating 23.53 per cent of male and 2.08 of female are falling within this education level.

Only 9 per cent of the entire sample group found having their educational qualification, equivalent to the level of intermediate. 14.71 per cent and 39.68 per cent of male, 10.42 per cent and 8.33 per cent of female and 13.33 per cent and 4.67 per cent of total respondents from the states of Assam and West Bengal are forming this group. However, in national scenario, only 3.46 per cent of the secondary teachers are falling in this education-category.

The survey observed that a substantially higher percentage (49.34 per cent) of teachers are graduates (which can be considered as optimum level of education for secondary school teachers) in consonance with 42.88 per cent in the national scenario. 37.25 per cent and 53.97 per cent of male, 56.25 per cent and 62.50 per cent of female and 43.33 per cent and 53.33 per cent of total respondents from the states of Assam and West Bengal, respectively, are having graduate-degrees. The picture which evolved, juxtaposing the percentage of teachers from the two states at this level reveals that comparatively more teachers from West Bengal and females from both the states are having this optimum level of education when compared to their respective counter respondent groups.

Exactly one-third (*i.e.*, 33.33 per cent) of the respondent group at this level with 26.67 per cent from Assam and 40 per cent from West Bengal are found having post-graduate level – education, while in national sketch, in an average 27.43 per cent of the secondary school teachers are having education up to this level. This finding is sufficient enough to give up the preconceived notion of the so-called mainstream regarding inferior educational status of the tribal teachers.

This group of teachers, with post-graduate level of education incorporates 24.51 per cent and 42.06 per cent of male and 31.25 per cent and 29.17 per cent of the female group of respondents from the states of Assam and West Bengal respectively.

Juxtaposition reveals that more males and fewer females from West Bengal are having post-graduate education in comparison to their respective counterparts from the state of Assam.

Academic Performance

In search of teachers' status – especially their academic status, the study delved into the deep of their academic performance during their studenthood. Though there is no such guaranty that a good student should always be a good teacher and reverse, however the society expects that the academic carrier of a teacher, irrespective of denomination, should be uniformly fair. Due to sequel of socio-economic causes, it was hardly possible to the tribal teachers to reflect their actual academic performance during their studenthood.

Table 6.6 gives us a detailed picture about the academic performance of the respondent groups. From the previous Table, it was observed that none of the respondents from West Bengal, possessing a qualification of "Matriculation", where as 16.67 per cent of the respondent was found from Assam with such level of education, including 24 male and 1 female teachers.

While the only female – matriculate teacher from Assam passed in IInd division, 4 male teachers also got IInd division in matriculation. Only a male teacher got Ist division and the rest (nineteen in number) passed in IIIrd division. It should be noted here that none of these teachers continued their studies due to varied socio-economic and environmental circumstances as described by them.

The study observed 27 teachers [20 from Assam and 7 from West Bengal], who are higher secondary or intermediate passed.

Among the 20 teachers from Assam, 15 were male and five were female. Out of the fifteen male respondents, 2,6, & 7 stood in Ist, IInd and IIIrd division respectively at their matriculation level however at higher secondary level, only three of them received second division and rest fifteen were placed in IIIrd division. None of them at higher secondary level did able to qualify in first division.

In case of female respondents, all of them passed in IIIrd division at matriculation examination but in their successive level one passed in IInd division and rest four in IIIrd division at their higher secondary level.

Seven teachers from West Bengal who have had an educational level of higher secondary, includes five males and two females. Among the males, one got 1st division and 4 got second division at their matriculation stage and during higher secondary, 4 got second division and one-third division.

Almost all the respondents from both the states opined that they were not in a position to carryout their education either due to non-availability of nearby colleges, or due to socio-economic condition as because they were absorbed in teaching profession.

Table 6.6: Academic Performance of the Respondents During Their Studenthood

Assam		*Matriculation*			*Higher Secondary*			*Graduation*			*Post Graduation*			*Grand Total*
		1st	*2nd*	*3rd*	*1st*	*2nd*	*3rd*	*1st*	*2nd*	*3rd*	*1st*	*2nd*	*Pass*	
Matriculate	Male	1	4	19										
	Female	0	1	0										
	Total	1	5	19										25
	Male	2	6	7	0	3	12							
H.S. Passed	Female	0	0	5	0	1	4							
	Total	2	6	12	0	4	16							20
	Male	3	16	19	7	22	9	1	4	33				
Graduate	Female	1	8	18	0	0	27	0	2	25				
	Total	4	24	37	7	22	36	1	6	58				65
Post Graduate	Male	8	16	1	6	13	6	2	5	18	0	25	0	
	Female	0	11	4	3	8	4	1	9	5	6	9	0	
	Total	8	27	05	9	21	10	3	14	23	6	34	0	40
Grand Total		15	62	73	16	47	62	4	20	81	6	34	0	
			150			125			105			40		

(*Contd.*)

(Contd.)

West Bengal		Matriculation			Higher Secondary			Graduation			Post Graduation			Grand Total
		1st	2nd	3rd	1st	2nd	3rd	1st	2nd	3rd	1st	2nd	Pass	
Matriculate	Male	0	0	0										
	Female	0	0	0										
	Total	0	0	0										0
H.S. Passed	Male	1	4	0	0	4	1							
	Female	2	0	0	1	1	1							
	Total	3	4	0	1	5	1							7
Graduate	Male	46	11	11	3	59	6	24	41	3				
	Female	8	7	0	12	3	0	5	9	1				
	Total	54	18	11	15	62	6	29	50	4				83
Post Graduate	Male	48	5	0	9	42	2	14	39	0	0	51	2	
	Female	7	0	0	1	5	1	2	5	0	0	7	0	
	Total	55	5	0	10	47	3	16	44	0	0	58	2	60
Grand Total		112	27	11	26	114	10	45	94	4	0	58	2	
			150			150			143			60		

Among the graduate teachers, including 38 male and 27 female from the sample group of Assam, it was seen that at the matriculation level only 4 of them placed in Ist division where as 24 got IInd division and rest 37 (*i.e.*, 56.92 per cent) passed their matriculation with a IIIrd division.

In higher secondary level, when only 10.77 per cent of them got first division, 33.85 per cent received IInd division and rest 55.38 per cent passed in third division.

At the graduation level, only 1.54 per cent of the graduate respondents from Assam obtained a first class followed by 9.23 per cent who got IInd class and rest, the grand majority with 89.23 per cent of the teachers passed without any division.

Their gender wise performance reveals that 7.89 per cent of male and 3.70 per cent of female, 42.1 per cent of male and 29.63 per cent of female and 50 per cent of male and 66.67 per cent female were placed in 1st, 2nd and 3rd division respectively at their matriculation level. At the higher secondary level only 18.42 per cent and 57.89 per cent of graduate male passed their higher secondary education in Ist and IInd division respectively while 23.68 per cent of male and all the female graduate teachers from Assam passed in III division during their higher secondary level.

Further it was observed that among them only 2.63 per cent of male and none of the female was Ist class graduate. 10.53 per cent of male and 7.41 per cent of female were 2nd class graduate and 86.84 per cent of male and 92.59 per cent of female were graduate without having any class.

The scenario reveals that from the state of Assam, male sample showed a comparatively better carrier/academic performance than that of their female counter parts during their very level of study.

Only a little more than a quarter (*i.e.*, 26.67 per cent) of the respondent group from Assam have had a post-graduate qualification among whom only 20 per cent, 22.5 per cent, 7.5 per cent and 15 per cent stood first class during matriculation, higher secondary, graduation and post graduation levels respectively. The percentage of the total respondents who stood at second division in the respective academic levels are 67.5 per cent. 52.5 per cent, 35 per cent and 85 per cent, which is further followed by 12.5 per cent, 25 per cent, 57.5 per cent and 0 per cent of the Postgraduate respondents who stood in IIIrd class in their respective academic levels.

The educational qualification of the sample group from West Bengal reveals that only 4.67 per cent respondent group from the state are non-graduate, having an educational qualification up to 12th grade including 5 male and 2 female.

During matriculation, among them, one male, two females and three in total passed in first division and four males were placed in second division. However, none of them were IIIrd class matriculate. Among this group of teachers, only one female did able to pass H.S. in first division. Five teachers, including 4 male and one female stood in second division in higher secondary level and rest one male passed in third division.

The basic reason due to which they did not continue their studies as per their version, was the financial crunch, lack of colleges within the accessible range and overall, an early absorption in jobs.

From the Table 6.6, it can further be observed that majority of the respondents are graduate including 55.33 per cent of the respondent group from West Bengal.

Out of the graduate secondary teachers, 65.05 per cent stood in first division, including 46 male and 8 female, 21.69 per cent stood in second division, including 11 male and 7 female and rest 13.25 per cent stood in third division, incorporating 11 male respondents during their matriculation.

From this group of respondents, 18.07 per cent stood in first division, including 3 male and 12 female, 74.70 per cent placed in second division, incorporating 59 male and 3 female and rest 7.23 per cent were placed in third division, including 6 men during their higher secondary or intermediate level.

However at the graduation level, 34.94 per cent of them received a first-class degree incorporating 24 males and five females. Most of the graduate teachers forming almost 60.24 per cent of this group were second-class graduates, incorporating 41 male and 9 female. However a marginal part (4.82 per cent) of this group of respondents passed their graduation, without any class – including 3 male and one female.

Fortunately, a better percentage (40 per cent) of the respondents was found having a post-graduate qualification. This group includes 53 male and 7 female respondents.

While analyzing their academic performance at different levels, it was found that at the matriculation level, all of them were placed either in first or in second division and none passed their matriculation in third division. Further analysis in this level reveals that 91.67 per cent of them were matriculated in first division including 48 male and 7 female. Rest 8.33 per cent was placed in second division and all of them were male.

At the +2 standard, 16.66 per cent of them including only 9 males and 1 female could able to keep hold their position and achieved a first division. However majority (78.33 per cent) of them (42 male and 5 female) were placed in second division at this level and only 5 per cent of them (2 male and 1 female) possessed a third division higher secondary/intermediate certificate.

At the latter stage, (*i.e.*, during graduation) a little more than a quarter (26.67 per cent) of them including 14 male and 2 female got a first class bachelor degree, while majority of them (73.33 per cent) received IInd class bachelor degree. 39 male and 5 female were found in this group. While none were found placed in IIIrd class. This may be due to the reason that in West Bengal, there is not such class offered by the universities and those who failed to achieve at least the minimum percentage for IInd class are considered 'fail' in most of the universities.

Their performance at the post graduate level reveals that almost all, except two got in second class. 51 males and 7 females comprising 96.67 per cent of the entire group were found to have 2nd class in postgraduate level. Only two male teachers were found in this group who passed their post graduation without any class.

Constraints of Education: Distance from Institution During School Days

One of the standing problems, which become synonymous with the tribal education, is the massive rate of dropout. Various studies [*viz.* Ambasht (1970), Singh (1984), Pandey (1993), Sujatha (1987) etc.] observed that distance of the school & other educational institutions from the natural habitations of the tribal people is quite much which hinder the tribal education. Keeping this is view an attempt was made to explore, to what extent the teachers from the tribal communities was affected during their studenthood due to the very cause.

Table 6.7: Average Distance between the Institution and Residence of the Respondents, During their Student Hood

Assam		*Sec. School Level*	*H.S. School Level*	*College Level*	*University Level*
Matriculate	Male	8.53 Km 0.5 to 40 Km.			
	Female	2.18 Km 0.5 to 5 Km			
	Average	5.36 0.5-22.5 Km.			
H.S. Passed	Male		10.15 Km. 0.5 to 40 Km		
	Female		2.60 Km. 0.5 to 7 Km		
	Average		6.38 Km 0.5-23.5 Km.		
Graduate	Male			38.7 Km. 2 to 49 Km	
	Female			33.5 Km. 0.5 to 45 Km	
	Average			36.1 1.25-47 Km)	
Post Graduate	Male				270.80 Km 96 to 342 Km
	Female				218.57 Km 6 to 300 Km
	Average				244.69 51 to 312 Km.

(Contd.)

(Contd.)

Assam		*Sec. School Level*	*H.S. School Level*	*College Level*	*University Level*
West Bengal Matriculate	Male	6.5 Km. 0.2 to 28 Km.			
	Female	2.0 Km. 0.0 to 6 Km.			
	Average	4.25 Km 0.0 to 17 Km.			
H.S. Passed	Male		10.15 Km. 0.5 to 40 Km.		
	Female		7.50 Km. 0.0 to 28 Km		
	Average		8.83 Km. 0.25 to 34 Km		
Graduate	Male			58.8 Km. 16 to 120 Km	
	Female			19.5 Km. 0.0 to 22 Km	
	Average			39.15 Km 8 to 64 Km	
Post Graduate	Male				300.16 Km 42 to 411 Km
	Female				296.05 Km 40.5 to 388 Km
	Average				298.11 Km 41.25 to 399.5 Km

Table 6.7 shows the average distance of the institutions with different levels, (where the respondent attended last and pursued their education) from the native place (in Km.) of the respondents during their studenthood.

Constraints During Secondary Schooling

While the mean distance of the secondary schools from the native place of the respondents of Assam was 5.36 Km., with a variation of minimum 0.5 Km. and a maximum of 22.5 Km. The same in case of the respondents from West Bengal was found to be 4.25 Km. with a minimum of 0 Km. to a maximum of 17 Km. This reveals that the secondary education for the respondents from West Bengal was comparatively more-accessible, in terms of mean distance of the secondary schools from the habitation of the respondents.

The comparative sketch towards education for the males from two states shows that while in the State of Assam it is 8,53 Km., it is only 6.5 Km. for West Bengal, with a variation range of minimum of 0.5 Km. and 0.2 Km. and maximum of 40 Km. and 28 Km. respectively for the states Assam and West Bengal.

The same in case of female respondents from the two state was with a mean of 2.18 Km. and 2 Km. with a variation range, minimum of 0.5 Km. and 0 Km. and maximum of 5 Km. and 6 Km. for the states, Assam and West Bengal respectively. This reveals that for the females of both the states, it was easier to avail secondary education, when compared to their male counterparts; when this comparison is made between the respondent groups from the two states, it was observed that both for males and females from West Bengal, it was easier to avail secondary education, when the distance of secondary schools from their residence is taken into consideration.

Constraints During Higher Secondary Schooling

It was observed that while the mean distance of the higher secondary schools from the native place of the respondents from Assam was 6.38 Km., varying from 0.5 Km. minimum and 23.5 Km. maximum, it was 8.825 Km., varying from 0.25 Km. (minimum) to 34 Km. (Maximum) in case of West Bengal.

This picture reveals that higher secondary education for the respondents from Assam were comparatively easy accessible, when the average distance between the institution and home is taken into consideration. This average distance varied for the females for both the states, however, no difference was found from the responses of the males and in both the state, and this mean distance for male was found to be 10.15 Km. with a variation ranging from minimum of 0.5 Km. to a maximum of 40 Km.

In case of female teachers, this mean distance was 2.60 Km, ranging from 0.5 Km. to 7 Km. in the state Assam and in West Bengal it was 7.5 Km., ranging from 0 Km. to 28 Km. Naturally it can be said that higher secondary education for the female respondents was comparatively easy accessible, compared to their counter gendergroup from West Bengal.

Constraints During Graduation

Table 6.7, further reveals that while the mean distance between college and home for the respondents from Assam was 36.1 Km. ranging from a minimum of 1.25 Km. to a maximum of 47 Km., the same in case of the respondents from West Bengal was 39.15 Km., ranging from 8 Km. to 64 Km.

So it can be said that as like the education at higher secondary level, access towards college education (during graduation) was also comparatively easier for the respondents from Assam.

While taking the male group of respondents into consideration, one can find that in case of Assam the mean distance was 38.7 Km., ranging with a minimum of 2 Km. to a maximum of 49 Km.; where as in case of West Bengal for male, it was 58.8 Km., ranging from 16 Km. to 120 Km.; naturally it may be said that for the male sample group from Assam, College education was comparatively easy–accessible than that of their counter group of respondents from West Bengal

A different picture can be observed when the female groups from these states are taken into consideration. It is the female respondent group from West Bengal who were supposed to face a mean distance of 19.5 Km. to attend education at Bachelors level, varying from 0 to 22 Km. and thereby facing less constraints than that of the female respondent group from Assam, from whom this distance was 33.5 Km, ranging from 0.5 Km. to 45 Km.

Constraints During Post-Graduation

From the same Table, it may further be observed that during Post Graduation, the sample group from Assam was supposed to cross a mean distance of 244.69 Km., ranging from 6 Km. to 300 Km. to attend the post-graduate institutions however this distance was 298.105 Km. for the sample group from West Bengal. It reveals that for the sample group from West Bengal, it was too some extent difficult to avail education at post graduation level, so far the mean distance from university and their residence is concerned. For them this distance varied from a minimum of 41.25 Km. to maximum of 399.5 Km.

This distance was 270.80 Km. with a variation range of 96 Km to 324 Km for the male group from Assam, however it is 300.16 Km. for the male group from West Bengal, ranging from 42 Km. to 411 Km.

For the female it was 218.57 Km. ranging from 6 Km. to 300 Km. from Assam and 296.05 Km. with a minimum variation of 40.5 Km. to a maximum variation of 388 Km. for their counter part from West Bengal.

Schooling and Further Education

Schooling and educational institution stands as a symbol of status for any individual in Indian socio-educational fabric, though not designated. In this case the reputation of the institution acts as the status indicator. A person who studied in well-known and prestigious institutions enjoys comparatively higher status than that who did pursue his studies from a mediocre institution. Most of the cases, the tribals suppose to study in such mediocre institutions having less name and fame, not only for the reason that they are not capable to be admitted to such institutions in terms of their merit. The underlining fact is that the 'Prestigious institutions' are mostly centralized in urban areas and are often quite expensive, which compel them to peruse education from ordinary institutions.

Table 6.8 presents a clear picture of the location of institutions of different levels, where the respondents carried out their studies.

From the state of Assam, while out of 150 respondents, 36.67 per cent, 18 per cent and 49.33 per cent studied up to the matriculation level in the schools situated in urban, sub-urban and rural areas respectively, in the West Bengal this proportion was 0.67 per cent, 6 per cent and 93.33 per cent in the same order.

Juxtaposition reveals that while majority of the sample from Assam studied in schools located either in urban or in sub-urban areas, In West Bengal, bulk of our sample (93.33 per cent) studied in rural schools.

Table 6.8: Location of Institutions Where the Respondent Teachers Studied During their Studenthood

		Assam				*West Bengal*				*Grand Total*
		Urban	*Sub Urban*	*Rural*	*Total*	*Urban*	*Sub Urban*	*Rural*	*Total*	
Up to Matriculation	Male	36	13	53	102	1	6	119	126	
	Female	13	14	21	48	0	3	21	24	
	Total	49	27	74	150	1	9	140	150	300
		(32.67%)	(18%)	(49.33%)	(100%)	(0.67%)	(6%)	(93.33%)	(100%)	(100%)
During H.S.	Male	52	20	6	78	1	104	21	126	
	Female	16	25	6	47	2	11	11	24	
	Total	68	45	12	125	3	115	32	150	275
		(54.4%)	(36%)	(9.6%)	(100%)	(2%)	(76.67%)	(21.33%)	(100%)	(91.67%)
During Graduation	Male	51	12	–	63	3	91	27	121	
	Female	29	13	–	42	8	7	7	22	
	Total	80	25	0	105	11	98	34	143	248
		(76.19%)	(23.81%)	(0%)	(100%)	(7.69%)	(68.53%)	(23.78%)	(100%)	(82.67%)
During Post Graduation	Male	25	–	–	25	4	47	2	53	
	Female	15	–	–	15	7	–	–	7	
	Total	40	0	0	40	11	47	2	60	100
		(100%)			(100%)	(18.33%)	(78.34%)	(3.33%)	(100%)	(33.33%)

So, rural schools played an important role to educate the respondents up to matriculation level in West Bengal, and the urban and sub-urban schools in the state of Assam played similar role. However, almost half (49.33 per cent) of the respondents from Assam studied in rural schools up to their matriculation level. So, it can be said that rural schools played an important role to educate the entire sample group from both the states.

16.67 per cent of the respondents from Assam continued their education up to matriculation level. Only 125 respondents continued their study beyond the level from this state. Among them majority (54.5 per cent) of the respondents passed higher secondary education from the institutions situated in urban areas and only 36 per cent and 9.6 per cent of them did studied in the institutions situated in sub-urban and rural areas respectively from this state.

On the other hand, in West Bengal, majority (76.67 per cent) of the respondents pursued their higher secondary education from the institutions situated in sub-urban areas, followed by 21.33 per cent and only 2 per cent studied in the institutions situated in rural and urban areas respectively, form this state.

So, while the sub-urban institutions took the responsibility to educate the respondents from West Bengal at +2 stage, it is the urban institutions, which played the similar role for educating our respondents from Assam.

Only 105 respondents from Assam pursued their education till the graduation level while the number is 143 for West Bengal.

Among the 105 respondents from Assam, 76.19 per cent were graduated from urban colleges while 68.53 per cent of the total of 143 respondent from West Bengal pursued graduation form sub-urban colleges. Only 23.81 per cent of the respondents pursued their graduation from sub-urban colleges and not even a single respondent studied in rural colleges from Assam. However, 23.78 per cent of the respondents from West Bengal studied in rural colleges and only 7.69 per cent of them carried out their study from urban colleges during graduation.

This finding reveals that while the urban colleges of Assam show the maximum enrollment of the respondent tribe teachers, in West Bengal, the colleges in the similar setting had the minimum enrollment of the respondents from the very state.

It was further observed that 26.67 per cent and 40 per cent of the respondents from the states of Assam and West Bengal respectively studied up to post graduate level and cent per cent of the respondents studied in the universities situated in the urban areas.

On the other hand, during post graduation, majority (78.34 per cent) of the respondents from West Bengal studied in the universities, situated in sub-urban areas. 18.33 per cent of them carried out their post graduation from the universities, situated in urban areas and rest 3.33 per cent studied their post graduate in the universities, situated in rural set up.

NOTES

1. Only study in this direction is reported by Roy, R. in 2001.
2. A brief perusal over the census reports (special tables for scheduled tribes) since 1961 establishes the fact.
3. A macro survey over the state of tribe teachers in eastern and northeastern region of India helps conclude the statement.

7

Linguistic, Religions and Family Status

Linguistic Status vis-a-vis Constraints of Education

Language is not merely the medium of instruction rather it is the major way of communication. Especially in pedagogical atmosphere it become an important factor for the students as because the perception of the content fully depend upon the medium of instruction. The tribal communities in India follow more than hundred languages and dialects. They are, at the same time born and mostly brought up in their own linguistic environment and develop sufficient command over their mother tongue. Their education hinders when the tribal students are compelled to peruse their education in some other (State) language with which they are less familiar. This effects their education. Even if they are introduced with education through their own language at the outset of education however the medium is withdrawn in the successive class-grades.

While delving the linguistic status of the respondents, in terms of the medium of instruction they followed in the different levels of education, it was observed that from the state of Assam, the medium of instruction were mostly English, Assamese, Bengali, Khasi, Mizo and Manipuri. However, from West Bengal the languages were Bengali, English, Bengali and English both, Alchiki and/or santhali. It should be specified that from both the states, the respondent group possessed a varied linguistic groups, so far their mother-tongues are concerned. But some how they were compelled to accept only a hand-counted few languages as their medium of instruction at different levels of studies, which are shown in Table 7.1.

It was observed that, from Assam, during school level (which further includes higher secondary study), 9.80 per cent of male and 37.5 per cent of female respondent, together comprising 18.67 per cent of total respondents from this state, took up English as their medium of instruction. Where as in West Bengal, only 4.76 per cent of male respondent and none of the female took up this very language, forming a total of 4 per cent of the respondent group from West Bengal in the school level.

Table 7.1: Medium of Instruction During Studenthood

Assam		*English*	*Assamese*	*Bengali*	*Khasi*	*Mizo*	*Manipuri*	*Gr. Total*
School Level	M	10 (9.80%)	49 (48.05%)	18 (17.65%)	11 (10.78%)	8 (7.84%)	6 (5.88%)	102
	F	18 (37.5%)	11 (22.92%)	07 (14.58%)	4 (8.33%)	05 (1.42%)	3 (6.25%)	48
	T	28 (18.67%)	60 (40%)	25 (1667%)	15 (10%)	13 (8.67%)	9 (6%)	150 (100%)
College Level	M	42 (66.67%)	17 (26.98%)	1 (1.59%)	2 (3.17%)	1 (1.59%)	0 (0%)	63
	F	26 (61.91%)	8 (19.05%)	3 (7.14%)	2 (4.76%)	3 (7.14%)	0 (0%)	42
	T	68 (64.76%)	25 (23.81%)	4 (3.81%)	4 (3.81%)	4 (3.81%)	0 (0%)	105 (70%)
University Level	M	18 (72%)	6 (24%)	0 (0%)	1 (4%)	0 (0%)	0 (0%)	25
	F	11 (73.33%)	4 (26.67%)	0 (0%)	0 (0%)	0 (0%)	0 (0%)	15
	T	29 (72.5%)	10 (25%)	0 (0%)	1 (2.5%)	0 (0%)	0 (0%)	40 (26.67%)

(Contd.)

(Contd.)

West Bengal		*Bengali*	*English*	*Bengali & English*	*Alchiki/and or Santhali*	*Gr. Total*
School Level	M	109 (86.51%)	6 (4.76%)	11 (8.73%)	0 (0%)	126
	F	20 (83.3%)	0 (0%)	1 (4.17%)	3 (12.5%)	24
	T	129 (86%)	6 (4%)	12 (8%)	3 (2%)	150 (100%)
College Level	M	102 (84.30%)	3 (2.48%)	16 (13.22%)	0 (0%)	121
	F	21 (95.45%)	1 (4.55%)	0 (0%)	0 (0%)	22
	T	123 (86.01%)	4 (2.82%)	16 (11.18%)	0 (0%)	143 (95.33%)
University Level	M	48 (90.57%)	1 (1.83%)	4 (7.55%)	0 (0%)	53
	F	6 (85.71%)	0 (0%)	1 (14.29%)	0 (0%)	7
	T	54 (90%)	1 (1.67%)	5 (8.33%)	0 (0%)	60 (40.00%)

In this context it was observed that in both states, a handful percentage of the respondents offered with the state language as their medium of instruction at the school level. While 48.05 per cent of male and 22.92 per cent of female respondents – together forming a group of 40 per cent from Assam studied in Assamese language in their school days, in the state of West Bengal, 86 per cent of the respondent group, incorporating 86.51 per cent of male and 83.3 per cent of female studied in Bengali medium in their school days.

It is clear from the Table 7.1 that influence of state language as the medium for the respondents in the school level is substantially higher in West Bengal, compared to Assam.

While 16.67 per cent of the respondent group including 17.65 per cent of male and 14.58 per cent of female from Assam opted Bengali as the medium if instruction during school days; 8 per cent of the respondents from West Bengal, including 8.73 per cent of male and 4.17 per cent of female carried out their school level education both in Bengali and English language in a bilingual fashion.

Only 2 per cent of the respondent group from West Bengal, including 12.5 per cent of female respondents and none of the male respondent carried out their studies in indigenous languages. *Viz.*, Alchiki and/or Santhali in this level where as in Assam almost (32 per cent) one third of the respondent had the opportunity to opt for own languages (Khasi, Mizo, Manipuri) as their medium of instruction in the very level. It can be observed that 10 per cent (incorporating 10.78 per cent male and 8.33 per cent female), 8.67 per cent (including 7.84 per cent of male and 10.42 per cent female) and 6 per cent (incorporating 5.88 per cent of male and 6.25 per cent of female) carried out their studies in school level in Khasi, Mizo and Manipuri language respectively.

The extent of indigenous languages as medium of instruction is mostly found in Assam compared to West Bengal

At the college level, scope of choice towards medium of instruction reduced to some extent and it was observed that from Assam, majority (64.76%) pursued their college education in English medium, including 66.67 per cent of male and 61.91 per cent of female while 23.81 per cent pursued education at this level in Assamese medium, incorporating 26.98 per cent of male and 19.05 per cent of female respondents. Uniformly 3.81 per cent of the respondents pursued education in Bengali, Khasi and Mizo medium comprising a group of 11.43 per cent of the total respondents from the state. None in this level was found carried out their education in Manipuri language.

On the other hand, from West Bengal 86.01 per cent, 2.81 per cent and 11.18 per cent of the respondents pursued their college education in Bengali, English and both in Bengali and English medium incorporating 84.30 per cent, 2.48 per cent and 13.22 per cent of male and 95.45 per cent, 4.55 per cent and 0 per cent of female in the respective mediums in the same order.

Comparing the level of education in both the states, one can find a declining trend of availability of medium of instruction in indigenous language and a domination of English and respective state language can be observed as a common feature in this context during graduation.

This declining trend continues even in post graduation level where 72.5 per cent of the postgraduate respondents from Assam pursued education in English medium, followed by 25 per cent and only 2.5 per cent who pursued their education in Assamise and Khasi languages respectively.

Similar trend is visible even in West Bengal, where 90 per cent (including 90.57 per cent male and 85.71 per cent of female) respondents pursued post graduation in Bengali medium, followed by 8.33 per cent (including 7.55 per cent male and 14.29 per cent female) respondents, for whom the medium of instruction was both English and Bengali, further followed by only 1.67 per cent of the respondents who carried out their post graduation in English medium.

Influence in English as the medium of instruction is therefore scanty at higher education level for the respondents from West Bengal, compared to their counterparts from Assam. This is due to the multi-lingual environment in the state of Assam where English language is taken as a lingua franca and accepted at higher education by almost all ethnic groups. However, in West Bengal the domination of state language (*i.e.* Bengal) is a common phenomenon, which influenced even the higher education. This may be due to differing state policy in language in the states.

Religious Status

Religion may be regarded as the beliefs and patterns of behaviour by which humans try to deal with what they view as important problems that cannot be solved through the application of known technology, techniques of organization. It acts as a reagent to enhance learning of the different aspects of traditions. Finally religion plays an important role in maintaining community solidarity. One notable feature of the tribals in some parts of India is frequent shift from one religion to another which occur mostly to get-rid-of several social stigmas. Tables 7.2, 7.3 and 7.4 are reflecting the religions status of the respondents.

Table 7.2 presents religion wise distribution of the respondents from both the states. Here, it is worth-mentioning that, this religion-wise distribution does not indicate the respondents' ascribed – rather indicates their present religion, as they reported.

Table 7.2: Religion (*i.e.* Present Religion)

Assam	*Hindu*	*Christian*	*Prislitarian/ Others/ Buddhist*	*No response*	*Total*
Male	24 (23.53%)	72 (70.59%)	4 (3.92%)	2 (1.96%)	102 (100%)
Female	13 (27.08%)	34 (70.84%)	1 (2.08%)	0 (0%)	48 (100%)
Total	37 (24.67%)	106 (70.67%)	5 (3.33%)	2 (1.33%)	150 (100%)

West Bengal	*Hindu*	*Christian*	*Sari/Sarna*	*Prislitarian*	*No response*	*Total*
Male	69 (54.76%)	22 (17.46%)	35 (27.78%)	0 (0%)	0 (0%)	126 (100%)
Female	14 (58.33%)	3 (12.5%)	5 (20.83%)	1 (4.17%)	1 (4.17%)	24 (100%)
Total	83 (55.33%)	25 (16.67%)	40 (26.67%)	1 (0.665%)	1 (0.665%)	150 (100%)

The Table reveals that, 23.53 per cent male and 27.08 per cent of female, comprising almost a quarter (24.67 per cent) of the entire respondent group from Assam belonging to Hindu religion where as 70.67per cent of the respondents, including 70.59 per cent of male and 70.84 per cent of female from this state were found follower of Christianity. Only 3.33 per cent of the total respondent group, incorporating 3.92 per cent of male and 2.08 per cent of female are following Buddhism or Prislitarian or 'any other' religion. However, 1.33 per cent of the respondents did not respond towards the question. All the members from this silent group were male.

In the state of West Bengal, 54.76 per cent of male and 58.33 per cent of female, aggregately constituting 55.33 per cent of the total respondent group was found following the Hindu religion. Christianity was followed by 17.46 per cent of male, 12.5 per cent of female and a total of 16.67 per cent of the respondents.

Indigenous religion Sari/Sarna or the like was followed by 27.78 per cent of male and 20.83 per cent of the female respondents together comprising a group of 26.67 per cent of the respondent from West Bengal. Only 0.665 per cent of the entire respondents reported following prislitarian religion. Just 0.665 per cent did not replied to the question

A comparative picture from this table reveals that while substantially higher proportion of the respondents from Assam is following Christianity, marginally higher proportion of the respondent group from West Bengal were found Hindu.

Table 7.3: Ascribed Religion

Assam	*Hindu*	*Christian*	*Prislitarian/ Others/ Buddhist*	*No Response*	*Total*
Male	51 (50%)	11 (10.78%)	24 (23.53%)	16 (15.69%)	102 (100%)
Female	20 (41.67%)	6 (12.5%)	2 (4.16%)	20 (41.67%)	48 (100%)
Total	71 (47.34%)	17 (11.33%)	26 (17.33%)	36 (24%)	150 (100%)

West Bengal	*Hindu*	*Christian*	*Sari/Sarna*	*Prislitarian*	*No response*	*Total*
Male	20 (15.87%)	7 (5.56%)	80 (63.49%)	19 (15.08%)	0 (0%)	126 (100%)
Female	3 (12.5%)	4 (16.67%)	16 (66.67%)	0 (0%)	1 (4.16%)	24 (100%)
Total	23 (15.33%)	11 (7.33%)	96 (64%)	19 (12.67%)	1 (0.67%)	150 (100%)

Table 7.3 represent the distribution of the respondents in terms of their ascribed religion, where it is found that from Assam 47.34 per cent of the total respondents, (including 50 per cent of male and 41.67 per cent of female) who ascribed Hindu religion, and it is only 11.33 per cent, including 10.78 per cent of male and 12.5 per cent of female respondents who ascribed Christianity. 23.53 per cent of male and only 4.16 per cent of female, comprising 17.33 per cent of the total group from the state ascribed Prislitarian or religions other than Hindu and Christian.

A little less than a quarter of the respondents (24 per cent) did not respond towards this question including 15.69 per cent of male and 41.67 per cent of female.

Zooming the view to state West Bengal, it was found that majority of the respondents (64 per cent) ascribed Sari or Sarna religion, including 63.49 per cent of male and 66.67 per cent of female.

This group is followed by the group ascribed Hindu religion, including 15.87 per cent of male and 12.5 per cent of total female group from the state and thereby forming 15.33 per cent of the entire respondents from the state.

12.67 per cent of the respondents said to have ascribed Prislitarian religion and all the members from this group are male.

Only 7.33 per cent of the respondent group informed to have ascribed Christianity. 5.56 per cent of female and 16.67 per cent of the total female from the state West Bengal are forming this very group. However, only 0.67 per cent of the respondents did not respond about their ascribed religion.

The table reveals that from Assam, in terms of ascribed religion, where Hindus are the largest group, it is Sari/Sarna group from West Bengal.

Comparing the Table 7.2 and Table 7.3, we can observe that 54.67 per cent of the respondents from Assam and 68 per cent from West Bengal were converted from their ascribed religion. 58 male, 24 female and 82 respondents in total from Assam and 83 male, 19 female and 102 respondents in total from West Bengal was found converted. These converted group of respondents from both the states spelt numerous factors and forces. Response towards a question regarding reasons of conversion are systematically classified in seven broad categories and are presented in Table 7.4.

Table 7.4: Reasons of Conversion of Religion

Gender	Marriage	Economic	Social	Educational Opportunity	Scientific	No Response/ ignorance	Personal/ other	Total
				Assam				
Male	0	5	11	13	4	18	7	58
	(0)	(8.62)	(18.79)	(22.41)	(6.90)	(31.03)	(12.07)	(100)
Female	8	0	3	1	0	3	9	24
	(33.33)	(0)	(12.5)	(4.17)	(0)	(12.5)	(37.5)	(100)
Total	8	5	14	14	4	21	16	82
	(9.76)	(6.10)	(17.07)	(17.07)	(4.88)	(25.61)	(19.51)	(100)
				West Bengal				
Male	1	2	2	53	2	6	17	83
	(1.20)	(2.41)	(2.41)	(63.86)	(2.41)	(7.23)	(20.48)	(100)
Female	11	1	4	0	0	0	3	19
	(57.9)	(5.26)	(21.05)	(0)	(0)	(0)	(15.79)	(100)
Total	12	3	6	53	2	6	20	102
	(11.77)	(2.94)	(5.88)	(51.96)	(1.96)	(5.88)	(19.61)	(100)

9.76 per cent of the converted respondents from Assam and 11.77 per cent from West Bengal emphasized on the reasons related to matrimonial. 33.33 per cent and 57.9 per cent of the female respondent from the states, Assam and West Bengal respectively, opined that they were converted due to marriage, while the reason remains same for only 1.2 per cent of male converted respondent. From the table, it is further observed that this conversion took place, due to marriage mostly in case of the female respondents.

The causes of conversion were a fact mostly due to economic constraints for 6.1 per cent and 2.94 per cent of the respondents from the states Assam and West Bengal respectively. Due to this fact, 8.62 per cent and 2.41 per cent of male from the respective two states were converted and only 5.26 per cent of the female respondents from West Bengal were also converted due to these constraints.

Further analysis of data reveals that while 17.07 per cent of the respondents were converted from their ascribed religion due to different social causes, from Assam, for only 5.88 per cent of the respondents from West Bengal the basic causes of conversion remain the same. Further, 18.97 per cent and 2.41 per cent of male and 12.5 per cent and 21.05 per cent of the female from the states of Assam and West Bengal, respectively were converted from their ascribed religion due to different social causes.

While 17.07 per cent of the respondent gave up their ascribed religion from Assam, in order to avail educational opportunities, it is 51.96 per cent of the respondents from West Bengal who also gave up their ascribed religion for the same reason. This happened mostly in case of the male respondents in both the states than that of the female respondents. From the Table 5.9 it is found that 22.41 per cent of male respondents from Assam and 63.86 per cent of male respondents from West Bengal took up some other religion to avail more educational opportunity. Considering the extent, it happened mostly in West Bengal than that of Assam.

Among the converted teachers only 4.88 per cent and 1.96 per cent of the respondents from Assam and West Bengal, respectively, views the reason of their conversion from ascribed religion as they feel that their achieved religion is more scientific than that of their ascribed one. One notable thing is that all of them were male.

31.03 per cent of male and 12.5 per cent of female converted respondents, forming a group of a quarter of the entire converted respondents from Assam and 5.88 per cent from West Bengal did not respond towards this question. However, 19.51 per cent respondents from Assam and 19.61 from West Bengal stressed on either personal or some other reasons, due to which they changed their ascribed religion.

12.07 per cent and 20.48 per cent of male and 37.5 per cent and 15.79 per cent of female respondents from the states of Assam and West Bengal respectively were found falling in this response category.

Family Status

The most important component of gestalt status in India as well as in other country depends mostly upon the family status of an individual. Human family is a group composed of a woman, her dependent children and at least one adult male joined through marriage or blood relationship. The tribal family may take many forms, ranging all the way from a single married compel with their children to a large group composed of several brothers and sisters with the sister's children. The particular form taken by the family is related to particular social, historical and ecological circumstances. The traditional tribal families are mostly extended in nature however nuclear families also exist. Where families are small and relatively independent, individuals are isolated from the aid and support of kin and fend for themselves in many situations. By contrast, the community structured family – mostly known as extend family includes several adults within the same large household – must find ways of controlling various kind of tensions that invariably exist between their members. Tables 7.5, 7.6 and 7.7 presents a brief sketch of the family status in terms of nature, size and number of sibling of their family.

Table 7.5: Nature of Family

State→	*Assam*			*West Bengal*			*Grand Total*
Type→ ↓Sex	*Nuclear*	*Extended*	*Total*	*Nuclear*	*Extended*	*Total*	
Male	42 (41.18%)	60 (58.82%)	102 (100%)	42 (33.33%)	84 (66.67%)	126 (100%)	228 (76%)
Female	34 (70.83%)	14 (29.17%)	48 (100%)	8 (33.33%)	16 (66.67%)	24 (100%)	72 (24%)
Total	76 (50.67%)	74 (49.33%)	150 (100%)	50 (33.33%)	100 (66.67%)	150 (100%)	300 (100%)

In terms of nature of the family, a bifurcation of the respondent groups is prominent which revealed that, while from the state of Assam 41.18 per cent of the male respondents are having family pattern which is nuclear in natures, 70.83 per cent of the female respondents from the same state are having similar nature of family. On the other hand, majority (58 82 per cent) of the male respondents are living in extended family. Only 29.17 per cent of their female counter group is also having an extended family structure. In total, it was observed that while 50.67 per cent of the respondents from Assam are living in nuclear family, the rest 49.33 per cent are staying in extended families.

On the other hand, from the state of West Bengal, while one-third of the respondents, both male and female, are having nuclear pattern of family, majority of (two-third) them are living in extended families.

Generally, in both the states while extended family pattern is quite a common phenomena among the tribal groups, however the forthcoming Table reveals that, though marginally, till majority of the respondents are deviating from their ancestral pattern of family. This is due to massive effect of modernization and some times due to a distant place of work where they are supposed to stay in family with nuclear pattern.

Table 7.6: Distribution of the Respondents in Terms of Their Family Size

State	*Assam*				*West Bengal*				*Grand Total*
Family size→ Sex	*1 – 3*	*4 – 6*	*7 & above*	*Total*	*1 – 3*	*4 – 6*	*7 & above*	*Total*	
Male	5 (4.90%)	54 (52.94%)	43 (42.16%)	102 (100%)	12 (9.52%)	68 (53.97%)	46 (36.51%)	126 (100%)	228 (76%)
Female	8 (16.67%)	28 (58.67%)	12 (25%)	48 (100%)	0 (0%)	19 (79.17%)	5 (20.83%)	24 (100%)	72 (24%)
Total	13 (8.67%)	82 (54.67%)	55 (36.66%)	150 (100%)	12 (8%)	87 (58%)	51 (34%)	150 (100%)	300 (100%)

Table 7.6 represents the family size of the respondents considering the number of members in the family. Here classification has been made as small family, medium and large family. From the table, it is observed that majority

of the respondents from Assam and West Bengal are having a medium size of family.

8.67 per cent of the respondents from Assam and 8 per cent from West Bengal are having small family and 36.66 per cent and 34 per cent of the respondents from the respective states are having larger families.

Sex wise distribution of these types of family reveals that while among the male 4.9 per cent, 52.94 per cent and 42.16 per cent are having smaller, medium and larger family from Assam, these figures are 9.52 per cent, 53.97 per cent and 36.51 per cent from West Bengal respectively.

On the other hand, while 16.67 per cent, 58.33 per cent and 25 per cent of the female from Assam are having smaller, medium and larger family respectively; these percentages are 0, 79.17 and 20.83 for the females from West Bengal.

So far the percentage of different types of family is concerned, a similar trend can be observed in this regard while majority of the respondents are having medium size family, followed by larger families, a marginal few are having smaller families. Other things being equal, one significant difference was that, while 16.67 per cent of the female respondents from Assam are having smaller family none found among the females from West Bengal, having smaller family. The Table shows a gradual transition of medium and smaller families from their traditional extended family to modern nuclear family.

Table 7.7: Number of Siblings of the Respondents

State→	*Assam*				*West Bengal*				*Grand Total*
Siblings→ ↓ *Sex*	*1 – 3*	*4 – 6*	*7& more*	*Total*	*1 – 3*	*4 – 6*	*7& more*	*Total*	
Male	2 (1.96)	44 (43.14)	56 (54.90)	102 (100)	20 (15.87)	61 (48.41)	45 (35.72)	126 (100)	228 (76)
Female	11 (22.91)	14 (29.17)	23 (47.92)	48 (100)	0 (0)	13 (54.17)	11 (45.83)	24 (100)	72 (24)
Total	13 (8.66)	58 (38.67)	79 (52.67)	150 (100)	20 (13.33)	74 (49.34)	56 (37.33)	150 (100)	300 (100)

Status often depends on the economic potentiality, which inversely varies with the increased number of family members – as it reduces the per capita income, basically when the younger member of the family, having restricted or no capacity to earn for the family are more in number. To have a reflection of the economic condition of their families during early school days, certain question has been designed. Responding towards the question, 52.67 per cent of the respondents from Assam and 37.33 per cent from West Bengal replied that they had a substantially higher number of siblings (seven and more). Definitely these group of respondents were lacking in terms of sufficient economic support from their parents, compared to 38.67 per cent and 49.34

per cent of the respondents from the respective states who had lesser number of siblings, varied with a minimum of four to a maximum of six.

Further grouping can be perused from the Table, where only 8.66 per cent of the respondents from Assam and 13,33 per cent from West Bengal had siblings, varying from one to three in number. This third group includes members with less percentage than that of other two comparable groups. We can assume that though less, but they did able to enjoy economic support from their family with comparatively greater extent.

In terms of sex of the respondents, it can be observed from the Table that only 1.96 per cent of male and 22.91 per cent of female respondents from Assam had a maximum number of three siblings where 15.87 per cent of male respondents had less number of siblings (with maximum of three) in this context. It should be noted here that none of the female sample from West Bengal did have less than four siblings. Naturally, it can be said that it is the female respondent group from West Bengal, for whom the economic situation during school days differed significantly compared to the other three groups of respondents (*viz.* Both the male group of respondents from Assam and West Bengal and also the female group of respondent from Assam).

Housing Status

Housing condition probably the most authentic indicator of the over all status of an individual within a certain cultural context. For the sake of the basic objective of the present study, the author encompassed his vision over several aspects of their house *viz.* the type of house, number of rooms there in and the specific location of the house which are analyzed in the Tables 7.8, 7.9, 7.10 respectively.

Table 7.8: Types of House

State	*Type of House*	*Own*	*Partly Own & Partly rented*	*Rented*	*Quarters*	*Others*	*Total*
Assam	Male	62 (60.78)	0 (0)	14 (13.73)	19 (18.63)	7 (6.86)	102 (100)
	Female	35 (72.92)	0 (0)	9 (18.75)	3 (6.25)	1 (2.08)	48 (100)
	Total	97 (64.67)	0 (0)	23 (15.33)	22 (14.67)	8 (5.33)	150 (100)
West Bengal	Male	64 (50.79)	6 (4.76)	26 (20.63)	30 (23.82)	0 (0)	126 (100)
	Female	15 (62.5)	0 (0)	7 (29.17)	2 (8.33)	0 (0)	24 (100)
	Total	79 (52.67)	6 (4)	33 (22)	32 (21.33)	0 (0)	150 (100)
Grand Total →		176 (58.67)	6 (2)	56 (18.67)	54 (18)	8 (2.66)	300 (100)

To determine the status of the respondents for the study, the types of houses, where they are staying was also taken into consideration. The type of house where the respondents are living is classified in Table 7.8, where from we can say that among the total group of respondents from both the states, 58.67 per cent are residing in their own house. 60.78 per cent and 50.79 per cent of the male, 72.92 per cent and 62.5 per cent of female and 64.67 per cent and 52.67 per cent of the total respondents from the states of Assam and West Bengal, respectively, are having their own house. So it can be said that more respondents from Assam are having their own house compared to the respondents from West Bengal. And again with a step forward it can be said that status of the respondents from Assam is higher than that of West Bengal in terms of the ownership of house.

From Table 7.8 we can further observe that a total of 2 per cent of the entire respondent group are staying in the house, which is partly owned and partly rented. Almost all of them are from West Bengal and are having their own house but are supposed to stay in some rented house, nearer to their working place, mostly due to long distance between school and their own residence.

Only a some of 15.33 per cent of the respondents incorporating 13.73 per cent of male and 18.75 per cent of female from Assam and 22 per cent of the respondents, incorporating 20.63 per cent of male and 29.17 per cent of female from West Bengal were found staying in rented house, comprising 18.67 per cent of the entire respondents from both the sates. Considering the respondent groups from two different states, it is observed that the percentage of respondent group staying in rented house is more in West Bengal compared to their counterparts from Assam, which further reveals that the status of the respondent group (both male and female) from Assam is comparatively higher than that of West Bengal.

From the Table it is further observed that while 18.63 per cent of male, 6.25 per cent of female and 14.67 per cent of the total respondents from Assam are residing in the quarters mostly provided by the institutions, where they are working, it is 23.82 per cent of male, 8.33 per cent of female and 21.33 per cent of the total respondents from West Bengal. In total, it was found that 18 per cent of the entire respondent group is staying in quarter, adjacent to school.

If we consider the availability of quarter as a facility in working condition, mostly it is the respondent group from West Bengal, availing this facility to a grater extent compared to their counterparts from Assam.

Only a marginal (2.66 per cent) percentage of the respondents from the entire respondent group was found staying in some other type of residences. The study did not find any such instances from West Bengal. However, 5.33 per cent of the total respondents from Assam, incorporating 6.86 per cent of male and 2.08 per cent of female said that they are staying in some other sort of houses not comming under previously mentioned forms.

Table 7.9: Number of Rooms in the House

State	Assam					West Bengal					Grand Total
No. of Rooms in House → Sex	4 & More	Three	Two	Single	Total	4 & More	Three	Two	Single	Total	
Male	29 (28.43)	62 (60.79)	7 (6.86)	4 (3.92)	102 (100)	25 (19.84)	45 (35.71)	43 (34.13)	13 (10.32)	126 (100)	228 (76)
Female	28 (58.33)	20 (41.67)	0 (0)	0 (0)	48 (100)	2 (8.33)	14 (58.34)	8 (33.33)	0 (0)	24 (100)	72 (24)
Total	57 (38)	82 (54.67)	7 4.665)	4 (2.665)	150 (100)	27 (18)	59 (39.33)	51 (34)	13 (8.67)	150 (100)	300 (100)

Status of an individual does not merely depend upon the type of, houses but also on the housing condition. Table 7.9 gives a brief perusal of the number of rooms the respondents are having in their house.

It was found that while from Assam 2.665 per cent, 4.66 per cent, 54.67 per cent and 38 per cent of the respondent are staying in house having single room, double rooms, three roomed and four or more rooms respectively, the percentages are 8.67, 34, 39.38 and 18 in the same order for the respondents from West Bengal.

Further analysis reveals that while 3.92 per cent of male from Assam are staying in single roomed residence, more than ten per cent (10.32 per cent exactly) of the male respondents from West Bengal are staying in such houses. None of the female from any state are staying in single-roomed house.

Observing the fact, it can be interpreted that in this respect, while the male group of teachers from West Bengal is holding a comparatively lower status than their male counter group from Assam, the females from both the states are having a comparatively higher status.

The study observed that 6.86 per cent of the male respondents from Assam are staying in two roomed houses, 34.13 per cent of the male respondents from West Bengal are staying in such houses. One third (33.33 per cent) of the female respondents from West Bengal are also staying in two roomed houses while none of their matching sample group from Assam are staying in 2 roomed houses.

60.79 per cent and 35.71 per cent of the male respondents and 41.67 per cent and 58.34 per cent of the female respondent group reported to have staying in three-roomed house from the states of Assam and West Bengal respectively. While comparatively more male teachers from Assam are staying in the house having three rooms, it is the male group from West Bengal staying in three-roomed houses, who are comparatively more in number as compared to their counter group from Assam.

The Table reveals that 28.43 per cent and 19.84 per cent of the male and 58.33 per cent and 8.33 per cent of the female respondents from the states of

Assam and West Bengal are staying in the houses having at least four rooms. These figures obviously goes in favour of the respondent groups, both male and female from Assam indicating their comparatively higher status than that of the respondents from West Bengal.

Table 7.10: Location of Home

State	*Location →* *Sex*	*Urban*	*Suburban*	*Village*	*Remote Village*	*Total*
Assam	Male	32 (31.37%)	19 (18.63%)	34 (33.33%)	17 (16.67%)	102 (100%)
	Female	23 (47.92%)	8 (16.665%)	14 (29.165%)	3 (6.25%)	48 (100%)
	Total	55 (36.67%)	27 (18%)	48 (32%)	20 (13.33%)	150 (100%)
West Bengal	Male	13 (10.32%)	9 (7.14%)	50 (39.68%)	54 (42.86%)	126 (100%)
	Female	0 (0%)	1 (4.16%)	16 (66.67%)	7 (29.17%)	24 (100%)
	Total	13 (8.67%)	10 (6.66%)	66 (44%)	61 (40.67%)	150 (100%)
	Grand Total	68 (22.67%)	37 (12.33%)	114 (38%)	81 (27%)	300 (100%)

While carrying out the study, it was observed that our sample group is spread over urban, sub-urban, rural and even in remote villages from the ten districts of the states of Assam and West Bengal. Though the tribal communities ordinarily reside in remote areas, but while carrying out the survey it was observed that the sample groups are normally spreaded over different areas.

36.67 per cent, 18 per cent and 45.33 per cent of the respondent groups from Assam are spreaded over urban, suburban and rural areas respectively, while out of 45.33 per cent respondents, 32 per cent are staying in villages and only 13.33 per cent of the respondents are staying in remote villages. In total 22.67 per cent, 12.33 per cent, 38 per cent and 27 per cent of the respondents are staying in urban areas, suburban areas, village areas and remote villages, respectively.

While 31.37 per cent and 10.32 per cent of the male respondents are staying in the houses situated in urban areas from Assam and West Bengal respectively 47.92 per cent of the female are also staying in urban locality from Assam. None of the females from West Bengal is having their house in urban locality. In an average 36.67 per cent of the respondent group from Assam and 8.67 per cent from West Bengal are residing in urban areas.

A juxtaposition of the respondents from these two states reveals that a greater number of respondents from Assam are living in urban areas compared to their counter respondent groups from West Bengal.

18.63 per cent and 7.14 per cent of the male respondent groups and 16.665 per cent and 4.16 per cent of the female respondents groups from the states of Assam and West Bengal respectively are found staying in suburban areas. In total 18 per cent of the total respondent group from Assam and 6.67 per cent from West Bengal are residing in the suburban areas of Assam and West Bengal.

The picture reveals that comparatively more teachers are residing in suburban areas in Assam than that of West Bengal.

Village Dwellers

In total 38 per cent of the entire sample group, including 32 per cent of the sample from Assam and 44 per cent of the respondents from West Bengal are staying in villages. The initial picture indicates that comparatively more respondents from West Bengal are village dwellers. Among the males, while one-third (33.33 per cent) of the respondents are living in villages, comparatively more males (39.68 per cent) are staying in villages from West Bengal. The trend among the female respondents reveals the same to a greater extent where 29.165per cent of female respondents are dwelling in villages and almost two-third (66.67 per cent) of them from West Bengal are living in similar set up. This picture advocates the fact that while the respondents from Assam are concentrated in urban areas, in West Bengal they are mostly spreaded over the rural set up.

16.67 per cent and 42.86 per cent of male, 6.25 per cent and 29.17 per cent of female and 13.33 per cent and 40.67 per cent of the total respondents from the states of Assam and West Bengal respectively, comprising 27 per cent of the entire respondent groups were found living in remote villages.

8

Economic Status

The most important component of the status coexists with the concept of economic condition – which often uttered as 'economic status'; in fact economic status is the key indicator of the overall status of an individual or of a family or even of a group or of a community. The indigenous tribal community in many a cases are more familiar with subsistence economy however the wave of modernization today compelling them to adopt the national economic system. Whatever it may be, the economic situation of a teacher depends upon salary he earns through teaching. The economic status of the respondents comes under the preview of the research and hence attempt had been made to explore the economic status of the tribal teachers in the following Tables where their economic situation, individual monthly income, family income & personal savings are analyzed.

Table 8.1: Economic Situation of the Respondents

State	*Assam*				*West Bengal*				*Grand Total*
Economy Sex	*Well Off*	*Average*	*Difficult*	*Total*	*Well Off*	*Average*	*Difficult*	*Total*	
Male	0 (0)	65 (63.73)	37 (36.27)	102 (100)	24 (19.05)	85 (67.46)	17 (13.49)	126 (100)	228 (76)
Female	2 (4.17)	37 (77.08)	9 (18.75)	48 (100)	5 (20.83)	19 (79.17)	0 (0)	24 (100)	72 (24)
Total	2 (1.33)	102 (68)	46 (30.67)	150 (100)	29 (19.33)	104 (69.34)	17 (11.33)	150 (100)	300 (100)

One of the basic and important components of status is the economic circumstance or situation. Delving towards this very dimension of status, certain question was asked to the respondents. In response towards the question, 68 per cent of the respondents from Assam described their present economic set up as average, followed by 30.67 per cent as poor and only 1.33 per cent as "well off" during the time of survey. Among the males from this state, economic situation was average to 63.73 per cent of the respondents followed by 36.27 per cent of the respondent, to whom it was poor. None of the male sample from this state described their economic setup as 'well off'. However 4.17 per cent of the female respondents from the state considered their economic setup as 'well off' while to most of them (77.08 per cent) it is average. Only 18.75 per cent of the respondents considered their economic set up as poor.

So, it may be interprited that irrespective of sex, majority of the respondents from Assam are having an average economic situation, as they considered. Only a marginal few perceived it as well off and almost one-third of the respondents considered their economic set up as poor.

Almost a similar trend was observed in West Bengal where majority (69.34 per cent) of the respondents described their economic situation as average. It was found that 67.46 per cent of male from this state and 79.17 per cent of female were with such opinion.

19.05 per cent of male as well as 20.83 per cent of female, together comprising 19.33 per cent of the respondent group from West Bengal described their economic situation as 'well off'. This group was further followed by 11.33 per cent of the total respondents from West Bengal among whom all where male, describing their economic situation as poor.

While juxtaposing the different response categories from both the states, it is observed that according to the perception of the respondent groups from the two states, comparatively higher percentage of respondents from West Bengal considered their economic situation as 'well off'. On the other hand, more respondents from Assam considered their economic situation as poor than that of their counterparts from West Bengal. To most of the respondents from both the states, the economic situation was average.

Table 8.2 presents the monthly income of the respondent group. Five income strata was specified in this context, consulting the salary range of the secondary school teachers, which varied to a large extent, due to educational qualification of the teacher and absorption of the teachers in different types of school in terms of management and control. We can consider these income ranges as highest, higher, middle, lower and lowest income groups. The ranges of these respective income groups are shown in Table 8.2, where it is observed that 24 per cent, 20.67 per cent, 37.33 per cent, 13.67 per cent and 4.33 per cent of the total respondent groups are falling in highest, higher, middle, lower and lowest income groups respectively. 10 per cent, 20 per cent, 42 per cent, 19.33 per cent and 8,67 per cent of the respondent groups from Assam and 38 per cent, 21.33 per cent, 32.67 per cent, 8 per cent and 0 per cent of the respondent groups are falling in the successive income groups from West Bengal.

Table 8.2: Monthly Income of the Respondents

State	Income Gr. Sex	8501/- & Above Highest	7001/- to 8500/- Higher	5501/- to 7000/- Middle	4001/- to 5500/- Lower	4000/- & less Lowest	Total
Assam	Male	11 (10.78%)	26 (25.49%)	36 (35.30%)	21 (20.59%)	8 (7.84%)	102 (100%)
	Female	4 (8.33%)	4 (8.33%)	27 (56.25%)	8 (16.67%)	5 (10.42%)	48 (100%)
	Total	15 (10%)	30 (20%)	63 (42%)	29 (19.33%)	13 (8.67%)	150 (100%)
West Bengal	Male	51 (40.48%)	26 (20.63%)	48 (38.10%)	1 (0.79%)	0 (0%)	126 (100%)
	Female	6 (25%)	6 (25%)	1 (4.17%)	11 (45.83%)	0 (0%)	24 (100%)
	Total	57 (38%)	32 (21.33%)	49 (32.67%)	12 (8%)	0 (0%)	150 (100%)
	Grand Total	72 (24%)	62 (20.67%)	112 (37.33%)	41 (13.67%)	13 (4.33%)	300 (100%)

Highest

Based on their monthly income, while 10.78 per cent of the male and 8.33 per cent of the female respondents from Assam are holding highest income status, ranging from a minimum of Rs. 8501/- and above, per month, comparatively more teachers from West Bengal, including 40.48 per cent of male and 25 per cent of female from West Bengal are found falling in this income category.

Higher

25.49 per cent of the male and 8.33 per cent of the female respondents from Assam was found to belong to the higher income status where the monthly income ranged from Rs. 7001/- to Rs. 8500/-. On the other hand, 20.63 per cent of the male and 25 per cent of the female respondents was found falling in the very income category form West Bengal. Among the respondents from this economic status, more males and fewer females from Assam are obtaining higher economic status, when compared to their counterparts from West Bengal.

Middle

The third slab in this context is the middle income group, ranging from a monthly income of Rs. 5501/- to Rs. 7000/- where 35.30 per cent and 38.10 per cent of male and 56.25 per cent and 4.17 per cent of female was found falling in this income category. It can be said that a substantially higher percentage of female respondents from Assam are falling in this income range, when compared to their counter respondent group from West Bengal. However, a marginally higher percentage of male respondents from West Bengal found falling in this very income group than that of their counterparts from Assam.

Lower

Those who are earning a monthly salary ranging from Rs. 4001/- to Rs. 5500/- are considered as lower income group. Table 8.2 reveals that while only 0.79 per cent of male respondent from West Bengal are falling in this income category, a substantially higher percentage of respondents (20.59 per cent) from Assam are also falling in this income category. However, in case of female respondents, a comparatively better percentage (45.83 per cent) of respondent from West Bengal can be observed, while comparing with their counter parts from Assam. Only 16.67 per cent of female respondents found falling in this income range.

Lowest

The respondents, whose monthly income is even less than Rs. 4000/- per month is considered in the lowest income range group. Here, it should be worthnoting that these teachers are mostly absorbed in privately managed schools, where the salary is not up to the mark. However, this group is quite scanty and none of the respondent from West Bengal was found falling in this category. In contrast, 7.84 per cent of male and 10.42 per cent of the female respondents and in total 8.67 per cent of the respondent from Assam was found falling in this income category.

Though both the state governments specified almost a similar salary scale of pay for the secondary school teachers, but this scale is not followed by the schools, managed privately, or by religious trusts. Naturally, the respondents who are absorbed in such type of schools are not getting adequate salary and mostly those teachers are falling in lower or lowest income range group. In addition to this factor, the salary scale is not up to the mark for those who are having less qualifications (*i.e.*, bellow graduate). Due to these causes, a disparity in the salary range of the respondent is visible.

Table 8.3 shows the distribution of the respondents in terms of their monthly family income, as they reported. It was observed mostly in case of female, they are not the only earning members of their respective families. Practically they are supplementing their family income, except only a few cases where they are the prime income source for their family, shouldering the financial responsibility. A categorization was done, keeping parity with Table 8.2, where we can find five income ranges – *viz.*, highest, higher, middle, lower and lowest – where the cut off points of income remain unchanged.

In terms of their monthly family income, 46 per cent of the entire samples are occupying the highest status. While only 20.33 per cent of the respondents having monthly family income, substantially high, varying within a range of Rs. 7001/- to 8500/-. Also 22.67 per cent of them are having a medium status, followed by 8.33 per cent having lower and is further followed by 2.67 per cent who are occupying the lowest economic status so far the monthly family income of the respondents are concerned.

Table 8.3: Monthly Income of the Respondent's Family

State ↓	Income→ Gr. ↓ Sex	8501/-& Above **Highest**	7001/- to 8500/- **Higher**	5501/- to 7000/- **Middle**	4001/- to 5500/- **Lower**	4000/- & less **Lowest**	Total
Assam	Male	32 (31.37%)	23 (22.55%)	19 (18.63%)	20 (19.61%)	8 (7.84%)	102 (100%)
	Female	26 (54.17%)	13 (27.08%)	8 (16.67%)	1 (2.08%)	0 (0%)	48 (100%)
	Total	58 (38.67%)	36 (24%)	27 (18%)	21 (14%)	8 (5.33%)	150 (100%)
West Bengal	Male	67 (53.17%)	21 (16.67%)	38 (30.16%)	0 (0%)	0 (0%)	126 (100%)
	Female	13 (54.17%)	4 (16.665%)	3 (12.5%)	4 (16.665%)	0 (0%)	24 (100%)
	Total	80 (53.33%)	25 (16.67%)	41 (27.33%)	4 (2.67%)	0 (0%)	150 (100%)
	Grand Total	138 (46%)	61 (20.33%)	68 (22.67%)	25 (8.33%)	8 (2.67%)	300 (100%)

Highest

It is revealed from Table 8.3, that while 31.37 per cent of the male respondents from state of Assam are occupying the highest economic status, it is 53.17 per cent for their counter group from West Bengal. It implies that more male teachers from West Bengal are occupying this highest economic status, so far their monthly family income is concerned. Incase of female respondents, quite an equal percentage (54.17 per cent) of the respondents from both the states are falling in this category.

In total, 38.67 per cent and 53.33 per cent of the respondents from the states of Assam and West Bengal, respectively, was found holding their position in this income group. Naturally it may be said that comparatively more respondents from West Bengal are occupying their position in this status group, than that of the respondents from Assam.

Higher

In terms of the monthly family income, 20.33 per cent of the respondents replied that their total family income varies within 7001/- to 8500/-. This group of respondents incorporates 24 per cent of the respondent group from Assam and only 16.67 per cent of the respondent group from West Bengal. While 22.55 per cent of the male and 27.08 per cent of the female respondents from Assam are having their higher range of family income, from West Bengal a uniform percentage of both male and female found falling in this income group. From the Table, it can further be found that comparatively more respondents from Assam, both male and female, are falling in this income groups when compared to their counter groups from West Bengal.

Middle

Considering the monthly family income of the respondents, it was found from the Table that 19.61 per cent of the male from Assam are having their monthly family income, ranging from 5501/- to 7000/- while 30.16 per cent of their counter group (*i.e.* Male) was found from West Bengal. This income group includes 16.67 per cent and 12.5 per cent of the female respondents from the states of Assam and West Bengal, respectively. In total, while 18 per cent of the total respondents from Assam are falling in this middle-income group, 27.33 per cent of the respondents from West Bengal are found falling in this income category.

Lower

It can be further perused from the Table 8.3 that while 14 per cent of the respondents from Assam are holding a lower income status, it is only 2.67 per cent of the respondent from West Bengal who are holding almost a similar status. While from Assam, 19.61 per cent of male and 2.08 per cent of female are having monthly family income ranging from 4001/- to 5500/- it is only 16.665 per cent of the female respondents from West Bengal, falling in the very income category. None of the male respondent from West Bengal is found in this income category

A comparative sketch reveals that while more respondents from Assam are falling in this income group, less number of respondents from West Bengal is found in this income group.

Lowest

The rest group includes the respondents whose monthly family income is a maximum of Rs. 4000/- and less as per their reporting. No such teachers, neither male nor female, were found from West Bengal.

From Assam only, 7.84 per cent of male respondent are found have a monthly family income of Rs. 4000/- and around per month. However, no female respondent from this state is found to fall in this category.

A total of only 2.67 per cent of the entire respondents are found to fall in this income category and all of them are employed in privately managed schools.

In case of the female respondents from either states, as the data in Tables 8.3 and 8.4 depicts, they are not the only earning members of their family and are supplementing their family income by their earning.

However, on the other hand the male respondents are the prime-earning members. Comparing the Table 8.2 and Table 8.3, 8 male respondents from Assam found falling in the lowest income range, having income even less than or around Rs. 4000/- per month.

Table 8.4: Personal Savings of the Respondents

State	*Savings →* *Sex* ↓	*4 Lakhs & above*	*3-4 Lakhs*	*Rs. 200001 to 300000/-*	*1-2 Lakhs*	*Less than 1 Lakhs*	*Total*
Assam	Male	2 (1.96%)	5 (4.91%)	7 (6.86%)	26 (25.49%)	62 (60.78%)	102 (100%)
	Female	1 (2.08%)	2 (4.17%)	6 (12.5%)	15 (31.25%)	24 (50%)	48 (100%)
	Total	3 (2%)	7 (4.67%)	13 (8.67%)	41 (27.33%)	86 (57.33%)	150 (100%)
West Bengal	Male	3 (2.38%)	4 (3.17%)	15 (11.90%)	37 (29.37%)	67 (53.18%)	126 (100%)
	Female	0 (0%)	0 (0%)	3 (12.5%)	1 (4.17%)	20 (83.33%)	24 (100%)
	Total	3 (2%)	4 (2.67%)	18 (12%)	38 (25.33%)	87 (58%)	150 (100%)
	Grand Total	6 (2%)	11 (3.67%)	31 (10.33%)	79 (26.33%)	173 (57.67%)	300 (100%)

Based on the personal savings of the respondents, five categories have been formed. For the sake of analysis this groups can be termed as 'Highest', 'above average', average, bellow average and lowest saving groups whose savings varies between – (*a*) more than four lakhs, (*b*) three to four lakhs, (*c*) more than two lakhs, but less than three lakhs, (*d*) one to two lakhs and (*e*) less than one lakhs. This categorization has been made to determine the economic status of the respondents.

Data pooled by socio-economic status scale reveals that:

Highest

Only two per cent of the entire respondents as well as the respondents from the two states are having a highest economic status, in terms of their personal savings, where the respondents said to have more than four lakhs rupees as their personal savings. 1.96 per cent of male and 2.08 per cent of female from Assam and 2.38 per cent of the male respondent from West Bengal was found falling in this 'savings' category.

This group includes a marginally less percentage of respondents from both the states.

Above Average

Only 3.67 per cent of the entire respondents including 4.67 per cent respondents from Assam and 2.67 per cent of the respondents from West Bengal reported to have an above average personal savings, varying from Rs. 300000/- to 400000/-.

Where, from Assam 4.91 per cent of male respondents and 4.17 per cent of female respondents are placed in this savings category, the figures are just 3.17 per cent and 0 per cent for male and female respectively from West Bengal.

This finding reveals that in terms of their number, both male and female respondents from Assam are holding higher economic status than that of their counter groups from West Bengal, when their 'personal savings' is taken into consideration.

Average

Only 10.33 per cent of the entire respondents reported to have a personal savings, ranging from Rs. 20000/- to 300000/- who are considered 'average' group. 8.67 per cent of the respondents from Assam, incorporating 6.86 per cent of male and 12.5 per cent of the female and 12 per cent of the respondents from West Bengal including 11.90 per cent of male and 12.5 per cent of female on other hand was found comprising this group.

It can be said from the responses given by the respondents in this context, that in total, more respondents from West Bengal are falling in this group. Though exactly equal percentage of female from both the states are found in the group however comparatively more male respondent from West Bengal belonging to this very group when compared to their counterparts from Assam.

Below Average

In total 26.33 per cent of the respondents said to have personal savings varied from rupees one lakh to two lakhs. This group incorporates 27.33 per cent of the respondents from Assam and 25.33 per cent of the respondents from West Bengal; 25.49 per cent and 29.37 per cent of male and 31.25 per cent and 4.17 per cent of female respondents from the states of Assam and West Bengal was found falling in this group. It is seen that more respondents from Assam are falling in this group. Again, less percentage of male and substantially higher percentage of female respondents from Assam are falling in this category, when compared to their respective counter parts from West Bengal.

Lower

Majority of the respondents (57.67 per cent) from both the states, 57.33 per cent from Assam and 58 per cent from West Bengal said having personal savings valued equal to or less than rupees one lakhs. While among the males, 60.78 per cent respondents from Assam and 53.18 per cent respondents from West Bengal are falling in this saving-group, among females, 50 per cent respondents from Assam and 83.33 per cent of the respondents from West Bengal reported belong to this group.

The column reveals that, though marginal, more percentage of total respondents from Assam belongs to this category.

More male respondents from Assam are holding a lower economic status while substantially higher percentage of female respondents from West Bengal are also holding a lower economic status when the personal savings of the respondents are taken into consideration.

9

Socio Political Status

Political Status

Teachers, being the social atoms, always having the right to participate in political activities, which is in the form of, may be a direct bearing with the professional organizations (such as teachers organizations) or may be completely far from that. The basic function of an ideal political organization is to maintain social order and to minimize social disorder. However political participation of the teachers, in India, some how bring some different sketch where the teacher spend much time and effort in the organizational activities and thus it puts a negative impact over the pedagogical activities. The present study aimed to explore the political status of the respondent tribal teachers in terms of their political participation, the nature and level of membership of political parties and their perception about the activities of political parties, which are illustrated in the following tables:

Table 9.1: Political Participation of the Respondents

State	*Assam*			*West Bengal*			*Grand Total*
Response / *Sex*	*Yes*	*No*	*Total*	*Yes*	*No*	*Total*	
Male	5 (4.90%)	97 (95.10%)	102 (100%)	71 (56.35%)	55 (43.65%)	126 (100%)	228 (76%)
Female	3 (6.25%)	45 (93.75%)	48 (100%)	5 (20.83%)	19 (79.17%)	24 (100%)	72 (24%)
Total	8 (5.33%)	142 (94.67%)	150 (100%)	76 (50.67%)	74 (49.33%)	150 (100%)	300 (100%)

Political participation was considered as a component of status and therefore to delve into the deep of the political status of the respondents, certain questions were designed. Responding towards such a question, while only 5.33 per cent of the respondents from Assam said to hold membership of political parties (or belong to political parties), majority (50.67 per cent) of the respondents from West Bengal respond in similar way. It was further observed that those who belong to political parties from West Bengal numbered almost ten times then their counter group from Assam.

The juxtaposition reveals that while the respondents from West Bengal belonging to political parties in massive rate, the rate of political participation of the respondents from Assam is too scanty in this context.

4.90 per cent and 56.35 per cent of male and 6.25 per cent and 20.83 per cent of female respondents from the states of Assam and West Bengal respectively, formed the groups who respond in an affirmative way towards the question.

It can further be observed from Table 9.1, that while more female respondents from Assam are possessing membership of political parties,. The sketch is just reverse in West Bengal where males are majority in holding membership of political parties, when compared to their counter-gender-groups from the respective states.

Table 9.2: Distribution of Respondents who Belongs to Political Parties

State	Assam					West Bengal					
Nature of Member-ship / Sex	Active	Ordinarily	Executive	Supporter	Total	Active	Ordinarily	Executive	Supporter	Total	Grand Total
Male	2 (40)	2 (40)	1 (20)	0	5/102 (100)	26 (36.62)	9 (12.68)	5 (7.04)	31 (43.66)	71/126 (100)	76/228
Female	1 (33.33)	2 (66.67)	0 (0)	0 (0)	3/48 (100)	1 (20)	2 (40)	0 (0)	2 (40)	5/24 (100)	8/72
Total	3 (37.5)	4 (50)	1 (12.5)	0 (0)	8/150 (100)	27 (35.53)	11 (14.47)	5 (6.58)	33 (43.42)	76/150 (100)	84/300

An immediate next question was brought to the respondents, who agreed to have a membership of political parties, regarding the nature of membership. Table 9.2 presents the distribution of such respondents in terms of their nature of membership.

37.5 per cent of the respondents from Assam, incorporating 40 per cent of male and 33.33 per cent of female respondents said that they are the active members. In West Bengal, these figures are 35.53 per cent, 36.62 per cent and 20 per cent respectively.

The sketch reveals that more males are having active membership compared to the females from both the states while females from Assam show a higher percentage compared to their counter group from West Bengal in this regard.

While 50 per cent of the respondents from Assam, incorporating 40 per cent male and 66.67 per cent female, among those who are associated with political parties are just ordinary members, 40 per cent of such respondents from West Bengal, incorporating 12.68 per cent of male and 40 per cent of female respondents are also having an ordinary membership status.

While 12.5 per cent of the respondents are holding executive membership from Assam, from West Bengal it is only 6.58 per cent (even less than half).

43.42 per cent of the respondents from West Bengal are just supporter members of respective political parties of their choice including 43.66 per cent of male and 40 per cent of female respondents, and none such respondents are found in Assam.

Respondent group from West Bengal are having a comparatively higher participation in politics than that of Assam. However, in terms of nature of membership, respondents from Assam are comparatively in a better situation.

Table 9.3 presents the levels of membership of the respondents, belong to political parties. Five different levels are found, within which their membership varied. These levels starts with local till national, suffixing within this two are block, district and state level memberships.

It is already been clear that from the sample group, only eight respondents (5.33 per cent) from Assam and seventy-six respondents (50.67 per cent) from West Bengal belonging to political parties. Definitely this group of respondents, holding membership of political parties, are having some different sorts of political status. It should be accepted by each and every hand that status of an individual, belonging to a political party, depends on the level of membership the individual is holding.

Among the respondents who belongs to political parties from Assam, 12.5 per cent, 37.5 per cent, 25 per cent and 12.5 per cent of them reported having membership of various political parties at national, state, district, block and local level respectively.

Among the female respondents from this state, while two-third found holding a district level membership the rest one-third are having a local level membership.

However, among the male respondents from this state, while 40 per cent are holding a block level membership, rest of them are holding district, state and national level membership in an uniform proportion. Though no question was placed in front of them about the specific parties to which the respondents belong, however it can be observed from the Table that at least 20 per cent of the male respondents and 12.5 per cent of the total respondent from the state Assam are associated with national level political parties.

Zooming the view on West Bengal, it can be observed that out of a total of seventy-six respondents 44.74 per cent are holding local level membership. 35.53 per cent, 17.10 per cent and 2.63 per cent of the respondents from this group are holding membership at block, district and state levels respectively and none found having a membership at national level.

Among the males from this state, while 43.66 per cent 36.62 per cent, 16.90 per cent and 2.82 per cent of the total seventy-one respondents are having their membership at local, block, district and state level respectively, only 60 per cent, 20 per cent and 20 per cent of the females out of a total of five, said having membership at local, block and district level respectively.

Table 9.3: Level of Membership (Only those Who Belong to Political Parties)

State	Assam						West Bengal						Gr. Total
Level Sex	Local	Block	District	State	National	Total	Local	Block	District	State	National	Total	
Male	0 (0%)	2 (40%)	1 (20%)	1 (20%)	1 (20%)	5 (100%)	31 (43.66%)	26 (36.62%)	12 (16.90%)	2 (2.82%)	00 (0%)	71 (100%)	76 (100%)
Female	[illegible] (33.33%)	0 (0%)	2 (66.67%)	0 (0%)	0 (0%)	3 (100%)	3 (60%)	1 (20%)	1 (20%)	0 (0%)	0 (0%)	5 (100%)	8/ (100%)
Total	[illegible] (12.5%)	2 (25%)	3 (37.5%)	1 (12.5%)	1 (12.5%)	8 (100%)	34 (44.74%)	27 (35.53%)	13 (17.10%)	2 (2.63%)	0 (0%)	76 (100%)	84/ (100%)

Irrespective of gender, from this state, the percentage of respondents, comes down with an increased hierarchical order – so far their level of membership is concerned and none of the male respondents are found holding membership of a political party at it's national level. The status (political) of the female, as revealed from the Table indicates that there is no female respondent holding membership even at state level.

In the preceding Tables it is found that out of three hundred respondents, only eighty-four, (eight from Assam and seventy six from West Bengal) are associated with political parties. Rest two hundred and sixteen respondents are not associated with any political party.

To a certain question majority (87.5 per cent) of the respondents from Assam, holding membership of political parties opined that they do not think that political parties are exploiting the people like them, just only for their political interest, however 12.5 per cent of them did not respond towards the question.

Table 9.4: Respondents Reaction Towards Politics

State →		*Assam*			*West Bengal*			
	Sex → *Response ↓*	*Male*	*Female*	*Total*	*Male*	*Female*	*Total*	*Grand Total*
Belong to Political Party	Yes	0	0	0	4	0	4	4
	No	5	2	7	56	3	59	66
	Can't say	0	1	1	11	2	13	14
	Total	5	3	8	71	5	76	84
Do not belong to any Political Party	Yes	86	39	125	49	17	66	191
	No	3	2	5	6	2	8	13
	Can't say	8	4	12	0	0	0	12
	Total	97	45	142	55	19	74	216

However, among the counter respondent group who does not belong to an political party from this state (*i.e.*, Assam) 88.03 per cent said that they think that political parties are exploiting the people like them, just only for their political interest. This view was opposed by only 3.52 per cent of the respondents. While 8.45 per cent of the respondent did not respond towards this question.

Similarly, from the state of West Bengal, majority (78.57 per cent) of the respondents, holding membership of political parties negates the view saying that they do not think that political parties are exploiting the people like them just only for their political interest. However, majority (88.43 per cent) of the respondents, not associated with any political party, accept the view saying that political parties are exploiting the people like them, for their political interest.

Though less, till 4.76 per cent of the total group of respondents, even after holding membership of political parties accept the view of the majority of the respondents, detached from politics. Whereas only 6.02 per cent of the respondents who are not associated with any political parties says that they do not think political parties are exploiting the people like them.

However, 16.67 per cent of the respondents from West Bengal, who belongs to political parties and 5.56 per cent of those who does not belong to political parties did not respond towards this item.

Observing the responses towards the questions related to the political status, it can be said that extent of participation in political activities is significantly higher among the respondents from West Bengal. The female from Assam are comparatively more involved in political activities when compared to their counter-sex group from the very state.

In terms of nature of membership of political party, while a good percentage (43.42 per cent) of the respondent from West Bengal are supporter members, none such found from Assam.

Among the members of different political parties, 12.5 per cent occupying national level membership from Assam, while none such found from West Bengal.

Social Status

Social status basically depends upon the social upbringing of an individual and their sociability. Questions were designed regarding these two different aspects to delve into the deep of the social status of the tribal teachers.

Table 9.5: Up-bringing of the Respondents

State	*Assam*			*West Bengal*			*Grand Total*
Sex → *Types ↓* *of Area*	*Male*	*Female*	*Total*	*Male*	*Female*	*Total*	
Rural	64 (62.75%)	21 (43.75%)	85 (56.67%)	95 (75.40%)	19 (79.17%)	114 (76%)	199 (66.33%)
Suburban	13 (12.75%)	2 (4.165%)	15 (10%)	5 (3.97%)	0 (0%)	5 (3.33%)	20 (6.67%)
Urban	5 (4.90%)	14 (29.165%)	19 (12.665%)	2 (1.58%)	0 (0%)	2 (1.33%)	21 (7%)
Both in Rural & Urban	20 (19.60%)	11 (22.92%)	31 (20.665%))	24 (19.05%)	5 (20.83%)	29 (19.34%)	60 (20%)
Total	102 (100%)	48 (100%)	150 (100%)	126 (100%)	24 (100%)	150 (100%)	300 (100%)

Social upbringing and environment plays a pivotal role to determine the social status of individual. Keeping this in view a question was designed. From the data collected through status questionnaire, it is found that the respondents grew up in four types of environments – *viz.*, rural, suburban, urban and both rural and urban environments.

62.75 per cent of the male and 43.75 of the female respondents from

Assam, together comprising 56.67 per cent and 75.40 per cent of male and 79.17 per cent of female respondents from West Bengal together comprising a group of 76 per cent – further forming 66.33 per cent of the entire respondents from both the states, reported to be grown-up in rural areas.

A state wise juxtaposition reveals that comparatively more respondents from West Bengal mainly grew up in rural areas. While from Assam, it is the male respondent group, from West Bengal it is female respondent group who cuts out comparatively a larger proportion, when compared to their counter sex-group from respective states, who grew up in rural areas.

Out of the entire sample, while only 6.67 per cent grew up mainly in sub-urban areas, it is the 10 per cent of the respondent groups from Assam, incorporating 12.75 per cent of male and 4.165 per cent of the female respondents from the state, who grew up in sub-urban areas. On the other hand, a marginally less percentage (3.33 per cent) of the total respondents and 3.97 per cent of the male respondent said to have grew up in sub-urban areas. None of the female respondents from West Bengal replied to have grown up in sub-urban areas from West Bengal.

It is found from Table 9.5 that only 7 per cent of the entire respondents including 12.67 per cent of the respondents from Assam and just only 1.33 per cent from West Bengal grew up mostly in urban areas. While 4.90 per cent of male and 29.165 per cent of female respondents from Assam mainly grew up in urban areas, from West Bengal, these figures are just 1.58 per cent and nil respectively.

A comparative sketch reveals that more percentage of (male and female) respondents from Assam had the opportunity to be brought up in urban areas, than that of West Bengal.

More or less, one-fifth of the respondents said to have grown up both in urban and rural areas in different span of time.

The observation from Table 9.5 reveals that, in terms of the locality, where the tribal teachers mostly grew up, majority of the respondents from both the states are concentrated in rural areas, and the extent of this concentration in rural areas in comparatively much more in West Bengal than that of Assam.

State wise comparison reveals that male-concentration in rural areas from Assam is significantly higher than females and though not significant, but in West Bengal, the percentage of female respondents is to a little extent higher than male.

Table 9.6 gives us a clear picture of the respondents' perception about their participation in various social programmes.

24.67 per cent, 63.67 per cent and 11.66 per cent of the entire respondent group said that they use to participate in various social programmes however their participation varies in degree, *viz.*, always, often and rarely respectively.

Table 9.6: Participation in Social Programmes

State →	Assam			West Bengal			Grand Total
Sex → Parti- ↓ cipation	Male	Female	Total	Male	Female	Total	
Always	55 (53.92%)	1 (2.08%)	56 (37.33%)	17 (13.49%)	1 (4.17%)	18 (12%)	74 (24.67%)
Often	39 (38.24%)	41 (85.42%)	80 (53.34%)	93 (73.81%)	18 (75%)	111 (74%)	191 (63.67%)
Rarely	8 (7.84%)	6 (12.50%)	14 (9.33%)	16 (12.70%)	5 (20.83%)	21 (14%)	35 (11.66%)
Total	102 (100%)	48 (100%)	150 (100%)	126 (100%)	24 (100%)	150 (100%)	300 (100%)

While 37.33 per cent of the respondent from Assam said that they always use to participate in various social programmes, this percentage is just 12 per cent for West Bengal; including 53.92 per cent and 13.49 per cent of male and 2.08 per cent and 4.17 per cent of female from the states of Assam and West Bengal respectively.

It can be said that more male respondents are sociable to a greater degree than that of female from both the states. However the respondents from Assam are more in number, showing a greater extent of sociability than their counter group from West Bengal.

63.67 per cent of the entire respondent group, including 53.34 per cent of the respondents from Assam and 74 per cent of the respondent from West Bengal respond that they often use to participate in social occasions. This group can be considered having a moderate degree of sociability.

It can be said that the respondents having a moderate degree of sociability are more in number from West Bengal than that of Assam.

Comparing the sex-groups, it can be said that more percentage of female respondents posses a moderate degree of sociability when compared to their female counter-group from West Bengal. However the female group is marginally larger than the male group from West Bengal.

The respondents who respond that they rarely use to attend social programmes can be considered having lower degree of sociability.

One can find 11.66 per cent of the total respondents, including 9.33 per cent from Assam and 14 per cent from West Bengal, who possess a lower degree of sociability.

Females are quite larger in number, possessing the lower degree of sociability than their male counterparts from both the states, which can be perused from the Table 9.6. It can be further observed from the same table that in terms of total number of respondents, more respondents from West Bengal possess low degree of sociability than the respondents from Assam.

When the entire sample is taken into consideration, it is observed that majority of the respondents (63.67 per cent) are possessing a moderate degree of sociability, followed by almost a quarter of the total (24.67 per cent), having a higher degree of sociability. Only 11.66 per cent of the respondents found having lower degree of sociability.

10

Perception Towards Changing Cultural Pattern

Cultural Status

Culture consists of the abstract values, beliefs, and perceptions of the world that lie behind peoples, behaviour and that their behaviour reflects. These are shared by the members of a society, and when acted upon, they produce behaviour considered acceptable within the society.

Table 10.1: Status of the Cultural-environment of the Schools Where the Respondents are Teaching

State	*Assam*			*West Bengal*			*Grand Total*
Sex → *Rating*	*Male*	*Female*	*Total*	*Male*	*Female*	*Total*	
Reach	35 (34.31%)	1 (2.08%)	36 (24%)	3 (2.38%)	1 (4.17%)	4 (2.67%)	40 (13.33%)
Ordinary	58 (56.87%)	38 (79.17%)	96 (64%)	101 (80.16%)	16 (66.67%)	117 (78%)	213s (71%)
Poor	9 (8.82%)	9 (18.75%)	18 (12%)	22 (17.46%)	7 (29.16%)	29 (19.33%)	47 (15.67%)
Total	102 (100%)	48 (100%)	150 (100%)	126 (100%)	24 (100%)	150 (100%)	300 (100%)

Table 10.1 presents the respondent's rating over the cultural environment of the respective schools, where they are employed.

While considering the total group of respondents, it is observed that majority (71%) considered the cultural environment of their school as ordinary, followed by 15.67 per cent, to whom it was poor and only 13.33 per cent considered the same as reach.

24 per cent and 2.67 per cent of the respondents from the states of Assam and West Bengal respectively considered the cultural environment of their schools as reach and to majority (64 per cent from Assam and 78 per cent from West Bengal), the environment is ordinary; however 12 per cent of the respondent from Assam and 19.33 per cent from West Bengal rated the cultural environment of their institution as 'poor'.

A juxtaposition sketch in this regard reveals that while substantially higher percentage of the respondents from Assam rated the cultural environment of their institution as reach, more respondents from West Bengal considered the same as ordinary and poor, when juxtaposed with the respondents from the counter state.

One of the important finding of the study is that, while a substantially higher percentage of the female respondents rated their school environment as 'ordinary' from the state of Assam, for the state of West Bengal, a substantially higher percentage of the male rated the cultural environment of their school as ordinary. However, majority of the respondents, both male and female, from both the states considered the cultural environment of their institution as ordinary.

It is only 8.82 per cent and 17.46 per cent of the male and 18.75 per cent and 29.16 per cent of the female respondent from the states of Assam and West Bengal to whom, the cultural environment of the institute, where they are working, is poor. If it is considered that response as a symptom of dissatisfaction towards the cultural environment of their respective schools, the females are more dissatisfied from both the states, than that of their male counter parts, towards the cultural environment of their schools.

On the other hand, more male respondents from Assam and less from West Bengal are quite satisfied with the cultural environment of their respective institutions as they rated the same as reach.

Table 10.2: Rating of the Respondents Over the Status of the Culture and Environment of the Adjacent area in which their Schools are Situated

State	*Assam*			*West Bengal*			*Grand Total*
Sex → *Rating ↓*	*Male*	*Female*	*Total*	*Male*	*Female*	*Total*	
Reach	8 (7.84%)	0 (0%)	8 (5.33%)	11 (8.73%)	0 (0%)	11 (7.33%)	19 (6.33%)
Ordinary	88 (86.28%)	46 (95.83%)	134 (89.34%)	74 (58.73%)	14 (58.33%)	88 (58.67%)	222 (74%)
Poor	6 (5.88%)	2 (4.17%)	8 (5.33%)	41 (32.54%)	10 (41.67%)	51 (34%)	59 (19.67%)
Total	102 (100%)	48 (100%)	150 (100%)	126 (100%)	24 (100%)	150 (100%)	300 (100%)

Table 10.2 presents the rating of the respondents over the culture and environment of the adjacent area in which their schools are situated.

As like in Table 7.10, majority (74%) of the respondents rated the culture and environment of the adjacent area in which their schools are situated, as ordinary, followed by 19.67 per cent to whom it was poor and only 6.33 per cent consider the same as 'reach'.

While 89.34 per cent of the respondents from Assam, including 86.28 per cent of male and 95.83 per cent of female considered 'ordinary', it is 58.67 per cent of total respondents from West Bengal, incorporating 58.73

per cent of male and 58.33 per cent of female from the state who also rated in a similar way.

A juxtaposition of the response in this category indicates that, comparatively more respondents from Assam, both male and female, rated the culture and environment of the area in which their schools are situated as ordinary than that of the number of respondents from West Bengal. It can be further observed that substantially higher percentage of female considered the culture and environment of the adjacent areas as ordinary, in which their schools are situated, when compared to their male counterparts.

While to 6.33 per cent of total respondents, 5.33 per cent from Assam and 7.33 per cent from West Bengal, the culture and environment of the locality is 'reach', in which their schools are situated, it is 'poor' to 19.67 per cent of total respondents, including 5.33 per cent of the respondents from Assam and 34 per cent of the respondent from West Bengal.

Only 7.84 per cent and 8.73 per cent of the male respondents from Assam and West Bengal respectively rated the environment as reach while to 5.88 per cent and 32.54 per cent of the male respondents it is poor, from the states of Assam and West Bengal respectively.

None of the female respondents from any states considered the culture and environment as reach in which their schools are situated. However, only 4.17 per cent and 41.67 per cent of the female respondents from the states of Assam and West Bengal considered the same as poor.

Table 10.2 reveals that a substantially higher percentage of respondents from West Bengal, both male and female, considered the culture and environment as 'poor' in which their schools are situated, when compared to their counter-groups from Assam.

Table 10.3: Rating of the Respondents Over the Cultural Environment of their Own Community

State	*Assam*			*West Bengal*			*Grand Total*
Sex → / *Rating ↓*	*Male*	*Female*	*Total*	*Male*	*Female*	*Total*	
Reach	32 (31.37%)	25 (52.09%)	57 (38%)	73 (57.94%)	6 (25%)	79 (52.67%)	136 (45.33%)
Ordinary	59 (57.84%)	22 (45.83%)	81 (54%)	53 (42.06%)	18 (75%)	71 (47.33%)	152 (50.67%)
Poor	11 (10.79%)	1 (2.08%)	12 (8%)	0 (0%)	0 (0%)	0 (0%)	12 (4%)
Total	102 (100%)	48 (100%)	150 (100%)	126 (100%)	24 (100%)	150 (100%)	300 (100%)

In a certain item, the respondents were asked to rate over the cultural environment of their own community, with three options *viz.*, reach, ordinary and poor.

A little more than half of the entire respondents (*i.e.*, 50.67 per cent) considered the cultural environment of their own community as 'ordinary'.

54 per cent and 47.33 per cent of the total respondents, incorporating 57.84 per cent and 42.06 per cent of male and 45.83 per cent and 75 per cent of female from the state of Assam and West Bengal respectively, rated their community culture as ordinary.

It is 45.33 per cent of the total respondents who considered their community culture as 'reach'. 38 per cent of the total respondents, including 31.37 per cent of male and 52.09 per cent of female from the state of Assam and 52.67 per cent of the total respondents, incorporating 57.94 per cent of male and a quarter (25 per cent) of female from West Bengal rated the cultural environment of their community as 'reach'.

It is only 8 per cent of the respondents from Assam, including 10.79 per cent of male and 2.08 per cent of female respondents to whom the cultural environment of their community is poor. However, there is not a single respondent who considered their cultural environment of their own community as poor.

The observations from the Table 10.3 reveals that substantially more female and less male respondents and in total less respondents from the state of Assam considered the cultural environment of their own community as 'reach', when compared to their counter respondent group from West Bengal.

The cultural environment of their own community is ordinary to substantially more respondents from Assam. However, same is the rating of more female respondents and less male respondents from the state of West Bengal.

Though less, however comparatively more respondents, both male and female, from Assam considered the cultural environment of their community as 'poor', when compared to the respondent group from West Bengal. Not even a single respondent from West Bengal rated the cultural environment of their community as poor.

Table 10.4: Perception about the Cultural Pattern of the Community

State	*Assam*			*West Bengal*			*Grand Total*
Sex → *Response*	*Male*	*Female*	*Total*	*Male*	*Female*	*Total*	
Yes	92 (90.20%)	26 (54.17%)	118 (78.67%)	93 (73.81%)	21 (87.5%)	114 (76%)	232 (77.33%)
No	4 (3.92%)	21 (43.75%)	25 (16.665%)	32 (25.40%)	3 (12.5%)	35 (23.33%)	60 (20%)
Can not Say	6 (5.88%)	1 (2.08%)	7 (4.665%)	1 (0.79%)	0 (0%)	1 (0.67%)	8 (2.67%)
Total	102 (100%)	48 (100%)	150 (100%)	126 (100%)	24 (100%)	150 (100%)	300 (100%)

In response towards a question that whether they are thinking the cultural trend of their home and community is changing or not, majority (77.33 per cent) of the respondents (78.67 per cent from Assam and 76 per cent from West Bengal) including 90.20 per cent and 73.81 per cent of male and 54.17 per cent and 87.5 per cent of female from the states of Assam and West Bengal, respectively, accepted the issue, saying that a change is taking place, so far the cultural trend of their home and community is concerned.

However, 20 per cent of the total respondents, 16.655 per cent from Assam and 23.33 per cent from West Bengal negates the view. 2.67 per cent of the total respondents, 4.665 per cent from Assam and 0.67 per cent from West Bengal did not want to comment over the issue.

Taking the issue into consideration, it is clear that less percentage of male and more female from West Bengal are in favour of the issue; on the other hand more male and less female from West Bengal are against the issue, compared to their respective counter groups from the state of Assam. As such the issue remains as a controvercial one, so far the perception of the respondents from the states are covered.

Table 10.5: Respondents Rating Over their Present Cultural Pattern if Compared to the Cultural Pattern of their Previous Generation

State	*Assam*			*West Bengal*			*Grand Total*
Sex → *Rating*	*Male*	*Female*	*Total*	*Male*	*Female*	*Total*	
Very Rich	17 (16.67%)	8 (16.67%)	25 (16.67%)	44 (34.92%)	3 (12.5%)	47 (31.33%)	72 (24%)
Rich	31 (30.39%)	18 (37.5%)	49 (32.67%)	70 (55.56%)	20 (83.33%)	90 (60%)	139 (46.33%)
Moderate	40 (39.22%)	19 (39.58%)	59 (39.32%)	4 (3.17%)	0 (0%)	4 (2.67%)	63 (21%)
Poor	9 (8.82%)	1 (2.08%)	10 (6.67%)	7 (5.56%)	1 (4.17%)	8 (5.33%)	18 (6%)
Very Poor	5 (4.90%)	2 (4.17%)	7 (4.67%)	1 (0.79%)	0 (0%)	1 (0.67%)	8 (2.67%)
Total	102 (100%)	48 (100%)	150 (100%)	126 (100%)	24 (100%)	150 (100%)	300 (100%)

To delve into the deep of their cultural status, certain question was designed. Responding towards the question 24 per cent, 46.33 per cent, 21 per cent, 6 per cent and 2.67 per cent of the total respondents rated their present cultural pattern as very rich, rich, moderate, poor and very poor respectively, while comparing it to the cultural pattern of their previous generation.

16.67 per cent and 34.92 per cent of the males, 16.67 per cent and 12.5 per cent of the females and 16.67 per cent and 31.33 per cent of the total respondents from the states of Assam and West Bengal respectively, considered their cultural pattern as 'very-rich' while comparing the same with their previous generation, which reveals that more respondents from West Bengal are considering their present cultural pattern as reach. However comparatively less female respondents and more male respondents from West Bengal followed the same view, than that of the counter respondent group from Assam.

Substantially higher percentage of respondents, both male and female, from West Bengal considered their present cultural pattern as 'rich'; However, it is substantially lesser percentage of the respondents – both male and female – from West Bengal who considered their present culture pattern as 'average' while comparing the same with the culture-pattern of their previous generation(s).

Table 10.6: Perception about the Scope respondents are Having to Transmit Indigenous Knowledge of their Community Through their Teaching

State	Assam			West Bengal			Grand Total
Sex→ / Response	Male	Female	Total	Male	Female	Total	
Yes	83 (81.37%)	30 (62.5%)	113 (75.33%)	70 (55.56%)	13 (54.17%)	83 (55.33%)	196(65.33%)
No	19 (18.63%)	18 (37.5%)	37 (24.67%)	56 (44.44%)	11 (45.83%)	67 (44.67%)	104 (34.67%)
Total	102 (100%)	48 (100%)	150 (100%)	126 (100%)	24 (100%)	150 (100%)	300 (100%)

Table 10.6 presents the distribution of the respondents regarding their perception about the scope they are having to transmit indigenous knowledge of their own community, through their teaching.

Majority (65.33 per cent) of the respondents, 75.33 per cent of total including 81.37 per cent male and 62.5 per cent of female respondents from Assam and 55.33 per cent of the total respondents from West Bengal including 55.56 per cent of male and 54.17 per cent of female respondents responded that they think that they are having sufficient scope to transmit indigenous knowledge of their community among their students through teaching.

However, 34.67 per cent of the total respondents, 24.67 per cent from Assam and 44.67 per cent from West Bengal opined that they are not having such scope. 18.63 and 44.44 per cent of male and 37.5 per cent and 45.83 per cent of female from the state of Assam and West Bengal supported this view.

So, it may be said that, substantially more respondents from Assam while having the scope to transmit indigenous knowledge of their community among their students than that of their counter respondent group from West Bengal, it is the male group of respondents from both the states with a higher percentage, though not significant from West Bengal, to avail such scope.

In other hand, comparatively higher percentage of female respondents from Assam opined that they are not having such scope, if compared with their counter gender-group from the same state.

Table 10.7: Response about the Scope they are Having to Transmit the Indigenous Culture of their Community Through their Teaching

State	*Assam*			*West Bengal*			*Grand Total*
Sex → / *Response*	*Male*	*Female*	*Total*	*Male*	*Female*	*Total*	
Yes	76 (74.51%)	30 (62.5%)	106 (70.67%)	54 (42.86%)	7 (29.17%)	61 (40.66%)	167 (55.67%)
No	26 (25.49%)	18 (37.5%)	44 (29.33%)	72 (57.14%)	17 (70.83%)	89 (59.33%)	133 (44.33%)
Total	102 (100%)	48 (100%)	150 (100%)	126 (100%)	24 (100%)	150 (100%)	300 (100%)

A similar question was asked to the respondents, regarding their scope to transmit their indigenous culture of their community through their teaching, where the groups bifurcated in two opinions. Their distribution is presented in Table 10.7.

The Table reveals that majority of the entire group of respondents (55.67 per cent) are having the scope to transmit indigenous culture of their community through their teaching whereas on the other hand, 44.33 per cent of the entire sample group negates this view.

Juxtaposing the respondent-groups from different states, it is found that while majority (70.67 per cent) of the respondents from Assam, incorporating 74.51 per cent of male and 62.5 per cent of female said having such scope, the respondents are minority (40.66 per cent) from the state of West Bengal, including 42.86 per cent of male and 29.17 per cent of female, who supported this view.

On the other hand, majority of the respondents (59.33 per cent), including 57.14 per cent of male respondents and 70.83 per cent of the female respondents from West Bengal negates the view saying that they are nor having any scope to transmit indigenous culture of their own community among the students – through their teaching.

29.33 per cent of the total respondents from Assam, including 25.49 per cent of male and 37.5 per cent of female also found supporting the view and reported, are not having any scope to transmit their indigenous culture through their teaching.

Table 10.8 represent the response of the respondents about the extent of interest of their students towards the indigenous knowledge and culture of the tribal communities.

Table 10.8: Perception about the Interest of the Students Towards Indigenous Knowledge and Culture

State	Assam			West Bengal			Grand Total
Sex → Response	Male	Female	Total	Male	Female	Total	
Quite Interested	49 (48.04%)	5 (10.42%)	54 (36%)	11 (8.73%)	0 (0%)	11 (7.33%)	65 (21.665%)
Interested	47 (46.08%)	28 (58.33%)	75 (50%)	78 (61.90%)	20 (83.33%)	98 (65.34%)	173 (57.67%)
Indifferent	4 (3.92%)	8 (16.67%)	12 (8%)	37 (29.37%)	1 (4.17%)	38 (25.33%)	50 (16.665%)
Not at all Interested	2 (1.96%)	7 (14.58%)	9 (6%)	0 (0%)	3 (12.5%)	3 (2%)	12 (4%)
Total	102 (100%)	48 (100%)	150 (100%)	126 (100%)	24 (100%)	150 (100%)	300 (100%)

The responses came on four points over the issue. It is observed that while majority (57.67 per cent) of the entire respondent group are considering that their students are interested towards their indigenous knowledge and culture, it is only 4 per cent of the entire respondents who said that their students are not at all interested towards the indigenous knowledge and culture of the tribal communities.

While 21.665 per cent of the respondents opined that their students are interested towards the indigenous knowledge and culture of the tribal communities to a greater extent, it is just 16.665 per cent of the respondents who considered that their students possess an indifferent attitude towards their knowledge and culture.

In one hand, 48.04 per cent of male and 10.42 per cent of female, together comprising a total of 36 per cent of the respondents from Assam and 8.73 per cent of male and none of the female from West Bengal, forming a total of only 7.33 per cent respondents holds the issue affermatively. In the other hand, who were with the opinion that the students of their schools are interested with a greater extent, towards the indigenous knowledge and culture of the tribal societies. This ultimately reveals that substantially higher percentage of respondents from Assam feel that their students are quite interested towards the knowledge and culture of the tribal communities.

It is mostly the females from both the states, to whom, their students are not at all interested towards the indigenous knowledge and culture of the tribal communities. Only 1.96 per cent of male from Assam and none of the male respondents of West Bengal supported this view.

So, in terms of gender, a variation in perception is visible about the interest of their students, while to the majority of the male respondents from both the states, the students of their schools are interested towards the indigenous knowledge and culture of tribal communities, it is the female respondents from both the states who does not consider the same.

A question was designed, seeking response from the respondents whether they are having any scope to develop their own community through their teaching or not. Responding towards this question, majority (69 per cent) of the total respondents affirmed that they are having sufficient scope to develop their own respective communities through their teaching. However 30.33 per cent of the total respondents negate this view. It is only 0.67 per cent of the total respondents who did not respond towards this question. Their response break-up is presented in Table 10.9.

Table 10.9: Response of the Tribal Teachers Towards their Scope to Develop their Community Through Teaching

State	*Assam*			*West Bengal*			*Grand Total*
Sex→ / *Response*	*Male*	*Female*	*Total*	*Male*	*Female*	*Total*	
Yes	85 (88.33%)	40 (83.34%)	125 (83.33%)	70 (55.56%)	12 (50%)	82 (54.67%)	207 (69%)
No	17 (16.67%)	7 (14.58%)	24 (16%)	56 (44.44%)	11 (48.83%)	67 (44.665%)	91 (30.33%)
Can not Say	0 (0%)	1 (2.08%)	1 (0.67%)	0 (0%)	1 (4.17%)	1 0.665%)	2 (0.67%)
Total	102 (100%)	48 (100%)	150 (100%)	126 (100%)	24 (100%)	150 (100%)	300 (100%)

Among the respondents from Assam while substantially higher percentage (83.33 per cent) of the respondents opined that they are having scope to develop their community through their teaching, comparatively lesser percentage (54.67 per cent) of the respondents from West Bengal accepted the view.

While only 50 per cent of the female respondents from West Bengal said to have scope to develop their community through their teaching it is 83.33 per cent of the female respondents from Assam who also think so.

83.33 per cent and 55.56 per cent of the male respondents from states, Assam and West Bengal respectively also respond in a similar manner.

It can be said that it is the respondent groups both male and female, from Assam who are substantially more in number to say that they can develop their community through their profession, compared to their counter respondent group from West Bengal.

On the other hand, substantially higher percentage (44.665 per cent) of respondents from West Bengal, including 44.44 per cent of male and 48.83 per cent of female respondents negates the issue, saying that they do not have the scope to develop their community through their teaching. Only 16 per cent of the total respondents, including 16.67 per cent of male and 14.58 per cent of female from Assam were found supporting this very view. Marginal percentage of the respondents from both the states did not reply this question and all of them were female.

Until an individual is really having a close connection with her/his community, it is simply impossible for the individual to work for the betterment of the community. As the sample groups are having a specific ascribed status and the study is meant for analyzing their status, a question was designed, asking them whether the respondents are really trying to uplift their community or not. The response break-up towards the very question is given in Table 10.10.

Table 10.10: Are you Really Trying to Uplift Your Community?

State	Assam			West Bengal			Grand Total
Sex → Response	Male	Female	Total	Male	Female	Total	
Yes	99 (97.06%)	45 (93.75%)	144 (96%)	103 (81.75%)	22 (91.67%)	125 (83.33%)	269 (89.67%)
No	0 (0%)	2 (4.17%)	2 (1.33%)	0 (0%)	0 (0%)	0 (0%)	02 (0.665%)
No Response	3 (2.94%)	1 (2.08%)	4 (2.67%)	23 (18.25%)	2 (8.33%)	25 (16.67%)	29 (9.665%)
Total	102 (100%)	48 (100%)	150 (100%)	126 (100%)	24 (100%)	150 (100%)	300 (100%)

Responding towards the very question, significantly higher percentage (89.67 per cent) of the entire respondent group responds in an affirmative way; only a marginal fraction (0.665 per cent) directly negates the same. 9.665 per cent of the total respondents did not respond towards the question.

Now it is a question to the reader whether it can be assumed that those who did not respond towards the item are in a position or not, to uplift their respective communities.

State-wise analysis of data revealed that 96 per cent of the total respondents, including 97.06 per cent of male and 93.75 per cent of the female respondents from Assam are really trying to up lift their communities where as from West Bengal, these figures are 83.33 per cent, 81.75 per cent and 91.67 per cent respectively.

Considering the number of respondents it can be said that while more respondents from Assam are trying to uplift their communities, it is the male respondents from Assam and female respondents from West Bengal, more in number, compared to their respective counter groups, who reported trying to uplift their communities.

While none of the respondents from West Bengal was found saying that they are not trying to uplift their communities, it is only 1.33 per cent of the respondents from Assam, including 4.17per cent of female respondents who respond in the similar way.

2.94 per cent of male and 2.08 per cent of female respondents, together comprising a group of 2.67 per cent of the total respondents from Assam and 16.67 per cent of the total respondents, including 18.25 per cent of male and 16.67 per cent of the female respondents from West Bengal did not respond to this question. It can be taken granted that these groups are not actually trying to uplift their respective communities, may be, due to varied reasons.

In the status questionnaire, two specific questions were asked to the respondents for obtaining their reaction to their own social position and the position of their communities, which are presented in Table 10.11 and Table 10.12 respectively. The two questions were set with respect to a hypothetically constructed social ladder, the steps of which symbolized their social positions. The respondents were asked to place themselves on any step of the ladder and also to state whether such positions could be changed or not. Table 10.11 presents the distribution of the status of the respondents as perceived by them.

Table 10.11: Status of the Tribal Teachers as per their Perception

State	*Assam*			*West Bengal*			*Grand Total*
Sex → / *Response*	*Male*	*Female*	*Total*	*Male*	*Female*	*Total*	
Higher	0 (0%)	3 (6.25%)	3 (2%)	3 (2.38%)	5 (20.83%)	8 (5.33%)	11 (3.67%)
Middle	47 (46.08%)	29 (60.42%)	76 (50.67%)	92 (73.02%)	19 (79.17%)	111 (74%)	187 (62.33%)
Lower	55 (53.92%)	16 (33.33%)	71 (47.33%)	31 (24.60%)	0 (0%)	31 (20.67%)	102 (34%)
Total	102 (100%)	48 (100%)	150 (100%)	126 (100%)	24 (100%)	150 (100%)	300 (100%)

From Table 10.11, it was observed that a majority (62.33 per cent) of the total respondents from both the states (50.67 per cent from Assam and 74 per cent from West Bengal) considered themselves in the middle level of the social ladder. This status-position was opted by 46.08 per cent and 73.02 per cent of the male respondents and 60.42 per cent and 79.17 per cent of female respondents from Assam and West Bengal respectively.

This status group was followed by a group of 34 per cent of the total respondents, incorporating 47.33 per cent of the respondents from Assam and only 20.67 per cent of the respondents from West Bengal, who placed themselves in the lowest step of the hypothetical social ladder. 53.92 per cent and 24.60 per cent of the male respondents from the states, Assam and West Bengal respectively, placed themselves in the lowest step of the social ladder while only one-third (33.33 per cent) of the female respondents from Assam opted for a similar status. None of the female respondents from West Bengal was found opting the lower status, as observed from Table 10.11.

It is only 3.67 per cent of the entire respondent group, who considered a 'higher' status for them. Only 2 per cent of the total respondents from Assam including 6.25 per cent of the female respondents and 5.33 per cent of the respondents from West Bengal, incorporating 2.38 per cent of male and 20.83 per cent of the female respondents was found considering a similar status for themselves. Not even a single male respondent from Assam considered him in this very status group.

Tabulated data reveal that substantially higher percentage of respondents from West Bengal, both from the male and female groups opted for a medium status for themselves, compared to their counter respondent groups from Assam.

However on the other hand, it is the respondent groups from Assam, who opted for a lower status for themselves than that of their counter respondent groups from West Bengal.

Marginally higher percentage of the respondents in total, including significantly higher percentage of female respondents from West Bengal considered themselves in the high-status group compared to their counter respondent group from Assam who also opted for a similar status group.

The average deviation of the males and females in the extreme status group was found to be 31.7 per cent and 23.995 per cent respectively.

Table 10.12: Status of the Respondents' Communities as Perceived by the Respondents

State	Assam			West Bengal			Grand Total
Sex→ Status	Male	Female	Total	Male	Female	Total	
Higher	0 (0%)	0 (0%)	0 (0%)	0 (0%)	0 (0%)	0 (0%)	0 (0%)
Medium	42 (41.18%)	11 (22.92%)	53 (35.33%)	18 (14.29%)	9 (37.5%)	27 (18%)	80 (26.67%)
Lower	60 (58.82%)	37 (77.08%)	97 (64.67%)	108 (85.71%)	15 (62.5%)	123 (82%)	220 (73.33%)
Total	102 (100%)	48 (100%)	150 (100%)	126 (100%)	24 (100%)	150 (100%)	300 (100%)

Table 10.12 presents the distribution of the status of the respondent's respective communities as perceived by the respondents. It can be observed from the Table that while 3.67 per cent of the total respondents opted higher status for themselves none of the respondents from any state considered the status of their community as 'higher'. (Ref. Table 10.11). This signifies that considering the status-position, they're in a markable difference between the respondents and their communities.

This markable difference in terms of percentage still prevails when the respondent groups assigned a medium status – for themselves and for their communities It was found that while majority of the respondents (62.33 per cent) in total opted for medium status, it is only 26.67 per cent of the respondents who assigned such status to their communities.

41.18 per cent and 14.29 per cent of the male, 22.92 per cent and 37.5 per cent of the female and 35.33 per cent and 18 per cent of the total respondents from the states – Assam and West Bengal, respectively, considered the status of their respective communities as 'medium'. The corresponding figures for the respective respondent-groups for a similar status are quite higher (as shown in Table 9.5) which indicates that percentage of the respondents who opted for a medium status for them is substantially higher than that of those who placed their respective communities under such a status category.

From the Table it was further observed that 58.82 per cent and 85.71 per cent of the male, 77.08 per cent and 62.5 per cent of the female and 64.67 per cent and 82 per cent of the total respondents from the states Assam and West Bengal, respectively, reported that their respective communities are holding a lower status, according to their view. A substantially higher percentage of male respondents and marginally less percentage of female respondents from West Bengal reported that their respective indigenous communities are holding the 'lower' status, if compared to their counter respondent groups from Assam.

However, in total, it is the respondent group from West Bengal, comparatively larger than the respondent group from Assam, assigned lower status to their communities.

The juxtaposition in the 'lower-status' between the respondents and their communities revealed that the respondents from both the gender and state categories shows that while good number of respondents assigned 'lowest status' for their respective communities, it is lesser percentage of respondents who assigned similar status for themselves. A different picture can be perused if Table 10.11 and 10.12 is juxtaposed in terms of the other response categories ('*viz.* Higher & medium'). Comparatively higher percentage of respondents opted for 'higher' and 'medium' status for themselves than those who assigned similar status to their community – people.

Table 10.13: Subject's Perception about Upward Mobility of Status

State	*Assam*			*West Bengal*			*Grand Total*
Sex → *Response*	*Male*	*Female*	*Total*	*Male*	*Female*	*Total*	
Very hard	28 (27.45%)	9 (18.75%)	37 (24.67%)	35 (27.78%)	6 (25%)	41 (27.33%)	78 (26%)
Hard	51 (50%)	32 (66.67%)	83 (55.33%)	68 (53.97%)	11 (45.83%)	79 (52.67%)	162 (54%)
Cannot Say	23 (22.55%)	7 (14.58%)	30 (20%)	23 (18.25%)	7 (29.17%)	30 (20%)	60 (20%)
Easy	0 (0%)	0 (0%)	0 (0%)	0 (0%)	0 (0%)	0 (0%)	0 (0%)
Very easy	0 (0%)	0 (0%)	0 (0%)	0 (0%)	0 (0%)	0 (0%)	0 (0%)
Total	102 (100%)	48 (100%)	150 (100%)	126 (100%)	24 (100%)	150 (100%)	300 (100%)

Table 10.13 represents the respondent's perception about upward mobility of status.

While replying towards another question in the sequels, the respondent group's perception varied in types. The specific question was that, whether it is easy or hard to change the status of an individual in its upward direction. In total 26 per cent of the respondents replied that to them, it is 'very hard' to change one's status through upward mobility. To 54 per cent of them, it is 'hard' to change one's status through upward mobility. One fifth of the total respondent did not reply towards this question. The rest two-response categories (*viz.* – 'easy' & 'very easy') were not opted by any of the respondents.

The brief perusal of Table 10.13 reveals that 24.67 per cent and 27.33 per cent of the respondents from the states Assam and West Bengal respectively, opined that it is very hard to assume upward mobility in the social status. This respondent group includes 27.45 per cent and 27.78 per cent of male and 18.75 per cent and 25 per cent of the female respondents from the respective states.

Upward mobility of status was hard to 50 per cent and 53.97 per cent of male, 66.67 per cent and 45.83 per cent of female and 55.33 per cent and 52.67 per cent of the total respondents from the states Assam and West Bengal respectively. In an average 54 per cent of the total respondents from both the states considered that it is hard to change the status of an individual towards upward direction.

However, 20 per cent of the entire sample did not respond towards the item, 22.55 per cent and 18.25 per cent of male, 14.58 per cent and 29.17 per cent of the female from the states, Assam and West Bengal simply passed out the item. To none of the respondents of any states, it is easier to change the status of an individual towards upward direction.

The juxtaposition of the respondent groups from the two different states reveals that, social mobility is very hard to a little more percentage of respondents from West Bengal, than that of the respondent groups of Assam. Though majority of the respondent groups are with this opinion from both the states. However marginally higher percentage of the respondents (55.33 per cent) from Assam considered that it is really hard to change social status, if compared with their respective counter respondent group from West Bengal.

Table 10.14: Perception of Respondents about their Respective Community's Attitude Towards Developtment

State	*Assam*			*West Bengal*			*Grand Total*
Sex → *Attitude*	*Male*	*Female*	*Total*	*Male*	*Female*	*Total*	
Positive	77 (75.49%)	43 (89.58%)	120 (80%)	105 (83.33%)	21 (87.5%)	126 (84%)	246 (82%)
Indifferent	21 (20.59%)	5 (10.42%)	26 (17.33%)	19 (15.08%)	1 (4.17%)	20 (13.33%)	46 (15.33%)
Negative	4 (3.92%)	0 (0%)	4 (2.67%)	2 (1.59%)	2 (8.33%)	4 (2.67%)	8 (2.67%)
Total	102 (100%)	48 (100%)	150 (100%)	126 (100%)	24 (100%)	150 (100%)	300 (100%)

Table 10.14 represents the perception of the respondents about their respective communities' attitude towards development.

75.49 per cent and 83.33 per cent of male, 89.58 per cent and 87.5 per cent of female and 80 per cent and 84 per cent of the total respondents from the states Assam and West Bengal considered that their respective communities are holding a positive attitude towards development. Comparatively more respondents from West Bengal were found possessing this sort of attitude, than that of the respondents from Assam. More females considered the attitude of their respective communities as 'favourable' than that of the males. In total, 82 per cent of the total respondents are having this sort of view.

On the other hand 20.59 per cent and 15.08 per cent of the male, 10.42 per cent and 4.17 per cent of the female and 17.33 per cent and 13.33 per cent of the total respondents from the states – Assam and West Bengal respectively, said that their respective communities are having an indifferent attitude towards development. This reveals that according to the respondent's perception, the attitude of the tribal communities from West Bengal is too some extent favourable towards development.

Only 2.67 per cent of the total respondents reported that their indigenous communities are not in favour of development because of their negative attitude. However not a single female respondent was found falling in this response category.

Table 10.15: Perception of the Tribal Teachers about their Community's Attitude Towards Education

State	*Assam*			*West Bengal*			*Grand Total*
Sex → *Attitude*	*Male*	*Female*	*Total*	*Male*	*Female*	*Total*	
Positive	86 (84.31%)	42 (87.5%)	128 (85.33%)	93 (73.81%)	18 (75%)	111 (74%)	239 (79.67%)
Indifferent	14 (13.73%)	5 (10.42%)	19 (12.67%)	28 (22.22%)	2 (8.33%)	30 (20%)	49 (16.33%)
Negative	2 (1.96%)	1 (2.08%)	3 (2%)	5 (3.97%)	4 (16.67%)	9 (6%)	12 (4%)
Total	102 (100%)	48 (100%)	150 (100%)	126 (100%)	24 (100%)	150 (100%)	300 (100%)

From the Table 10.15, it can be perused that 84.31 per cent and 73.81 per cent of male, 87.5 per cent and 75 per cent of female & 85.33 per cent and 74 per cent of the respondents in total from the states Assam and West Bengal respectively together comprising a group of 79.69 per cent of the total respondents, reported that their respective communities are having a positive attitude towards education. Juxtaposition in this response categories reveal that this attitude is more favourable towards education among the tribal communities in Assam, when compared with Bengal, subject to considering the perception of the respondents.

The Table further reveals that more females from both the states considered that their respective communities are having positive attitude towards education, than that of their counter gender-group.

However 13.73 per cent and 22.22 per cent of male, 10.42 per cent and 8.33 per cent of female and 12.67 per cent and 20 per cent of the total respondents from the states, Assam and West Bengal respectively, together comprising a group of 16.33 per cent of total respondents reported that their respective indigenous communities possess an indifferent attitude towards education.

A marginal percentage of respondents (only 4 per cent in total) including 2 per cent of the respondents from Assam and 6 per cent of the total respondents from West Bengal, reported that their respective communities are possessing negative attitude towards education. Juxtaposition of the groups reveal that more respondents from West Bengal opined that their respective communities are possessing negative attitude towards education.

Table 10.16: Perception of the Respondents about the Attitude of their Communities Towards Administration

State	*Assam*			*West Bengal*			*Grand Total*
Sex → *Attitude*	*Male*	*Female*	*Total*	*Male*	*Female*	*Total*	
Positive	40 (39.22%)	25 (52.08%)	65 (43.33%)	14 (11.11%)	0 (0%)	14 (9.33%)	79 (26.33%)
Indifferent	16 (15.68%)	11 (22.92%)	27 (18%)	83 (65.87%)	17 (70.83%)	100 (66.67%)	127 (42.34%)
Negative	46 (45.10%)	12 (25%)	58 (38.67%)	29 (23.02%)	7 (29.17%)	36 (24%)	94 (31.33%)
Total	102 (100%)	48 (100%)	150 (100%)	126 (100%)	24 (100%)	150 (100%)	300 (100%)

The Table reveals that while 26.33 per cent of the total respondents considered that their respective communities are possessing positive attitude towards administration, it is 42.34 per cent and 31.33 per cent of the respondents to whom the attitude of their community – people is indifferent and negative respectively.

The state wise data reveals, while majority of the respondents, (66.67 per cent) from West Bengal said that their respective communities are possessing indifferent attitude towards different levels of administration. Only 18 per cent of the respondents from Assam reported similar attitude of their communities.

On the other hand, as many as 43.33 per cent of the respondents, of which 39.22 per cent of male and 52.08 per cent of female from Assam reported that their respective indigenous communities are having positive attitude towards administration. The figures are 11.11 per cent, 0 per cent and 9.33 per cent respectively in West Bengal. It reveals that, according to the respondents from different states, the tribal communities from Assam are having positive attitude towards administration, which is not a fact in case of the tribal communities from West Bengal. Only a marginal section of them are having positive attitude towards administration.

In total 38.67 per cent of the respondents from Assam and 24 per cent from West Bengal said that their communities are possessing negative attitude towards administration.

Hence, it can be said that the attitude of the tribal communities towards administration (i.e. government) from Assam is divided into two extreme ends, whereas in West Bengal, one can find an uniform attitude, tends toward negative direction, so far the opinion of the respondents of the present study is concerned in connection with the attitude of their communities towards administration.

11

Association among Status Components

Status and Training

It should be accepted by almost each and every hand that persuasion of training should definitely influence the status of any professionals. The teachers are not the exception. So, in this phase, attempts was made to explore whether their exist any association of the status of respondent tribal teachers as they perceive, with that of their persuasion of professional training or not.

χ^2 test has been employed over the entire sample group as well as over the groups from the two states, (*viz.*, Assam and West Bengal separately).

Table 11.1: Association between Status and Training (Total Sample)

Status \ *Training*	*Trained*	*Not trained*	*Total*
Higher	8 (5.17)	3 (5.83)	11
Middle	103 (87.89)	84 (99.11)	187
Lower	30 (47.94)	72 (54.06)	102
Total	141	159	N = 300

$\chi^2 = 20.491$; df = 3; P lies above 0.01

Association between the two variables *i.e.*, status and Training is highly significant at .01 level. The χ^2 value over the entire sample group of respondents reveals that highly significant (at 0.01 level) association exists between this two variables 'status' and 'persuasion' of training. It is further observed that professionally trained teachers are holding higher status than that of their non-trained counterparts.

Table 11.2: Association between Status and Training (Sample from Assam)

Status \ Training	*Trained*	*Not trained*	*Total*
Higher	3 (.92)	0 (2.08)	03
Middle	31 (23.31)	45 (52.69)	76
Lower	12 (21.77)	59 (49.23)	71
Total	46	104	150

χ^2= 16.766; df= 3; P lies above.01 level; Association is highly significant at .01 level.

While the respondents from the state Assam are taken into consideration, similar picture has been observed so far the status of the respondents from Assam and their persuasion of training is concerned.

Table 11.3: Association between Status and Training (Sample from West Bengal)

Status \ Training	*Trained*	*Not trained*	*Total*
Higher	8 (5.07)	3 (2.93)	08
Middle	72 (70.3)	39 (40.7)	111
Lower	18 (19.63)	13 (11.37)	31
Total	95	55	150

χ^2 = 0.484; df= 3; P lies between .9 and .8; Association is not significant.

However, the data obtained from the respondent group from West Bengal reveals no significant association between their 'perceived' status and 'persuasion of training' as the obtained c^2 value (= 0.484) is not significant at any standard level.

Juxtaposition of the χ^2 values obtained from two state groups of respondents reveals that respondent group from the state Assam indicates significantly stronger association between two factors under consideration than that as reflected by the respondent group from West Bengal.

Association between Status and Economic Situation

Economic situation is another important indicator of status and in the study attempt was made to explore the status profile of the respondents in terms of their economic circumstances. χ^2 test was administered for the purpose.

The obtained χ^2 value for the entire group of respondents establish strong association between the variables – the perceived status of the respondents and their economic situation which is significant at 0.01 level of confidence (χ^2 = 87.245 at 4 df).

Attempt was also made to observe the association of the concerned variables separately from the respondents from the two states, where it was found that strong association exists between the perceived status of the respondents and their economic situation from both the states and these association in both the dimensions of status are significant at 0.01 level of confidence (with a χ^2 value of 135.729 from Assam and 21.825 from West Bengal at df 4).

Table 11.4: Association between Status and Economic Situation (Total sample)

Status \ Economic Situation	Well off	Average	Difficult	Total
Higher	8 (1.14)	3 (7.55)	0 (2.31)	11
Middle	22 (19.32)	144 (128.41)	21 (39.27)	187
Lower	1 (10.54)	59 (70.04)	42 (21.42)	102
Total	31	206	63	300

χ^2 = 87.245; df = 4; P lies above.01 level

Table 11.5: Association between Status and Economic Situation (Sample from Assam)

Status \ Economic Situation	Well off	Average	Difficult	Total
Higher	2 (0.04)	1 (2.04)	0 (0.92)	3
Middle	0 (1.01)	69 (51.68)	7 (23.31)	76
Lower	0 (0.95)	32 (48.28)	39 (21.77)	71
Total	2	102	46	150

χ^2 = 135.729; df = 4; P lies above.01 level

Table 11.6: Association between Status and Economic Situation (Sample from West Bengal)

Status \ Economic Situation	Well off	Average	Difficult	Total
Higher	6 (1.55)	2 (5.55)	0 (0.91)	8
Middle	22 (21.46)	75 (76.96)	14 (12.58)	111
Lower	1 (5.99)	27 (21.49)	3 (3.51)	31
Total	29	104	17	150

χ^2 = 21.825; df = 4; P lies above.01 level

Status and Experience

In any profession, experience is one of the important component and indicator of professional status. In that sense, experience in a certain profession either enhance or reduces the professional status in it's qualitative aspect.

Keeping this in view an attempt has been made to find out the reply to the question statistically whether there exists any association between the two variables – 'the perceived status' and 'length of experience of the respondents' of the present study or not.

The respondent group was classified on the basis of their experience as well as on basis of their status as they perceived.

Table 11.7: Association between Status and Experience (Total Sample)

Status \ Experience	Less than 5 years	5-10 years	More than 10 years but less than 15 years	15-20 years	More than 20 years	Total
Higher	4 (3.52)	5 (3.19)	2 (3.19)	0 (1.43)	0 (1.1)	11
Middle	82 (59.84)	41 (54.23)	21 29.92)	18 (24.31)	25 (18.7)	187
Lower	10 (32.64)	41 (29.58)	25 (16.32)	22 (13.26)	5 (10.2)	102
Total	96	87	48	39	30	300

$\chi^2 = 54.075$; df = 8; P lies above.01 level

The obtained χ^2 value for the entire group of respondents from the two states reveal that association exists between two variables – *i.e.*, the 'perceived status' of the respondents and their 'experience' and it was observed that the association is significant at 0.01 level of confidence.

However while the χ^2 test was administered separately on the respondent groups from the two states, keeping in view the two variables – *i.e.*, the perceived status and their experience, it was observed that the association between the two variables is almost significant at 0.05 level among the respondents from both the states, and nowhere this association is significant at 0.01 levels.

Table 11.8: Association between Status and Economic Situation (Assam)

Status \ Experience	Less than 5 years	5-10 years	More than 10 years but less than 15 years	15-20 years	More than 20 years	Total
Higher	1 (0.34)	1 (1.02)	1 (0.48)	0 (0.62)	0 (0.54)	3
Middle	14 (8.61)	19 (25.84)	7 (12.16)	14 (15.711)	22 (13.68)	76
Lower	2 (8.05)	31 (24.14)	16 (11.36)	17 (14.67)	5 (12.78)	71
Total	17	51	24	31	27	150

$\chi^2 = 15.092$; df = 8; P lies between 0.1 and.05 level P is almost significant at 0.05 level.

Table 11.9: Association between Status and Economic Situation (West Bengal)

Status \ Experience	Less than 5 years	5-10 years	More than 10 years but less than 15 years	15-20 years	More than 20 years	Total
Higher	3 (4.21)	4 (1.92)	1 (1.28)	0 (0.43)	0 (0.16)	8
Middle	68 (58.46)	22 (26.64)	14 (17.76)	4 (5.92)	3 (2.22)	111
Lower	8 (16.33)	10 (7.44)	9 (4.96)	4 (1.65)	0 (0.62)	31
Total	79	36	24	8	3	150

$\chi^2 = 19.081$; df = 8. P lies between .02 and .01 level and significant at 0.05 level but not at.01 level.

Status and Religion

Religion is the predominant factor of statusprofile of any individual or even for a group. It may be an ascribed feature, or an adopted symbol for almost all the human societies spreaded over the universe. Being the downtrodden sections of the population, the most notable feature of the Indian tribes in some regions is to shift frequently form one religion to another, due to various physical facilities and lucrative positions, which further influence their status as a whole.

To explore association between the perceived status and religion of the respondents, χ^2 test has been administered on the entire group as well as on the state-groups.

The results obtained from Tables 11.10, 11.11 and 11.12 denotes that, while this association between two variables under consideration are significant at 0.05 level for the entire group of respondents with a χ^2 value of 13.886 at the df 6, the association is not significant, neither for Assam, nor for West Bengal, at any standard levels.

Table 11.10: Association between Status and Religion (Total sample)
Total Sample (N = 330 – 3 = 297)

Status \ Religion	Hindu	Christian	Sari/Sarna	Prislitarian	Total
Higher	4 (3.23)	3 (3.53)	1 (1.08)	0 (0.16)	8
Middle	82 (75.56)	71 (82.48)	29 (25.19)	5 (3.78)	187
Lower	34 (41.21)	57 (44.99)	10 (13.74)	1 (2.06)	102
Total	120	131	40	6	297

χ^2 = 13.886; df =6; P lies between .05 and .02 level
[* 3 of the respondents did not respond about their religion.]

Table 11.11: Association between Status and Economic Situation
(Sample from Assam; N = 150 – 2 = 148)

Status \ Religion	Hindu	Christian	Sari/Sarna	Prislitarian	Total
Higher	0 (0.25)	1 (0.72)	0 (0)	0 (0.03)	1
Middle	18 (19.00)	54 (54.43)	0 (0)	4 (2.57)	76
Lower	19 (17.75)	51 (50.85)	0 (0)	1 (2.40)	102
Total	37	106	0	5	148

χ^2 = 2.146; df = 6; P lies between .95 and .90
[* 2 of the respondents did not respond about their religion.]

Table 11.12: Association between Status and Economic Situation (Sample from West Bengal; N = 150 – 1 = 149)

Status \ Religion	Hindu	Christian	Sari/Sarna	Prislitarian	Total
Higher	4 (3.9)	2 (1.17)	1 (1.88)	0 (0.05)	7
Middle	64 (61.83)	17 (18.62)	29 (29.80)	1 (0.75)	111
Lower	15 (17.27)	6 (5.20)	10 (8.32)	0 (0.20)	31
Total	83	25	40	1	149

$\chi^2 = 2.079$; df = 6; P lies between 0.95 and 0.90.

[* One of the respondents was silent about religion.]

Status and Social Participation

One of the important dimensions of status is social status – which is expected to be reflected by social participation of the social atoms. For the present study, response was gathered from the tribal teachers about their social participation in various social occasions. On the basis of their rating over their status and social participation, it was observed that, their exists association between these two variables, which is neither significant at any standard level for the entire respondent group, not for the respective state groups.

However, the juxtaposition of the association for different groups implies that this association among the respondent group from West Bengal is higher than the respondent groups from Assam, which is further higher than the association exists for the entire respondent group.

Table 11.13: Association between Status and Social Participation (Total sample; N = 300)

Status \ Social Participation	Always	Often	Rarely	Total
Higher	4 (2.71)	6 (7.0)	1 (1.28)	11
Middle	44 (46.13)	120 (119.06)	23 (21.82)	187
Lower	26 (25.16)	65 (64.94)	11 (11.9)	102
Total	74	191	35	300

$\chi^2 = 1.236$; df = 4; P lies between 0.8 and 0.9

Table 11.14: Association between Status and Social Participation (Sample from Assam; N = 150)

Status \ Social Participation	Always	Often	Rarely	Total
Higher	2 (1.12)	1(1.6)	0(0.28)	3
Middle	30(28.37)	40(40.53)	6(7.09)	76
Lower	24(26.51)	39(37.87)	8(6.63)	71
Total	56	80	14	150

$\chi^2 = 2.02$; df = 4; P lies between 0.7 and 0.8

Table 11.15: Association between Status and Social Participation (Sample from West Bengal; N = 150)

Status \ Social Participation	Always	Often	Rarely	Total
Higher	2(0.96)	5(5.92)	1(1.12)	8
Middle	14 (13.32)	80(82.14)	17(15.54)	111
Lower	2(3.72)	26(22.94)	3(4.34)	31
Total	18	111	21	150

$\chi^2 = 5.012$; df = 4; P lies between 0.2 and 0.3.

Status and Political Participation

The Tables 11.16, 11.17 and 11.18 reveal that in terms of the political participation and their perceived status, the respondent group from both the states (*i.e.*, the Assam and West Bengal) does not show markable significant association, though political participation in social life is obviously an indicator of political status.

The present study observed, no significant relationship exists between the two variables – 'overall status' of the respondent groups (*i.e.*, the total respondent group and the respective-state-groups) and their 'participation in political activities'.

Table 11.16: Association between Status and Political Participation (Total Sample; N = 300)

Status \ Political Participation	Yes	No	Total
Higher	8(8.36)	3(2.64)	11
Middle	146(142.12)	41(44.88)	187
Lower	74(77.52)	28(24.48)	102
Total	228	72	300

$\chi^2 = 0.182$; df = 3; P lies below 0.95.
Association between the two variables is not significant at any level.

Table 11.17: Association between Status and Political Participation (Sample from Assam; N = 150)

Status \ Political Participation	Yes	No	Total
Higher	2(2.04)	1(0.96)	3
Middle	53(51.68)	23(24.32)	76
Lower	47(48.28)	24(22.72)	71
Total	102	48	150

$\chi^2 = 1.172$; df = 3; P lies between 0.70 and 0.80.
Association between the two variables is not significant at any standard level.

Table 11.18: Association between Status and Political Participation
(Sample from West Bengal; N = 150)

Status \ Political Participation	Yes	No	Total
Higher	6(6.72)	2(1.28)	8
Middle	93(93.24)	18(17.76)	111
Lower	27(26.04)	4(4.96)	31
Total	126	24	150

$\chi^2 = 0.703$; df = 3; P lies between 0.80 and 0.90.
Association between the two variables is not significant at any level.

Status and Location of Schools

The respondent groups for the study placed themselves in a hierarchical ladder to indicate their status. Data was also obtained about the location of their respective schools. It is fact that place of work is one of the important component of the professional status of any professionals. Keeping this in view χ^2 test was administered on the state groups as well as on the entire sample group to explore, whether there exists any significant association between two variables, *i.e.*, the 'status' as they perceive and 'professional status' in terms of their location of schools.

Table 11.19: Association between Status and Location of Schools
(Total Sample; N = 300)

Status \ Location	Urban	Suburban	Rural	Total
Higher	4(3.04)	2(1.1)	5(6.86)	11
Middle	39(51.74)	11(18.7)	137(116.56)	187
Lower	40(28.22)	17(10.2)	45(63.58)	102
Total	83	30	187	300

$\chi^2 = 26.315$; df = 4; P lies above .01.
Association between the two variables is significant at.01 level of confidence.

The chi-square test reveals significant association between the perception of the status of the respondents and the location of their schools, while the total group of respondents (N = 300) are taken into consideration as the chi square value is 26.315 at df 4 against the table value of 13.277. This association is significant at 0.01 level.

Table 11.20: Association between Status and Location of Schools
(Sample from Assam; N = 150)

Status \ Location	Urban	Suburban	Rural	Total
Higher	3(1.48)	0(0.36)	0(1.16)	3
Middle	36(37.49)	9(9.12)	31(29.39)	76
Lower	35(35.03)	9(8.52)	27(27.45)	71
Total	74	18	58	150

$\chi^2 = 3.265$; df = 4; P lies between 0.5 and 0.3.
Association between the two variables is not significant.

Table 11.21: Association between Status and Location of Schools (Sample from West Bengal; N = 150)

Status \ Location	Urban	Suburban	Rural	Total
Higher	1(0.48)	2(0.64)	5(6.88)	8
Middle	3(6.66)	2(8.88)	106(95.46)	111
Lower	5(1.86)	8(2.48)	18(26.66)	31
Total	9	12	129	150

χ^2= 32.871; df = 4; P lies above.01 level.

Association between the two variables is significant at 01 level of confidence.

Again, the chi square test does not reveal any significant association between the perception of the status of the respondents from Assam and the location of their schools, as because the obtained chi-square vale is 3.265 at df 4 which is quite less than the table value of 13.277. So, this association for the respondent group from Assam is not significant at any standard level. However, the χ^2 value for the very factor (*i.e.*, the perception of status and location of schools) reveals significant association in case of the respondent group from West Bengal, where the obtained chi-square value is 32.871 at df 4 and hence the association is significant at 0.01 level of confidence.

Status and Cultural Environment of the Tribal Communities

Rating has been obtained through the status question about the cultural environment of the respective communities to which the respondents belong. Further attempt has been made here to find out the association between the factors – 'status of the respondents' as they perceive and their 'perception about the cultural environment of their indigenous community'.

Table 11.22: Association between Status and Cultural Environment of the Tribal Communities. (Total Sample; N = 300)

Status \ Cultural Environment	Reach	Ordinary	Poor	Total
Higher	2(4.99)	8(5.57)	1(0.44)	11
Middle	80(84.77)	101(94.75)	6(7.84)	187
Lower	54(46.24)	43(51.68)	5(4.08)	102
Total	136	152	12	300

The table reveals that so far as the opinion of the entire respondent-group is concerned, significant association (at 0.05 level) exists between their status and the cultural environment as perceived by the respondents (χ^2 = 7.644 at df = 4)

This observation differs when the respondent groups from the two states considered separately.

Table 11.23: Association between Status and Cultural Environment of the Tribal Communities. (Total Sample from Assam; N = 150)

Status \ *Cultural Environment*	*Reach*	*Ordinary*	*Poor*	*Total*
Higher	0(1.14)	2(1.62)	1(0.24)	3
Middle	26(28.88)	44(41.04)	6(6.08)	76
Lower	31(26.98)	35(38.34)	5(5.68)	71
Total	57	81	12	150

$\chi^2 = 5.107$; df = 4; P lies between 0.3 and 0.2.

It was further observed that as per the response of the respondents from Assam, the association between their 'status' and 'cultural environment of their community' is not significant ($\chi^2 = 5.107$ at df = 4).

Table 11.24: Association between Status and Cultural Environment of the Tribal Communities. (Sample from West Bengal; N = 150)

Status \ *Cultural Environment*	*Reach*	*Ordinary*	*Poor*	*Total*
Higher	2(4.21)	6(3.79)	0(0)	8
Middle	54(58.46)	57(52.54)	0(0)	111
Lower	23(16.33)	8(14.67)	0(0)	31
Total	79	71	0	150

$\chi^2 = 2.857$; df = 4; P lies between 0.7 and.05.

As per the response obtained from the respondents from West Bengal, as like the state Assam, the association between the factors is not significant ($\chi^2 = 2.857$ at df 4).

The juxtaposition of the association between the factors under study indicates that the association is very less so far the responses of the state groups are concerned and in West Bengal it is even less than that of Assam.

Status and Culture of Previous Generations

The study aimed to find out the association of the status and the culture of their previous generations, as they perceived.

Table 11.25: Association between Status and Culture of Previous Generation (Total Sample; N = 300)

Status \ *Cultural Environment*	*Very Rich*	*Rich*	*Moderate*	*Poor*	*Very Poor*	*Total*
Higher	0(2.64)	0(5.1)	2(2.31)	6(0.66)	3(0.29)	11
Middle	43(44.88)	97(86.64)	33(39.27)	9(11.22)	5(4.99)	187
Lower	29(24.48)	42(47.26)	28(21.42)	3(6.12)	0(2.72)	102
Total	72	139	63	18	8	300

$\chi^2 = 86.821$; df = 8; P lies above.01 level.

Table 11.26: Association between Status and Culture of Previous Generation (Sample from Assam; N = 150)

Cultural Environment / *Status*	*Very Rich*	*Rich*	*Moderate*	*Poor*	*Very Poor*	*Total*
Higher	0(0.5)	0(0.98)	0(1.18)	1(0.2)	2(0.14)	3
Middle	8(12.67)	25(24.83)	31(29.89)	7(5.07)	5(3.55)	76
Lower	17(11.83)	24 (23.19)	28(27.93)	2(4.73)	0(3.31)	71
Total	25	49	59	10	7	150

$\chi^2 = 40.007$; df = 8; P lies above.01 level.

Table 11.27: Association between Status and Culture of Previous Generation (Sample from West Bengal; N = 150)

Cultural Environment / *Status*	*Very Rich*	*Rich*	*Moderate*	*Poor*	*Very Poor*	*Total*
Higher	0(2.51)	0(4.8)	2(0.21)	5(0.43)	1(0.05)	8
Middle	35(34.78)	72(66.6)	2(2.96)	2(5.92)	0(0.74)	111
Lower	12(9.71)	18(18.6)	0(0.83)	1(1.65)	0(0.21)	31
Total	47	90	4	8	1	150

$\chi^2 = 95.133$; df = 8; P lies above .01 level.

It was observed from Tables 11.25, 11.26 and 11.27 that there exists association between the two variables under consideration – for the entire respondent group as well as for the respondent groups from the states, Assam and West Bengal. It was further observed that these associations are significant at 0.01 level of confidence.

Training and Location of School

With a view to explore the association between the two components of status, *viz.*, 'training' and 'location of school', χ^2 test has been carried out over the entire sample group as well as over the respondent groups from the two states.

Table 11.28: Association between Training and Location of School (Total Sample; N = 300)

Location of School → / *Training*	*Urban*	*Suburban*	*Rural*	*Total*
Trained	47(39.01)	12(14.1)	82(87.89)	141
Non-trained	36(43.99)	18(15.9)	105(99.11)	159
Total	83	30	187	300

$\chi^2 = 4.423$; df = 3; P lies between.05 and.02.

The χ^2 test over the entire sample group reveals that though there is association between the location of the schools, where the respondents are employed, and their persuasion of professional training, however this association is not significant at any standard level.

Table 11.29: Association between Training and Location of School (Sample from Assam; N = 150)

Training \ Location	Urban	Suburban	Rural	Total
Trained	41(22.69)	5(5.52)	0(17.79)	46
Non-trained	33(51.31)	13(12.48)	58(40.21)	104
Total	74	18	58	150

$\chi^2 = 46.8456$; df = 3; P lies above 0.01 level.

While zooming the view over the state Assam, different picture has been observed. The respondents from the state Assam make it clear that significant association exists between the persuasion of training and the location of their work-field.

Table 11.30: Association between Training and Location of School (Sample from West Bengal; N = 150)

Training \ Location	Urban	Suburban	Rural	Total
Trained	6(5.7)	7(7.6)	82(81.7)	95
Non-trained	3(3.3)	5(4.4)	47(47.3)	55
Total	9	12	129	150

$\chi^2 = 0.775$; df = 2; P lies between 0.7 and 0.5.

However in the state West Bengal the obtained χ^2 value does not show significant association between the persuasion of training and location of the school as the value is not significant at any level. Association is significant at .01 level.

Location of School and Location of Home

Habitation and place of work are definitely influencing the status profile of any professional. It was observed that, either in terms of their location of the house or in terms of the location of schools/institutions, the sample respondent tribal teachers from both the states, Assam and West Bengal are scattered over different types of areas; considering the nature of the area, those are classified in three categories, *viz.*, urban, suburban and rural areas.

Table 11.31: Association between Location of School and Location of Home (Total Sample; N = 300)

Location of Home \ Location of School	Urban	Suburban	Rural	Total
Urban	30(18.81)	11(10.24)	42(53.95)	83
Sub-urban	11(6.80)	10(3.70)	9(19.50)	30
Rural	27(42.39)	16(23.06)	144121.55)	187
Total	68	37	195	300

$\chi^2 = 40.229$; df = 4; P lies above 0.01 level

The χ^2 value of the total respondent groups reveals that strong and significant (at 0.01 level of confidence) association exists between these two factors. (χ^2 value is 40.229 at df 4).

Table 11.32: Association between Location of School and Location of Home (Sample from Assam; N = 150)

Location of School / *Location of Home*	*Urban*	*Suburban*	*Rural*	*Total*
Urban	29(27.13)	11(13.32)	34(33.55)	74
Sub-urban	8(6.60)	7(3.24)	3(8.16)	18
Rural	18(21.27)	9(10.44)	31(26.29)	58
Total	55	27	68	150

χ^2 = 10.008; df = 4; P lies between 0.05 and 0.02 level.

The χ^2 value (=10.008 at df 4) of the respondents from Assam reveals that significant (at 0.05 level) association exists between the two factors, under consideration.

Table 11.33: Association between Location of School and Location of Home (Sample from West Bengal; N = 150)

Location of School / *Location of Home*	*Urban*	*Suburban*	*Rural*	*Total*
Urban	1(0.78)	0(0.60)	8(7.62)	9
Sub-urban	3(1.04)	3(0.80)	6(10.16)	12
Rural	9(11.18)	7(8.60)	113(109.22)	129
Total	13	10	127	150

χ^2 = 12.982; df = 4; P lies between 0.02 and 0.01 level.

Again the χ^2 value (= 12.982, at df 4) of the respondents from West Bengal reveals that significant (at 0.05 level and almost at 0.01 level) association exists between the location of school and habitation.

Juxtaposition reveals that the respondents of West Bengal show higher association between the two factors compared to that of the respondents from Assam.

12

Problems Faced by Tribe Teachers

The teachers from tribal denomination use to face sequel of problems in their day-to-day activities. So far the sources of these problems are concerned, these can be classified in two broad categories. Where some problems occur within the institutional periphery, the sources of other problems are deep-rooted in the society outside the school environment. Within the institution, problems, which they use to face, arc mostly caused by the various human components of the institution, *viz.*, the colleagues, students, non-teaching staffs and the school administrators.

However, in terms of nature of the problems faced by the tribal teachers either within their institutional periphery or even outside their institution, the problems can broadly be classified under eight types. These are as follows:

Professional Problems

Substantially higher percentage of respondents from Assam (as much as 84.67 per cent) are facing problem due to excessive workload than that of their counter respondent group from West Bengal. The underlining cause may be that in Assam a good number of respondents are absorbed in privately managed schools where the load of work is more.

The most crucial and composite problem stands with the respondents is denial of professional facilities. It is mostly the tribal teachers from Assam in general and trained respondents in specific who are more in number to face the problem. While possession of professional training help respondents from West Bengal to get-rid-of the very problem (though marginal in terms of the number), the trained respondents from Assam are worst effected by the problem.

The colleagues and students mostly, and sometimes the school administration 'often' create problem in the pedagogical activities of tribal teachers. Comparatively more respondents from West Bengal are facing the problem of this kind. The female respondents in general and the non-trained female tribal teachers in specific are the worst sufferer of this problem.

Due to lack of academic recognition the tribal teachers often suffer. Juxtaposition reveals that significantly higher percentages of respondents from West Bengal are facing the very problem. While none of the trained male respondents from Assam are facing problem related to lack of academic recognition, all of the non-trained respondents from West Bengal are facing the very problem. Among those who are facing the problem, majority from Assam always facing the problem of this kind whereas among such respondents from West Bengal, majority are often facing problem due to lack of academic recognition.

The most common and widespread problem is group-conflict among the teachers, which according to the respondents, a standing problem to them. While colleagues are responsible and are creating this very problem, even when the tribal teachers are trying to maintain distance from the conflicting groups. The problem of group-conflict is more acquit among the respondents from Assam. The school administrations apart from the colleagues are also indulge the respondents in West Bengal.

More respondents from Assam reported effected due to the different socio-cultural milieu if compared to their counter respondent group from West Bengal. The problem is mostly caused by their non-tribal folks in the institutional and extra institutional periphery.

Social Problems

Comparatively more respondents from Assam and female respondents from West Bengal are often affected due to non-cooperation from various human counterparts in their work-field – compared to their counter respondent groups.

A grand majority of the respondents from both the states are often facing problem due to faultfinding tendency of their colleagues and school administration. The problem mostly stands with the respondents from Assam and persuasion of professional training hardly help the respondents to get rid of the very problem.

It is the respondent group from West Bengal, who are, in a larger scale with the opinion that the extra institutional society as well as their colleagues and school administration are often trying to exploit them in various ways. Some times this tendency also prevail among the non-teaching staffs. Irrespective of sex, the extent of exploitation is quite higher among the non-trained tribal teachers.

Anther problem stands with tribal teachers is isolation form various corners, *viz.*, the school administration, colleagues and sometimes by the non-teaching staffs and society. The non-trained respondents are much more affected due to the problem of isolation. More respondents from West Bengal are often facing problem of isolation due to their tribal denomination.

Due to ethnocentric mentality of so called mainstream and socio-cultural milieu, the tribal teachers are facing a sort of hatred from the non-tribals. In an average the non-trained respondents from both the states are affected and are experiencing this very problem. Juxtaposition reveals that more respondents from West Bengal are often facing the hatred tendency from the non-tribal members.

Juxtaposition sketch reveal that comparatively much more respondents from West Bengal in general and female respondents in specific reported that the extra institutional society as well as the institutional factors are often creating problem on the way of their social adjustment. It is mostly the tribal teachers, working beyond their native place are facing problem in their way of social adjustment.

Though today teaching is considered as a noble job however as many as 12 per cent of the respondents from Assam and 24.41 per cent of the tribal teachers from West Bengal experienced lack of social regard from the society and institution basically due to their ascribed status. While delving into the deep of the cause, it was observed that the problem is emerging due to ethnocentric mentality of the other social groups. From Assam the problem is more acquit for the non-trained where as in West Bengal training is not become an intervening factor in this context.

52 per cent of the respondents from Assam and 28.08 per cent of the tribal teachers from West Bengal are with the opinion that lack of social awareness of the human factors inside and outside the school environment often creates problem to them. The non-trained respondents are more in number from both the states to check the very problem.

Cultural Problems

36 per cent of the respondents from Assam and 64.98 per cent of the respondents from West Bengal reported often facing problem due to ethnocentric mentality of the non-tribal folks, and sometimes by the tribal people from other tribes. Among the effected respondents while majority 'always' facing this kind of problem from Assam such respondents from West Bengal 'often' face the very problem.

Comparatively more respondents from Assam are suffering due to oppression form other ethnic communities. The problem occurs even in tribal belts where a tribal teacher from some different tribe is teaching. All the possible factors within and outside the institutional atmosphere causing the problem to the respondents. So far the frequency of occurrence of the problem is concerned, majority of the effected respondents from Assam while always facing oppression from the other ethnic communities, such respondents from West Bengal reported 'often' facing the very problem.

Teachers as professionals are holding a uniform status so far their achieved status is concerned. However, the present study observed that due to different ascribed status 24 per cent of the tribal teachers from Assam and 29.67 per cent of the respondents from West Bengal always victimized due to the neglecting tendency of their non-tribal colleagues, students, non-teaching staffs and also by their school administrators. Juxtaposition reveals that comparatively more respondents from West Bengal are supposed to face a neglecting tendency. This may be due to the reason that majority of the respondents from West Bengal are working in rural institutions where the socio-economic fabric in this context is more stringent.

38 per cent and 12.7 per cent of the respondents from Assam and West Bengal respectively, reported often facing problem due to community and racial conflict mostly caused by the society outside the school and the non-teaching staffs and colleagues, within the school environment. While the respondents from Assam are affected due to community and racial conflict – to a large scale, among the effected respondents from West Bengal, female, trained male and non-trained female respondents are more in number to come across the very problem compared to their respective counter groups.

The study observed that 21.33 per cent of the respondents from Assam and 56.75 per cent of them from West Bengal reported facing problem due to cultural hegemony which clearly reveals that the respondents from West Bengal are more in number to face the very problem, often caused by all the possible factors within and outside the institutional periphery. While more male from Assam checked the very problem it is the females from West Bengal who are more in number, experiencing the problem. Professional training rarely helps the tribal teachers to get rid of the problem.

11.33 per cent of the respondents from Assam and 22.82 per cent of the respondents from West Bengal was with the opinion that the rigid communal attitude of the colleagues and non-teaching staffs of the institution and sometimes, the greater society within which the school is situated, often causing problem to their day-to-day activities. The extent of this problem is affecting comparatively more female and non-trained respondents than that of their counter respondent-groups from the respective states. As observed, possession of professional training plays a vital role to overcome the very problem.

Political Problems

Politicization of education is one of the notable problems at the school level, which is affecting the interest of the teachers from the tribal communities. However, this problem is affecting more tribal teachers from West Bengal, may be due to massive political rivalry. It is mostly the non-trained respondents, often affected where, their colleagues apart from the extra institutional environment enhances the problem.

Over 12.67 per cent of the respondents from Assam and 49.61 per cent of the respondents from West Bengal reported that their academic activities are often hampered due to political interference. However, in West Bengal the extra-institutional societies as well as their colleagues are also boosting the problem. The extent of this problem is much more in West Bengal.

Psychological Problems

As the study observes the tribal teachers from both the states are astounded and often put into mental pressure mostly by their school administration. The effect of the problem is much among the respondents from West Bengal in general and the non-trained respondents in particular from the very state.

Basically more non-trained respondents from the two states and more respondents from Assam are often affected due to a psychological problem to gain confidence due to the unfavourable attitude from the various human components. The extra institutional environment acts as a reagent in this context.

Most of the tribal communities are having sufficient scope to nurture their creative potentialities within their indigenous social setup where they perceive social education through their brain, heart and hands. While working in the schools beyond their indigenous community in their professional atmosphere, naturally they are considering lack of creativity as a problem, which is mostly stands with the students and colleagues. Juxtaposition reveal that tribal teachers from West Bengal are more in number to face the very problem-situation.

Problems Related to the Curtailment of Freedom

As much as 83.33 per cent of the respondents from West Bengal was with the opinion that their right to express disagreement in connection with different school related issues are 'often' denied by their colleagues and school administrators. The respondents from Assam are less in number to face this sort of problem. In an average, more non-trained respondents from both the states are facing the problem of this kind. While significantly more female from Assam are affected due to this problem, marginally more (percentage) of male are facing this problem from West Bengal.

While 15.33 per cent of the respondents from West Bengal reported often victimized by their colleagues, non-trained staffs and school administrators for protesting against malpractice, more than a quarter of the respondents (26 per cent) from Assam also reported facing similar problem and for them the extra institutional society also act as a factor apart from the institutional factors to create such problem. Irrespective of state and gender, more non-trained respondents are victimized than that of their trained counterparts.

46.67 per cent of the respondents from Assam and 28.97 per cent of the respondents from West Bengal reported 'often' facing problem due to lack of sense of nationalism and democratic attitude of their colleagues, non-teaching staffs and school administration, apart from the extra institutional society. Irrespective of the state and gender, the non-trained respondents are more in number to face this very problem.

Linguistic Problem

42 per cent of the respondents from Assam and 23.32 per cent of the respondent from West Bengal reported facing linguistic problem during conversation with their colleagues, students, non-teaching staffs and school administrators, which further affecting their pedagogical activities as well as their personality in a recurring manner. By nature, the problem is further adversely affecting their communication skill. The respondents those who are facing linguistic problem are mostly working in the schools, quite far from their natural habitation. As per their version, others use to laugh at their pronunciation. Juxtaposition reveals that the extent of the problem is comparatively much more in Assam, probably due to multi-linguistic environment.

Problem Due to Value Conflict

36.67 per cent of the respondents from Assam and 46.84 per cent of the respondents from West Bengal reported often facing problem due to value conflict and value erosion of the colleagues, students, non-teaching staffs, school administration and also by the people living outside the school environment. The non-trained respondents from both the states are more in number to face this very problem.

Apart from the listed problems, a few more problem are also coming on the way of the respondents, especially to those who are working in the schools not directly controlled by the government. Delayed salary, poor salary scale, threat of sudden termination from job, economic hardship due to high cost of living, underquality students, unavailability of retirement benefits are few of those.

PART III: PSYCHOGRAPHY OF TRIBE TEACHERS

13

Status of Tribe Teachers
The Socio-Economic Dimension

On the basis of the analysis and interpretation of the data presented in previous Chapters, the major findings of the study are given in the following order:

Socio-Economic Status

Gender

In terms of gender of the tribe teachers, participation of educated male in teaching profession is significantly higher than the female respondents from the tribal communities in both the states – Assam and West Bengal. Participation of educated females in teaching profession, particularly in secondary schools, is substantially higher in the state of Assam, compared to that of West Bengal.

Marital Status

A grand majority of the tribal teachers (83.34 per cent), working in the secondary schools of Assam and West Bengal were found married during the time of investigation. In an average, only sixteen per cent of the respondents from the two states was found unmarried. Comparatively more respondents from Assam was found married, compared to their counter group of respondents from West Bengal. This observation can be generalized for the respondents from either sex. Only a marginal and negligible percentage of the respondents, specially, those from Assam households a marital status – either widow/widower or separated.

Institutional Status

Majority of the entire respondent group (62.33 per cent) is engaged in the schools situated in rural areas, followed by the respondents, working in urban-schools. In an average, only 10 per cent of the respondents are working in the secondary schools situated in suburban areas.

Majority of the respondents from both the states are working in co-educational institutions, followed by 16 per cent of the entire group of tribal teachers – who are working in 'boys' schools'. Only 14.67 per cent of the total respondents are teaching in 'girls schools'. While none of the female respondents are engaged in boys' schools in West Bengal, in Assam, none of the male respondents are working in girls' schools.

Majority (57 per cent) of the entire respondent group are teaching in secondary schools, followed by 35.33 per cent of the respondents, who are working in higher secondary schools. During the survey, only 7.67 per cent of the tribal teachers from Assam and West Bengal were found teaching in middle – schools.

The study observed that 1.33 per cent and 14 per cent, 67.34 per cent and 31.33 per cent and 31.33 and 39.33 per cent of the respondents are engaged in middle schools, secondary schools and higher secondary schools from the states Assam and West Bengal respectively.

Juxtaposition reveal that while comparatively more respondents from Assam are teaching in secondary schools, comparatively more respondents from West Bengal are teaching in higher-secondary schools – compared to their respective counter respondent groups engaged in teaching at the same level of schools.

It was also observed that the rate of female participation in teaching at higher secondary level is substantially higher in the state of Assam than that of West Bengal. Though marginal but the rate of female participation at secondary level of teaching is comparatively higher in West Bengal compared to Assam.

The respondents are mostly absorbed in 'government-aided schools', followed by the schools 'organized by religious trusts'. Only 11.33 per cent of the total respondents, incorporating 19.33 per cent of the respondents from Assam and 3.33 per cent of the respondents from West Bengal was found working in the schools fully controlled by the government. The extent of absorption of the tribal teachers in the government-aided schools is more in West Bengal than that of Assam. This observation remains unchanged even if the comparison is made on the basis of sex. The private schools are absorbing only 4.33 per cent of the total respondents and all of them are from Assam.

Cultural Environment of the Institution and Adjacent Area

To majority of the respondents from both the states, the cultural environment of their institution is 'ordinary'. While 24 per cent of the respondents from Assam and only 2.67 per cent of the respondents from West Bengal are quite satisfied with the cultural environment of their institution and rated the same as 'rich', to 12 per cent of the respondents from Assam and 19.33 per cent of the respondents from West Bengal, the cultural environment of their respective institution appears poor and they are quite dissatisfied with the cultural environment of their respective institutions.

While substantially higher percentage of the respondents from Assam rated the cultural environment of their institution as rich, to more respondents from West Bengal it is either ordinary or poor, if juxtaposed with their counter respondent group from the other state. Comparatively more male respondents from Assam and fewer respondents from West Bengal are quite satisfied with the cultural environment of their respective institutions.

Grand majority (74 per cent) of the entire respondents (N = 300) rated the culture and environment of the adjacent area within which their schools are situated – as 'ordinary' – followed by 19.67 per cent of the respondents to whom it was 'poor' and only 6.33 per cent considered the same as 'rich'. The scenario reveals that more female than that of male respondents considered the culture and extra-institutional environment as 'ordinary'. The number of respondents from West Bengal, who are quite dissatisfied with the extra-institutional environment, is quite higher, compared to the respondents from Assam with a similar opinion.

Experience

Even less than one-third of the entire group of respondents, incorporating 11.33 per cent of the respondents from Assam and 52.67 per cent of the respondents from West Bengal are having less than five years of teaching experience. Majority of the respondents from West Bengal are falling in this experience category. The comparison establishes that educated tribal youths from Assam are not that extent interested in teaching, compared to the tribal youths from West Bengal. This is due to lack of physical facilities in teaching profession, compared to other official or administrative jobs. However, the educated tribal youths from West Bengal has been taking teaching as their profession to uplift their social status. The underlining cause of these two different attitude towards teaching profession is that, in the North Eastern region of India, the society is holding much more materialistic outlook compared to Eastern India.

29 per cent of the entire respondents, incorporating 34 per cent of the respondents from Assam and 24 per cent of the respondents from West Bengal are engaged in teaching with an experience ranging from 5 to 10 years. 16 per cent, 13 per cent and 10 per cent of the total respondents having teaching experience of more than 10 years but less than 15 years, within fifteen to twenty years and more than 20 years, respectively.

Professional Status

While in India 91 per cent of the secondary-school teachers are trained, only 47per cent of the respondents of the present study was found possessing professional training. In the one hand, majority of the tribal teachers from Assam are non-trained, while on the other hand majority of the respondents from West Bengal are trained. In terms of persuasion of professional training, female tribal-teachers are quite advanced than that of their respective male counter groups from both the states. Female respondents from West Bengal are much advanced than that of the female respondents from Assam – so far persuasion of professional training is concerned.

Linguistic Status

While only 40 per cent of the respondents from Assam took up Assamese language as the medium of instruction during their school-days, to 86 per cent of the respondents from West Bengal the medium of instruction was Bengali at their school level. The scenario reveals that influence of state language as medium of instruction at school level was substantially higher in West Bengal, compared to Assam. This goes against the policy to introduce indigenous language for the tribal students at least at the school level. The experience says that the situation continues even today.

While only 2 per cent of the respondents from West Bengal have had the opportunity to start and to carryout their school education in their own indigenous languages, it is 32 per cent of the tribal teachers form Assam who did enjoy this opportunity to carry out or at least to start their school education in their own indigenous languages.

12.5 per cent of the female respondents from West Bengal started their school education with their mother-tongue or with some more akin tribal language as the medium of instruction (mostly Alchiki). However, none of the male respondents from Bengal had a similar opportunity.

Domination of English language or two respective state languages as the medium of instruction at the higher education was a common phenomenon in both the states. The respondents from both the states experienced the problem of non-availability of indigenous language in the higher education level.

Religious Status

During the survey, it was observed that grand majority of the respondents from Assam (70.67 per cent) are following Christianity, followed by 24.67 per cent of the respondents, who are Hindu. Only 3.33 per cent of the respondents from Assam were either Prislitarian or Buddhist or following some other religion. 1.33 per cent of the respondents from Assam were silent about their religion.

It was further observed that majority (55.33 per cent) of the respondents from West Bengal are Hindu by faith. The group was followed by 26.67 per cent of the respondents following Sari/Sarna or indegenious religion. 16.67 per cent and 0.665 per cent of the respondents are Christian and Prislitarian – respectively. 0.665 per cent of the respondents from West Bengal did not respond about their religion.

The comparative sketch of the religious status of the respondents from the two states reveal that Christianity is quite popular to the respondents from Assam where as marginally higher percentage of the respondents from West Bengal are following Hinduism.

So far as the ascribed religion of the respondents is concerned, majority (64 per cent) of the respondents from West Bengal were from Sari/Sarna or some indegenious religion fold. 54.67 per cent of the respondents from Assam and 68 per cent of the respondents from West Bengal were converted from their ascribed religion.

Among the respondents, who converted from the 'earlier religion' to the 'present religion', 9.67 per cent from Assam and 11.77 per cent from West Bengal reported that they gave-up their ascribed religion due to the causes related to matrimonial. Majority of these groups of respondents are female. The causes of conversion was a fact mostly due to economic constraints to 6.1 per cent and 2.94 per cent of the respondents from the state of Assam and West Bengal respectively. To 17.07 per cent and 5.88 per cent of the converted respondents from Assam and West Bengal, respectively, the conversion from their ascribed religion was due to different social causes. 17.07 per cent and 51.96 per cent of the converted respondents from Assam and West Bengal gave up their ascribed religion for availing educational opportunities. To 4.88 per cent and 1.96 per cent of the converted respondents from Assam and West Bengal, the underlining cause of changing ascribed religion is that, they consider their present religion more scientific than that of their ascribed religion. The causes of conversion of religion was not illustrated by 19.51 per cent of the converted respondents from Assam and 19.61 per cent of the respondents from West Bengal and they consider it completely a personal matter.

The present study did not observe any significant association between the religion and the status of the respondents from the two different states – Assam and West Bengal. However, significant association exists between the status and the religion of the respondents at 0.05 level when the entire group of respondents (N = 300) was taken into consideration.

Political Status

While the rate of political participation of the tribal teachers from West Bengal is substantially higher, the same in case of the respondents from Assam is quite scanty. In the state of Assam, rate of political participation is comparatively higher among the females, compared to their male counterparts. However, in West Bengal, the rate of participation in politics is substantially higher among the male respondents, if compared with their female counterparts.

Among the respondents, associated with political parties, more male respondents are having active membership, than that of the female respondents from both the states. More female respondents from Assam are holding active membership of different political parties than that of the female respondents from West Bengal.

Although the respondents from West Bengal are having comparatively higher rate of participation in politics than that of Assam, however, in terms of nature of membership, the respondents from Assam are comparatively in a better position. Among the respondents associated with political parties, 12.5 per cent from Assam reported holding membership at national level. None of the respondents from West Bengal found having membership of any political parties at such level.

Grand majority (72 per cent) of the entire group of respondents are not associated with any political parties and a bulk of them are with the opinion that political parties are exploitihg the people like them just only for the party's political interest; in contrast 8.45 per cent of such respondents was silent in this context. The respondents of the study do not signify any association between their 'political participation' and their 'percieved status'.

Family Status

Although extended pattern of family is a common phenomenon among the tribal groups from Assam as well as from West Bengal, but more than half (50.67 per cent) of the total respondents from Assam and exactly one-third (33.33 per cent) of the respondents from West Bengal reported living in nuclear family. From West Bengal, majority of the respondents are having extended pattern of family. The respondents from Assam, to a greater extent, deviated from their traditional pattern of family-structure. This is due to massive effect of modernization (rather westernization?) among the respondent-groups from North East region; though in a good number of cases, the respondents were under compulsion to live in nuclear family due to distant-place of work.

Majority of the respondents from both the states are having a medium size of family where the number of family members varies from 4 to 7. While as much as 16.67 per cent of the female respondents from Assam are having nuclear family, none of the female respondents was found from West Bengal who are living in nuclear family.

Social Upbringing

A grand majority of the respondents from both the states mainly grew up in rural areas. However further juxtaposition revals that, comparatively more respondents from West Bengal grew up in rural setup compared to their counter respondent groups from Assam. More respondents from Assam have had the opportunity to be brought-up mostly in urban areas, compared to the respondents from West Bengal. More or less one-fifth of the respondents reported to be grew up both in urban and rural setups.

Housing Status

While more respondents from Assam are having their own house, more respondents from West Bengal are staying in rented houses. Status of the respondents from Assam is comparatively much better than the respondents from West Bengal, so far their nature of house is concerned. In total, 18 per cent of the respondents are staying in rented quarters, provided by the institutions where they are employed.

Female respondents from both the states are holding comparatively a higher status than that of their respective male counter respondent groups – so far their housing condition is concerned. The male group of tribal teachers from West Bengal are holding comparatively lower status than the male – respondents from Assam in this very context.

In the state Assam, female respondents are holding comparatively higher status than that of their male counterparts, so far housing condition is considered as the indicator of status.

In terms of their location of house, comparatively more tribal teachers from Assam are living in urban areas whereas none of the female respondents from West Bengal reported staying in urban areas. While the male and female respondents from West Bengal are mostly staying in rural setup, the respondents from Assam are mostly centralized in urban areas. In the study it was further observed that there was a significant association between location of schools and location of house of the respondents. The association is comparatively higher among the respondents from West Bengal.

Sociability and Status

As per the perception of their own, male respondents from both the states are comparatively more sociable than the female respondents. Respondents having a moderate degree of sociability are more in number from West Bengal than that of Assam. Female respondents with a lower degree of sociability are more in number compared to the male respondents who also possess lower degree of sociability from both the states.

Among the total respondents, majority (63.67 per cent) are moderately sociable. 24.67 per cent of the entire group of respondents were highly sociable and only 11.66 per cent of the respondents found having low degree of sociability.

According to the perception of the respondents, the association between their status and social participation is not significant.

Status and Social Mobility

Comparatively more respondents from West Bengal and in an average 26 per cent of the respondents are with the opinion that, it is 'very hard' to assume upward social mobility and thereby to change social status; 54 per cent considered it hard. 20 per cent of the respondents did not agree to comment over the upward social mobility. However, none of the respondents from any state considered that upward mobility of social status is easy.

Economic Status

Assets

A massive difference has been observed between the indigenous tribal communities and the respondents from the respective states – so far the economic status determining assets are concerned. While the indigenous tribal communities from Assam considered the stone and wooden buttons, length of river banks under occupation, Jhum-land holdings, *Bhorot*, mithun (pet), stone utensils, cattle, winter-garments made up of animal skin, etc. as the assets for determining the economic status in their society, the same in case of the indigenous tribal communities from West Bengal are hand made ribbon for decorating hair, ancient antic and gold coins, thread and buttons made up of animal bone, old and large tree, fermentation chamber for preparing wine, cattle, land, house, brass utensils, farm-house (of the community), *Kori* and musical instruments, etc. However, the respondents from both the states show a similarity in this context and reported that bank balance, electrical and electronic gadgets, vehicles, piece of land, level of education, ornaments, modern dresses, utensils made up of steel and china-clay, fire gun, kitchen accessories, wealth, sofa set, colour television, refrigerator, telephone – are the assets which determine their status.

Economic Status of the Tribe Teachers During School Days

Status often depend upon the economic potentiality. Economic potentiality inversely reduce the per-capita income, specially when younger members of the family are more in number and are having no capacity to earn for the family. The study observed that majority of the respondents from Assam had even more than seven siblings. Comparatively less number of respondents from West Bengal had more than seven siblings. Naturally it may be a general conclusion that during their schooldays, comparatively more respondents from Assam faced economic hardship than the respondents from West Bengal. The economic situation of the female respondents from either state was comparatively better than that of the male respondents, during their school days.

Perception About Economic Status

Irrespective of gender majority of the respondents from both the states described their economic set-up as 'average'. Only a marginal few perceived their economic situation as 'well off' and it is 'difficult' to almost one-third of the respondents from Assam. Significantly higher percentage of respondents from West Bengal considered their economic situation as 'well off'. The study observed significant association between perception of status and economic situation of the respondents.

Monthly Income of the Respondents

Though both the sate-government prescribed almost a similar scale of pay for the secondary school teachers, however this prescribed scale of pay is not properly followed by the schools – especially those, which are managed privately or by religious trusts. Naturally the tribal teachers, who are absorbed in such type of schools, are not getting adequate salary and are falling in low-income range. In addition to this factor, the salary-scale is not up to the mark for those who are having less qualifications (*i.e.*, bellow graduate). Due to these causes, a variation in salary scale is prominent among the respondents.

Irrespective of these causes it was observed that comparatively more respondents from West Bengal is falling in highest income status with a minimum range of Rs. 8501/- per month, compared to the respondents from Assam. More male and less female respondents from Assam can be placed in high-income group (with a monthly income, ranging from Rs. 7001/- – 8500/- p.m.) than that of their respective matching groups from West Bengal.

Comparatively more respondents from Assam are falling in middle-income group (with a monthly income ranging from Rs. 5501/- – Rs. 7000/- per month) than that of the respondent group from West Bengal. Comparatively less respondents from West Bengal are falling in lower income group.

Monthly Family Income

Female respondents are not the only earning members of their respective families. Almost all of them actually supplementing their family income by their earning. Comparatively more respondents from West Bengal are falling in highest income group in terms of their monthly family income compared to the number of respondents from Assam, holding a similar income-range.

None of the respondents from West Bengal and none of the female respondents from Assam are falling in lowest – income status. In total, 2.67 per cent of the entire respondent group was found falling in low-income group and all of them are employed in privately managed schools.

Savings

The respondents from Assam, irrespective of their gender, are possessing comparatively better economic status in terms of their savings than that of the respondents from West Bengal.

Status *vis-a-vis* Income Situation

The χ^2 test reveals that strong and significant association exists between the status and the economic situation of the respondents.

Educational Constraints

44 per cent, 36.67 per cent and 10.67 per cent of the respondents in total (N = 300) pursued education mostly from their own house, hostel and mess respectively, during their student-hood. It is only 5.33 per cent of the respondents who pursued education mostly staying in their relative's house or the like.

In Assam, the rate of migration of the tribal peoples from their natural 'punjis' to the urban areas were substantially higher than that of West Bengal. Naturally though in both the states, educational facilities (especially higher education) are mostly centralized in urban areas, so it was West Bengal where it is comparatively more difficult to avail higher education for the tribal communities and scopes were limited to avail education from their own house.

19.33 per cent of the respondents, incorporating 9.99 per cent of the respondents from Assam and 28.67 per cent of the respondents from West Bengal required hostel facilities to pursue education during their student-hood, however they were denied to that very facility due to nonavailability. Only 36.67 per cent of the respondents were benefited with hostel facilities, mostly provided by the educational institutions and according to them, it would have been impossible to them to carryout their education if they were not provided with such facilities. The scenario reveals that hostel facilities, specifically for pursuing education at different levels, was quite inadequate for the tribal teachers, during their student days. Significantly more respondents from West Bengal did face this constraints in their way of pursuing education, compared to the number of respondents faced the similar problem from Assam. Even though more respondents from West Bengal were benefited by hostel facilities for the shake of pursuing education, the crisis is till more (in West Bengal) due to the natural habitation of the communities in the remot parts of West Bengal.

In terms of average distance between habitation and institution, secondary education for the respondents from West Bengal was comparatively easy accessible, due to comparatively higher population density and better communication facilities in the state. It was easier for the female respondents from both the states to attend secondary schools during their school days, than that of their male counterparts.

Education at higher secondary level was comparatively easy accessible for the respondents from Assam and for the female respondents in general, than that of their respective counter respondent groups, so far the average distance between residence and institution is concerned. The same at the college and university level was comparatively easy-accessible to the respondents, both the male and female, from Assam, compared to their respective counter respondent groups from West Bengal.

Rural schools from both the sates played an important role to educate bulk of the respondents. Among those who obtained higher secondary education, from Assam, majority of them studied in the urban institutions where as from West Bengal, most of the respondents pursued their higher secondary education from the institutions situated in suburban areas. Urban colleges from Assam and suburban colleges from West Bengal mostly extend the educational facilities to the respondents at their undergraduate level.

Academic Status

While in India only 27.43 per cent of the secondary school teachers are having post-graduate qualification, exactly one-third (*i.e.*, 33.33 per cent) of the sample group of respondents, incorporating 26.67 per cent of the respondents from Assam and 40 per cent of the respondents from West Bengal was found having a post-graduate qualification. This very finding is sufficient enough to give-up the pre-conceived notion of so called mainstream regarding the inferior academic status of the tribal teachers at secondary level. Juxtaposition of the academic status reveal that the tribal teachers from West Bengal are superior in terms of their academic status than their counter respondent groups from Assam. Comparatively more male respondents from West Bengal and more female respondents from Assam are having a post-graduate level of education, compared to their respective counter respondent groups from the concerned states.

So far academic excellence of the respondent groups are concerned, male tribal teachers show comparatively better academic performance than that of their female counterparts from Assam. In an average, the respondents from West Bengal are more qualified than the respondents from Assam.

More tribal teachers from West Bengal in general, and more female tribal teachers from both the states-in specific, were having optimum academic status (in terms of their educational qualification) for teaching at secondary schools – if compared with their respective counter sex-groups.

Cultural Environment of the Community

As perceived by the respondents, more than half of the total respondents considered that cultural environment of their respective community is 'ordinary', followed by a group of 45.33 per cent of the respondents to whom it is 'rich' and only 4 per cent considered that the cultural environment of their own indigenous community as 'poor'. Among the total group of respondents, substantially more female respondents and comparatively less male respondents considered the cultural environment of their community as 'rich'. While not even a single respondent from West Bengal considered the cultural environment of their indigenous community as 'poor' to 8 per cent of the respondents from Assam the same is 'poor'.

Less percentage of male and more female respondents from West Bengal reported that the culture-pattern of their community is in the process of change. On the other hand, more male and less female respondents were with the opinion that the 'culture-pattern' of their respective indigenous communities is not changing at all.

While comparing their present 'culture-pattern' with that of their previous generations, among the entire respondents, 24 per cent considered that their present culture-pattern is very rich; to 46.33 per cent it is 'rich' to 21 per cent it is 'moderate', to 6 per cent it is 'poor' and only 2.67 per cent considered that their 'present' 'culture-pattern' is very poor. Subsequently higher percentage of the respondents, both male and female from West Bengal considered their present culture-pattern as 'rich' compared to the respondents from Assam who also made a similar rating, while comparing the same with the culture-pattern of their previous generations.

Transmission of Indigenous Knowledge

Comparatively more respondents from Assam while having scope to transmit indigenous knowledge of their communities among the students, than that of their counter respondents group from West Bengal, it is the male respondents from both the states, with a higher percentage, who are having such scope. Only 40.66 per cent of the respondents from West Bengal are with this opinion.

Responding towards a certain question, majority (57.67 per cent) of the respondents reported that their students are interested towards their culture. 50 per cent of the respondents from Assam and 65.34 per cent of the respondents from West Bengal formed this group. On the other hand, 4 per cent and 16.67 per cent of the entire group of respondents reported that their students are not at all interested and are having indifferent attitude towards the indigenous knowledge and culture of the tribal communities, respectively.

Majority of the respondents from both the states and comparatively more respondents from Assam was with the opinion that they are having sufficient scope for developing their respective community through their teaching. However, 44.67 per cent of the total respondents negate the view.

Grand majority of the respondents (89.67 per cent) from both the states and comparatively more respondents from Assam says that they are really trying to uplift their community. It was further observed that comparatively more male respondents from Assam and more female respondents from West Bengal reported trying to uplift their indigenous community, compared to their respective matching groups.

Status as Perceived by the Tribal Teachers

As many as 62.33 per cent of the respondents from both the states considered a 'medium status' for themselves according to their perception. Substantially more respondents from West Bengal assigned a medium status for themselves. However, 34 per cent of the total respondents, incorporating 47.33 per cent of the respondents from Assam and only 20.67 per cent of the respondents from West Bengal assigned a 'lower status' for themselves. Comparatively more respondents from Assam, both male and female, reported holding a lower status-if compared with the number of respondents from West Bengal, who are also holding a similar status as per their perception.

Only 3.67 per cent of the total respondents reported holding 'higher status'. The group includes 2 per cent of the respondents from Assam and 5.33 per cent of the respondents from West Bengal – which reveals that substantially more tribal teachers from the either sex-groups from West Bengal opted for a higher status for themselves.

50.67 per cent of the respondents from Assam, 74 per cent of the respondents from West Bengal and 62.33 per cent of the total respondents perceived that they hold a medium status. Where as according to the perception of 34 per cent of the respondents, including 47.33 per cent of the respondents from Assam and 20.67 per cent of the respondents from West Bengal – they hold a lower status in the society, which reveals that comparatively more respondents from Assam opted for a lower status than that of the number of respondents from West Bengal, who opted for a similar status.

Status of the Respondents Within their Own Community

In accordance with the perception of the respondents, grand majority (73.33 per cent) says that the tribal communities are holding a lower status. Substantially higher percentage of male respondents and marginally less percentage of female respondents from West Bengal are of this opinion, compared to their respective counter respondent groups from Assam. The notable observation come out from the study, where a handful number of respondents from both the states assigned lower status for their respective indigenous communities and it is less percentage of respondents (34 per cent) who assigned a similar status for themselves. In contrast, 62.33 per cent of the respondents opted 'middle' status for themselves; it is only 26.67 per cent of the respondents who assigned 'middle' status for their respective indigenous communities.

In consonance with these findings and in accordance with the responses obtained through the participatory observation and discussion with the indigenous community groups from both the states, it may be assumed that a sizable proportion of the respondents are mostly de-rooted from their ascribed status groups. Their occupational status and it's influence make them the '*Diku's*' (i.e. the outsider from their indigenous community groups) and tragic fact is that the respondent teachers are not conscious about this phenomenon. Where as all the teacher respondents considered themselves as the member of tribal communities, none of the respondents from the sampled indigenous tribal communities consider the teacher respondents from their respective communities as the member of their core indigenous communities, rather considered them as the outsider '*master babu*'.

Actually with a very negligible exception a tendency among the teacher respondents from both the states has been observed where irrespective of their gender, they are opting/opted spouse from outside of their tribal fold and are trying to be defused in the main-stream.

In spite of the finding obtained from the indigenous tribal groups, the response obtained from the tribal teachers proved significant association between the status of the teacher and the cultural environment of the respective tribal community to which a tribal teacher belongs. However, the association between the factors 'status of the respondents' and 'cultural environment of the community' is not significantly associated when the state Assam is taken into consideration. That is why it can be concluded that the tendency to be defused in the mainstream society is comparatively more among the respondents from Assam.

Aspiration for Professional Education and Constraints of Education

Grand majority of the trained respondents from both the states pursued professional education after joining in teaching job, where as only 29.08 per cent of the respondents pursued professional education as 'fresher candidates' – *i.e.*, this latter group of teachers pursued professional training before taking the teaching as their profession.

Majority of the trained respondents reported that they were aspirant for professional education and pursued the same spontaneously. Substantially more trained respondents from West Bengal received professional training spontaneously, compared to the trained respondents from Assam. However, even less than one-third of the trained respondents in total (31.21 per cent) confessed that they pursued professional training under compulsion and all of them received training for teaching only after joining in the profession.

In total, 81.56 per cent of the trained respondents were supposed to appear in either written test or interview while seeking admission in professional training programmes. Comparatively more respondents from West Bengal constitute this group. Only 18.44 per cent of the respondents did face, neither test, nor interview while seeking admission to the professional training course; comparatively more trained respondents from Assam constitute this very group. Naturally, conclusion can be drawn that persuasion of professional training was comparatively (more) easier from the respondents from Assam.

Majority of the trained respondents from West Bengal and all the trained respondents from Assam feels that professional training are quite worth-while for developing professional skills – so far the teaching profession is concerned. Grand majority of the trained respondents (82.98 per cent) are eager to receive more professional trainings. In an average, the respondents from West Bengal are well equipped with professional training than that of the counter respondent group from Assam.

The Non-Trained Respondents

Majority of the non-trained respondents (69.33 per cent) from Assam and all of the non-trained respondents from West Bengal are eager to pursue professional training. However, a marginal few (13.21 per cent) of the non-trained incorporating 20.19 per cent of the non-trained respondents from Assam are not willing to receive any more professional training.

Majority of the respondents (81.73 per cent) from Assam and cent percent of them from West Bengal are eager to pursue professional training.

Those who are willing to pursue professional training are with the impression that training helps to develop better teaching skills. However, 18.27 per cent of the non-trained respondents from Assam negate this view.

Significant and positive association exists between the status and persuasion of professional training. Professionally trained teachers are holding higher status than that of their non-trained counterparts.

Interest Towards Profession

48 per cent of the respondents were predetermined to take-up teaching as their profession. This group of respondents includes 53.33 per cent of the respondents from Assam and 42.67 per cent of the respondents from West Bengal. On the other hand, more than a quarter of the respondents took up teaching as their profession after failing to join to their desired profession. To 12.66 per cent of the respondents, joining to teaching profession was quite incidental.

Majority of the respondents group is completely devoted in their profession, including 61.33 per cent and 55.33 per cent of the respondents from the states Assam and West Bengal respectively, without pursuing any other occupation. However, though marginal, but to 5.33 per cent of the respondents, teaching is not the only profession – they are pursuing some other occupation simultaneously with teaching. Irrespective of the intervening environmental variables, the tribal teachers from Assam are committed to teaching to a greater extent.

Majority of the tribal teachers (76.67 per cent), incorporating 72 per cent of the respondents from Assam and 81.33 per cent of the respondents from West Bengal are willing to continue with their existing profession and are not willing to change the profession even if they are offered with some other occupation with same salary and equal facilities.

More female respondents from both the states are willing to continue with their existing profession which establishes the fact that 'occupational rest-ness' is predominantly a 'female-characteristic' among the tribals.

10.33 per cent of the respondents, including 10.67 per cent of the respondents from Assam and 10 per cent of the respondents from West Bengal are not willing and 13 per cent of the respondents are absolutely dissatisfied with their profession – which reflects that though less but some tribal teachers are not properly adjusted in their profession.

Professional Relationship

The study reveals that in some of the schools, almost all the teachers are form tribal communities where as in some other schools the teachers from tribal and non-tribal communities are almost equal in number. It is worth noting that in most of the schools the number of tribal teachers is very few and present study come across mostly such type of schools.

The majority of the tribal teachers from both the states possess favourable attitude towards their colleagues and are trying to keep up a congenial and permissive professional relationship with colleagues. However, the extent of the professional relationship differs in terms of sex, state and location to which they belong. Juxtaposition reveals that more male respondents from Assam, female respondents from West Bengal and respondents from rural areas from both the states are having significantly warmer professional relationship with their colleagues compared to their respective counter respondent groups. The professional relationship with the colleagues is much better among the unmarried tribal teachers, than that of their married counter parts from both the states.

On the other hand, almost 10.33 per cent of the total respondents (10.67 per cent from Assam and 10 per cent from West Bengal) are not willing to continue with teaching profession and wants to shift to some other profession, with same emoluments, as because, according to their version, their colleagues, mostly the non-tribals are creating sequels of psychological, social, pedagogical and political problems to them.

Role of Government

Though less in practice, however theoretically government of India has taken a good number of policies which are supposed to be implemented through the respective state-governments as because education is coming under the perview of state-government by virtue of Indian Constitution. As like in other professions, special drive recruitment in teaching profession has been taken by the state governments. Constitutional amendment has reduced the tendency of frequent conversion of reserve posts for scheduled tribes and to make it 'open'. Policy has been taken to train the promising young educated persons from the tribal denomination to recruit them in the schools situated in the tribal belts. Facilities has also been made by the government to minimize the fees in various teacher's training colleges to attract the tribal trainees and thereby to boost the number of tribal teachers. Programmes has been initiated to integrate general education with the art and culture of the tribal communities in order to make education socially and culturally more acceptable, meaningful and interesting to the tribals and to improve the professional setup of the tribal teachers. Central Government has recently established a separate ministry to look after the tribal issues with a view to minimize the harassment, in case of their appointment.

Unfortunately, apart form the reservation facilities, implemented through roster system of appointment of teachers in various schools, the state governments (both the Assam and West Bengal) are quite silent to appoint sufficient number of tribal teachers in the schools especially situated in tribal belts. A change in roster system is desired to appoint adequate number of tribal teachers in the tribal areas. In fact, a rectification in appointment policy is desired so that the tribal teachers can contribute their share for proper upliftment of their communities.

14

Psychographic Status of Tribe Teachers

The Attitudinal Dimension

Attitudinal Status

Attitude towards Profession

After the extencive study it was found that the respondents from West Bengal possess significantly more favourable attitude towards their profession than that of the respondents from Assam. In this context, the male as well as the female respondents from West Bengal holds significantly more favourable attitude than that of their counter-matching respondents groups from Assam.

Both the trained, non-trained, urban and married group of respondents from West Bengal possess significantly high positive attitude towards their profession, if compared with their counter respondent groups from Assam.

Though the unmarried group of respondents from West Bengal possess marginally high positive attitude than that of their counter respondent groups from Assam but no significant difference exists between the unmarried groups of respondents from the two states, so far their attitude towards their profession is concerned.

Urban, suburban and rural respondents from West Bengal possess significantly high favourable attitude towards their profession, compared to their counter respondent – groups from Assam.

The respondents with different experience categories (except the teachers with less than 5 years of experience) from West Bengal does not differ significantly from the respective counter respondent groups, so far their attitude towards their profession is concerned. All these groups possess favourable attitude towards their profession.

The respondents from West Bengal with different religious-groups possess significantly more favourable attitude towards their profession compared to the respective counter respondents belonging to matching religious groups from Assam.

Female respondents and trained respondents from both the states possess significantly high positive attitude towards their profession – compared to the male and non-trained respondents from the respective states.

The unmarried group of respondents from both the states possess significantly high positive attitude towards their profession, compared to the married groups of respondents form the respective states.

Attitude towards Students

The respondents from West Bengal possess significantly positive attitude towards their students compared to the respondents from Assam.

The trained and the urban group of respondents from the states of Assam and West Bengal does not differ significantly so far their attitude towards their students is concerned.

Female respondents from both the states possess significantly more favourable attitude towards their students if compared with their respective male counterparts from both the states.

While from the state of Assam, the trained respondents possess though not significant but comparatively more favourable attitude towards their students then their non-trained counterparts; from the state of West Bengal it is non-trained group of respondents who possess significantly more favourable attitude towards their students than that of their trained counter parts from the very state.

The unmarried group of respondents possess comparatively more favourable attitude towards their students compared to the married respondents from both the states.

Attitude towards Colleagues

The respondent groups from the states does not differ significantly; so far their attitude towards their colleagues is concerned. Both the groups possess favourable attitude towards their colleagues.

The male respondents from Assam possess significantly high favourable attitude towards their colleagues than that of the male respondents from the state.

While the female respondents from Assam possess negative attitude towards their colleagues, the female respondents from West Bengal differs significantly in this context and are possessing positive attitude towards their colleagues.

Both the trained and non-trained group of respondents from Assam possess marginally more favourable attitude towards their colleagues – if compared to their matching respondent groups from West Bengal. However, neither of the cases, the difference is significant at any standard level.

Neither the married groups of respondents, nor the unmarried groups of respondents from the two states differ significantly – so far their attitude towards their colleagues is concerned.

The respondents working in the rural areas from Assam possess significantly more favourable attitude toward their colleagues, compared to the respondents working in the rural areas of West Bengal.

Among the respondents with less than five years of teaching experience, the group from West Bengal possess significantly more favourable attitude than that of the respondents from Assam.

Neither the Hindu respondents, nor the Christian respondents from the two states differ significantly so far their attitude towards their colleagues is concerned.

While the male respondents from Assam possess favourable attitude towards their colleagues, their counter female respondents possess negative attitude towards their colleagues.

Though the male respondents from West Bengal possess comparatively more favourable attitude towards their colleagues, but no significant difference exists between the two gender-groups from West Bengal in this context.

No significant difference exists between the trained and non-trained group of respondents from both the states, Assam and West Bengal – so far their attitude towards their colleagues is concerned.

The unmarried group of respondents from both the states possess a comparatively more favourable attitude towards their students, if compared with the married group of respondents from the respective states.

Attitude towards Government

Significant difference exists between the respondents from Assam and West Bengal. Respondents from West Bengal possess favourable attitude towards government where as the respondents from Assam possess negative attitude.

The male as well as female respondents from Assam possess negative attitude towards government where as their counter respondent groups possess favourable attitude towards government from the state West Bengal.

The trained and non-trained groups of respondents from Assam while possess negative attitude, the trained as well as the non-trained respondents from West Bengal possess positive attitude towards government. Significant difference exists between the trained and non-trained respondents from Assam and West Bengal in this context.

Significant difference exists between the married respondents from the two states. The respondents from West Bengal possess favourable attitude towards government where as the married respondents from Assam possess negative attitude towards government.

The respondents with less than five years of teaching experience from both the states possess favourable attitude towards the government. However the group of respondents from West Bengal possess significantly more favourable attitude in this context.

The experienced teachers from both the states possess negative attitude towards government.

While the Christian respondents from both the states possess favourable attitude towards government, the Hindu respondents from Assam possess negative attitude.

Though both the male and female respondents from Assam possess negative attitude towards government, however, significant difference exists between the two groups. The female respondents possess significantly more unfavourable attitude compared to the male counterparts from the state.

Significant difference exists between the male and female group of respondents from West Bengal so far their attitude towards the government is concerned. The male respondents possess favourable attitude towards the government where as the female respondents possess negative attitude.

While both the trained and non-trained respondents from Assam possess negative attitude, their counter respondent groups from West Bengal possess favourable attitude towards government. However, the trained and non-trained groups from both the states differ significantly in this context.

The attitude of the unmarried respondents from both the states is comparatively more favourable towards the government than that of their married counterparts.

Attitude towards Society

The respondents from West Bengal possesses significantly more favourable attitude towards the society. Similar sketch prevails when the male and female groups of respondents from the two states were juxtaposed.

Though not significant but the trained respondents from West Bengal, possess comparatively more favourable attitude towards the society compared to their trained counter respondents from the state Assam.

The non-trained respondents from West Bengal possess significantly more favourable attitude towards society than that of the non trained respondents from Assam.

The married as well as the unmarried group of respondents from West Bengal possess significantly more favourable attitude towards the society than that of their respective counter respondents groups from West Bengal. The observation prevails when the respondents from urban, suburban and rural areas from West Bengal was juxtaposed with their respective counter respondent groups from Assam. Keeping consonance, neither the respondents from different experience categories, nor from the different religious categories from the two states makes any difference in this observation.

The female respondents from both the states possess significantly more favourable attitude towards the society, compared to their respective male counter respondent groups.

While the trained respondents from Assam possess significantly more favourable attitude towards society compared to their non-trained counter respondents, it is the non-trained respondent group from West Bengal who possess significantly more favourable attitude towards society when compared to their trained counter respondent group from West Bengal.

The unmarried respondents from both the states possess significantly more favourable attitude towards society, if compared with their counter married respondents from the respective states.

As the study observed, marital status has its effect over the attitude of the tribe teachers towards the society.

Attitude towards Working Environment

The tribal teachers from both the states – Assam and West Bengal possess favourable attitude towards their working environment. However, the respondents from Assam possess significantly more favourable attitude compared to the respondents from West Bengal. The observation prevails even when the male and female respondent groups from the two states was juxtaposed separately.

Trained respondents from Assam possess significantly more favourable attitude towards their profession, compared to the trained respondents from West Bengal. On the other hand, the non-trained respondents from Assam though possess marginally more favourable attitude towards their profession than that of the non-trained respondents from West Bengal, but these non-trained groups of respondents from the two states does not differ significantly.

The respondents from Assam, irrespective of their marital status, possess more favourable attitude towards their profession if compared to their matching groups from West Bengal. However, where the married respondents from Assam possess significantly more positive attitude towards profession compared to the married respondents from West Bengal, the unmarried respondents from Assam and West Bengal does not differ significantly.

Among the respondents having teaching experience ranging from 15 to 20 years, the respondents from Assam possess significantly more favourable attitude towards the working environment compared to the respondents from West Bengal with a similar experience range.

The other groups from the two states formed on the basis of their location of schools, religion or from the other experience ranges, while partially juxtaposed, does not differ significantly – so far their attitude towards their working environment is concerned.

The female respondents from both the states, as the study observed, possess significantly more favourable attitude towards their environment compared to their male counterparts from the respective states.

Though the non-trained respondents from both the states possess more favourable attitude towards their working environment compared to the trained respondents from the states concerned, however, the difference in attitude is not significant.

The unmarried groups from both the states possess marginally more (but not significantly) favourable attitude towards their working environment, compared to the married group of respondents of the concerned states.

Composite Attitude

The respondents from both the states Assam and West Bengal possess positive attitude. However, the respondents from West Bengal possess significantly (at 0.01 level) more favourable attitude, compared to the respondents from Assam. This goes in consonance with the parallel juxtaposition results. While the attitude of the male groups and female groups of respondents from the two states are examined separately.

The trained respondents from West Bengal possess comparatively more favourable attitude than the trained respondents from Assam where as the non-trained respondents from West Bengal possess significantly (at 0.01 level) more favourable attitude if compared to the non-trained respondents from Assam.

The married respondents from West Bengal possess significantly more favourable attitude, compared to the married respondents from Assam.

The married respondents possess significantly more (at 0.01 level) favourable attitude, compared to the unmarried respondents from Assam. Similar observation prevails when the attitude of the respondents working in urban, suburban and rural schools of West Bengal is juxtaposed with the respective matching groups from Assam.

The Hindu as well as the Christian respondents from West Bengal possess significantly (at 0.01 level) more favourable attitude than that of the respondents following same religion from Assam.

While the female respondents possess comparatively more favourable attitude than the male respondent group from Assam, the female respondents from West Bengal possess significantly (at 0.01 level) more favourable attitude than that of the male respondents from the West Bengal.

The unmarried groups of respondents from both the states possess significantly (at 0.01 level) more favourable attitude, if compared with their married counter parts from the respective states.

15

Comparative Status of Tribe Teachers in Terms of Level of Creativity

Psychographic Status Based on Creativity

Society has a demand for innovation and inventors who can create a unique. The goal to create a unique society can only be achieved when the teachers of the society are creative enough. With an aim to explore the psychographic status of the tribal teachers, their 'creativity' and its level were studied. The study was made, not to classify the respondents rather emphasis was given to compare different groups and to find out the correlation of the components of creativity and also to point out the effect of other factors over creativity.

Though apparently it appears that the respondents from West Bengal are more creative than the respondents from Assam in terms of their mean creativity score over the Indian adaptation of Tarrance Text of Creative Thinking, but actually their exists no significant difference between the tribal teachers from the two different states and all the respondent groups from the states Assam and West Bengal holds almost a similar level of creativity.

The male respondents from West Bengal are more creative than the male respondents from Assam. Significant difference (at 0.05 level) exists between the male respondents from Assam and West Bengal so far their level of creativity is concerned.

The female respondents from Assam are having comparatively higher level of creativity than that of the female respondents from West Bengal. However, in this context, there exists no significant difference.

Though the trained respondents from West Bengal was found to be more creative than that of the trained respondents from Assam, however, the two groups does not differ significantly in terms of their level of creativity.

The non-trained respondents from West Bengal holds marginally higher level of creativity than that of the non-trained respondents from Assam, however, the difference is not significant.

The married groups of respondents from Assam hold marginally higher level of creativity than the married groups of respondents from West Bengal.

Here also, no significant difference exists between these two groups in terms of their level of creativity.

The unmarried respondents from West Bengal holds comparatively higher level of creativity than the unmarried respondents from Assam, but the difference between the two groups in terms of their level of creativity, is not significant.

In terms of their creativity the respondents working in urban areas in Assam and West Bengal does not differ significantly however the respondents from urban areas of West Bengal are comparatively more creative than the urban respondents from Assam so far the mean creativity scores are concerned.

No significant difference has been observed between the respondents from suburban areas from the two different states, though the respondents working in suburban areas of West Bengal having comparatively higher level of creativity.

Among the respondents from rural areas of the two states, the respondents from West Bengal are significantly more creative than the respondents from Assam.

Among the respondents from the two states, those who are having teaching experience, less than five years, no significant difference exists between them and they holds almost similar level of creativity.

The respondents from Assam, having teaching experience ranging from five years to ten years are more creative than their counter-respondents group from West Bengal having similar length of teaching experience. However, the difference in terms of the level of creativity of these two groups is not significant.

No difference exists between the respondents from the states of Assam and West Bengal, having teaching experience ranging more than ten years but less than fifteen years so far their level of creativity is concerned.

Though no significant difference exists between the respondents from the two states, with an experience ranging from fifteen to twenty years but among such respondents, the group from Assam possesses comparatively higher level of creativity and the respondents from both the states possess almost a similar level of creativity.

The respondents from the two states, who are by religion Christian, though does not differ significantly however, among them respondents from West Bengal are comparatively more creative than the respondents from Assam.

Among the respondents from Assam, females are more creative than male.

Among the respondents from West Bengal, though females hold comparatively higher level of creativity than male respondents, however, the difference is not significant.

Non-trained respondents from Assam are more creative than that of their trained counter respondent group.

The non-trained respondents from West Bengal hold significantly higher level of creativity than the trained respondents.

In the state of Assam, the unmarried respondents are more creative compared to the married respondents.

The unmarried group of respondents from West Bengal was found significantly more creative than their married counter respondent group. As such it may be assumed that training possesses adverse impact over the level of creativity of the tribe teachers.

Originality

The respondent groups of the two states hold almost a similar level of originality, one of the major components of creativity.

The male respondents from West Bengal possess comparatively higher level of originality though not significant at any standard level. On the other hand, the female respondents from Assam possess higher level of originality than that of the female respondents from West Bengal.

No significant difference exists between the trained respondents from two states so far their level of originality is concerned. Similar is the observation while the non-trained respondent groups from the two states were taken into consideration.

The suburban group of respondents from West Bengal possesses significantly higher (at 0.05 level) level of originality than that of the suburban respondents from Assam.

Among the respondents working in the schools situated in rural areas, the respondents from West Bengal are having significantly higher level of originality than that of the respondents from Assam.

Among the respondents having teaching experience ranging from 5-10 years, those who are from Assam, found hold significantly higher level of originality than the respondents from West Bengal.

The female respondents are possessing significantly higher level of originality than that of their male counterparts from the state Assam. However, in West Bengal, no such significant difference exists between the male and female respondents in connection with their level of originality.

Though the non-trained group of respondents from both the states Assam and West Bengal are possessing comparatively higher level of originality than their respective trained – counterparts, however in both the states, no significant difference exists between the trained and non-trained respondents in terms of their level of originality.

The unmarried respondents from both the states hold significantly higher level of originality compared to the married respondents from the respective states.

Flexibility

No significant difference exists between the respondents from Assam and West Bengal in terms of their level of flexibility; however, the respondents from Assam are marginally more flexible.

In the state Assam the female respondents are significantly more flexible than their male counterparts. Similarly, the non-trained respondents from the state Assam are significantly more flexible than the trained respondents from the very state. Where as in West Bengal the two gender groups and the groups formed on the basis of possession training holds almost similar level of flexibility.

Marital status does not make any difference in the level of flexibility of the tribe teachers in both the states.

Fluency

Significant difference (at 0.05 level) exists between the respondents from the states under consideration in connection with their level of fluency. The respondent groups from West Bengal are more fluent than the respondents from Assam.

The male respondents from West Bengal possess significantly higher level of fluency than that of their counter male respondents from Assam.

Though the female respondents from West Bengal holds comparatively higher level of fluency than the female respondents from Assam however the difference of the level of fluency in not significant at any standard level.

Significant difference exists between non-trained groups of respondents from the two states so far their fluency is concerned. The non-trained respondents from West Bengal possess significantly higher level of fluency than the non-trained respondents from Assam.

Correlational Observation of Creativity and its Components

The study observed that high positive and significant correlation exists between originality and flexibility, originality and fluency, originality and creativity, flexibility and fluency, flexibility and creativity and also between fluency and creativity. This goes in consonance with the observations of the studies in psychology carried out over various human groups.

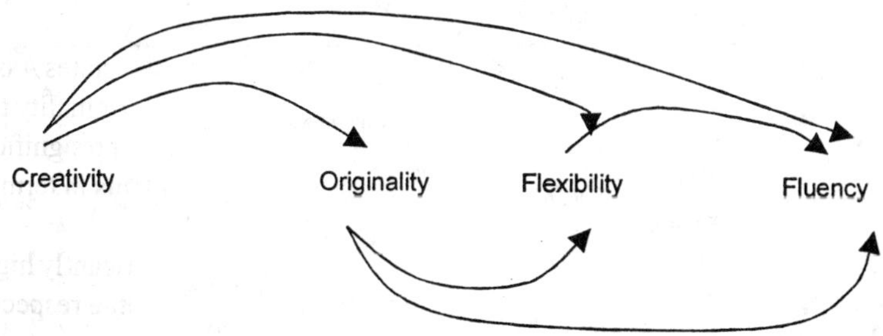

Other Findings over Creativity

The study observed that gender has its effect over the level of creativity and female respondents from both the states was found possessing comparatively higher level of creativity than that of their male counterparts.

Possession of training affects the level of creativity. The non-trained respondents from both the states possessed significantly higher level of creativity than that of their trained counterparts.

Habitation of the respondents (*i.e.* urban, suburban and rural) has its effect over their level of creativity, while the respondents from suburban areas possess comparatively higher level of creativity than those who are inhabiting in urban area, it is the respondent group from rural areas whose level of creativity is even less than that of the urban dwellers from both the states.

Marital status influence the level of creativity and the unmarried respondents possess substantially higher level of creativity than that of their married counterparts.

The study reveals that creativity varies with the experience in a haphazard way.

Significant difference exists between the respondents working in rural schools of Assam and West Bengal. Respondents working in rural schools of West Bengal are more flexible than the respondents from Assam who are also working in rural schools.

In Assam, the female respondents are more flexible compared to the male respondents whereas in West Bengal, no such difference was found between male and female group of respondents.

Trained respondents are more flexible than the non-trained respondents from both the states.

Where the unmarried respondents are significantly, much more flexible than the married respondents from West Bengal, no such difference is visible between married and unmarried respondents from Assam in this context.

State	*N*	*Sex*	*Training*	*Location*	*Marital Status*	*Ex-perience*	*Religion*	*Mean Creativity Score of the Groups*
West Bengal				Suburban				46.9167
West Bengal				Urban				45.6667
West Bengal					Unmarried			43.9211
Assam		Female						43.8958
Assam				Suburban				43.3889
West Bengal			Non-trained					41.9818
West Bengal		Female						41.9583
Assam				Urban				41.8243
Assam						Ex-2		41.6275
West Bengal							Christian	41.3200
Assam						Ex-1		41.2941

State	*N*	*Sex*	*Training*	*Location*	*Marital Status*	*Ex-perience*	*Religion*	*Mean Creativity Score of the Groups*
West Bengal						Ex-1		41.1013
Assam					Un-married			41.1000
Assam			Non-trained					40.3462
West Bengal	150(T)							40.1200
West Bengal						Ex-3		39.7917
			TOTAL				(N = 300)	39.7733
West Bengal		Male						39.7698
West Bengal							Sarna	39.6944
West Bengal						Ex-2		39.5556
Assam							Christian	39.5094
Assam						Ex-3		30.3760
Assam	150(T)							39.4267
West Bengal							Hindu	39.4096
Assam					Married			39.2101
Assam							Hindu	39.1081
West Bengal				Rural				39.1008
West Bengal			Trained					39.0421
West Bengal					Married			38.8304
Assam						Ex-4		37.3548
Assam			Trained					37.3478
Assam		Male						37.3235
Assam						Ex-5		36.5185
West Bengal								35.2500
Assam						Ex-4		35.1379

PART IV

16

Post Script

A perusal of situation of tribal education in India reveals that participation of the tribal population in general, and scheduled tribes in the states of Assam and West Bengal in particular in the teaching profession is very meager. Those who have attained the required qualification for participating in teaching profession from among the tribal denomination are hardly going for teaching profession. Educated people from tribal communities are preferring other jobs than that of teaching. This may be, due to the fact that socio-economic status of teacher is not very high in comparison to the status of other professionals. Among the tribal teachers, the study observed that the rate of participation of the male is significantly higher than that of females from both the states of Assam and West Bengal. However, juxtaposition reveals that the rate of female participation in teaching at higher-secondary level is much more higher in Assam than that of West Bengal and in contrast, the rate of female-participation at secondary schools is comparatively higher in West Bengal. The tribal teachers, irrespective of their gender or state, are mostly married and a negligible percentage of them from Assam holds a marital status – either widow/widower or separated. It is very interesting to note that none of the female tribal-teacher is engaged in boys' schools in West Bengal and none of the male tribal teacher is working in the girl's schools in Assam. On the other hand, a grand majority of the tribal teachers from both the states are absorbed in government-aided schools and very few teachers are absorbed in Government-schools. The notable observation came out from the study that due to lack of physical facilities compared to the administrative jobs, educated tribal youths from Assam are not that extent interested in teaching. However, their counterparts from West Bengal show a difference in this connection. 'To uplift their social status' – as per their version, educated tribals from West Bengal are opting teaching profession. The underlining cause of these differences in attitude towards teaching is that, in North Eastern India, the society is holding much more materialistic outlook compared to Eastern India.

The findings of the present study, regarding the linguistic status of the tribal teachers are somewhat different. Majority of them started school education with *Bangla* and *Assamisse* and not with their mother tongue. This goes against the policy to introduce indigenous tribal languages for the tribal students at least at the school level. Of course, a significant percentage of tribal teachers from Assam did enjoy the opportunity to carryout or at least to start their school education in their own indigenous languages. In terms of their religious status, a massive tendency of conversion is prominent among the tribal teachers from both the states where majority of the respondents gave up their ascribed-religious belief and took up some different religion.

The findings of the present study regarding the political status of the tribal teachers are usual in nature. The rate of political participation of the tribal teacher from West Bengal is substantially higher than that of Assam. But majority of the teachers are not associated with any political parties and they neither signify any association between their political participation and status, nor between their social-participation and status. Therefore, as the next step, studies may be initiated with the purpose of going into the details of the political process and their participation in the very process in connection with education. Grand-consensus of opinion prevailing in connection with upward social mobility and most of the respondents opined that it is very hard, and thereby to change the status. A contrast remains in context of their social up-bringing while majority of the tribal teachers from West Bengal grewup mostly in the rural setup. From Assam majority reported, mostly grewup in urban society. It seems to the author that to some extent, the respondents from two different states differ in terms of their perception of urban-rural areas. Female teachers hold comparatively higher status than their male counterparts from both the states – so far housing condition is considered as an indicator of status. The respondents signify a strong association between the nature – of their 'location of house' and 'location of schools'.

A massive difference has been observed between the indigenous tribal communities and the respondent tribal teachers, so far the perception of economic-status-determining assets are concerned. While the indigenous tribal communities from Assam considered the stone and wooden buttons, length of river banks under occupation, Jhum-land holdings, stone utensils, *bhorot*, 'mithun', cattle, winter-garments made up of animal skin etc. as the assets to determine their economic status in the society, the same in case of the indigenous tribal communities from West Bengal are-hand-made ribbon for decorating hair, ancient antic and gold coins, thread and buttons made up of animal bone, old and large tree, fermentation chamber for preparing wine, cattle, land, house, brass-utensils, farm-house, *Kori* and musical instruments as their economic status indicator. In this context, in search of status of tribal teachers it was observed that none of the respondents from any state spelt the assets as reported by their indigenous community, rather most of them considered bank balance, electrical and electronic gadgets, vehicles, piece of land in "proper area", level of education, ornaments, modern dress, utensils-made up of china-clay and steel, fire-gun, kitchen accessories, wealth, sofa-set, colour television, refrigerator, telephone as the assets which determine their status. The very observation advocates that most of the teachers from the tribal communities are de-rooted from their indigenous community. Apart from the fact, respondents from both the states signify a strong association between their status and economic situation. It is worthnoting in this context that though both the state government prescribed almost a similar scale of pay for the teacher but due to varied educational qualifications and absorption in different types of schools, heterogeneity is prevailing among the respondents in terms of their earning. Present study signifies noticeable association between status and economic situation of the tribal teachers.

The perception and experience of the tribal-teachers support the view to establish more hostel or residential institutions for the interest of 'tribal-education'. Academic qualification of the sample group advocates to give-up the preconceived notion of so-called-mainstream regarding the inferior academic status of the tribal teachers at secondary level and juxtaposition of the academic status further reveal that the tribal teachers from West Bengal are superior than the tribal teachers from Assam. More tribal teachers from West Bengal in general and more female tribal teachers from both the states in specific, are having optimum academic status for teaching at secondary schools, compared to their respective counter-groups. The respondents are quite aware about their social responsibility and grand majority of the respondents reported trying to uplift their community.

Majority of the respondents reported hold a medium status, which is completely of their own perception. More indepth study need to be initiated by the future researchers in this context, collecting data from the other relevant sources. In case of such research, the findings of the present study may be considered for the purpose of framing hypotheses; the status questionnaire developed for the present study may also be used for developing a status-scale. The future researcher need to be cautious about inter-state and inter-community variations among the tribals.

The study realized the necessity to motivate the educated tribals towards teaching profession by wideningup the scope of professional training. Recommendations of various committees and commissions in this context should be implemented as early as possible. In-depth survey should be carried out on specific region, state and community to assess the educational interest of the tribals. Effect of gender can also be a vergine dimension of tribal-study in this context. The study reveals that apart from various problems, the teachers from tribal communities want to develop a warm professional relationship with their colleagues. Occupational rest-ness, as the present study finds, appears as a predominantly female characteristics among the tribals. It has been observed that the state governments – neither in Assam nor in West Bengal is wholeheartedly trying to improve the status of tribal teachers; more initiatives are expected in this context.

So far the attitude of the respondents of the present study is concerned, difference is prevailing among various categories of teachers; and again, towards various dimensions of attitude. The notable finding of the study reveals that the tribal-teachers, for varied reasons, are mostly dissatisfied with the government. Heterogeneity, in terms of Psychographic status of the tribal teachers is prominent. Sex, training, marital status are the major parameters which aggravate such heterogeneity. However, in general the respondents from both the states possess a moderate degree of creativity. Significant association has been explored between the creativity and it's components, which goes in consonance with the earlier research findings. Scope remains open to take up in-depth study among the tribal teachers on this specific aspect.

In conclusion, the author modestly wants to submit that Anthropological approach has a profound importance in the study of educational problems in general and the tribals in particular. This novel approach, almost virgin in educational researches, will lead the future researchers to a new road of knowledge and lay a new vista in the coming decades in educational research.

Bibliography

Aberle, Devid F. (1961), *"Culture and Socialization" in Psychological Anthropology – Approaches to Culture and Personality*, Dorsey Press; Home Wood, pp. 381-99.

Adaval, S.B. ed. (1968), *Third Indian Yearbook of Education: Educational Research*; NCERT; New Delhi.

Adisai, G. (1978), A Comparative Study of Creative Thinking in Relation to Socio-Economic Status, School Climate and Classroom Behaviour of High School Students in India and Thailand, Unpublished Ph.D. Thesis in Education, M.S. University; Boroda.

Adiseshiah, M.S & Ramnathan, S. (1974), Educational Problems of Scheduled Caste and Scheduled Tribes in Tamil Nadu; An ICSSR Project Report carried out by Madras Institute of Development Studies; Madras.

Adiseshiah, M.S. & Tripathi, K.K. (1980), Temporal Orientation and Deprivation; *Journal of Psychological Research*, Vol. 24, pp. 144-51.

—— (1993), *Status of Tribal Woman in India: Educational Implications*; *Social Change.*

Agarwal, P.C. (1974), *A Study of Correlation of Achievement Motivation*; Unpublished Ph.D. Thesis in Education, Kurukshetra University; Kurukshetra.

Ahmed, Karuna (1979), Towards a Study of Education and Social change; *Economic and Political Weekly*; Vol.-XIV, No. 4, January 27.

Aiyappan, A. (1948), A Report on the Socio-Economic Conditions of the Aboriginal Tribals of the Province of Madras; Manager of Publications; Govt. of India; New Delhi.

Alexander, K.L. *et. al.* (1994), When expectations Work: Race and SES differences in School Performance; *Psychological Abstracts*, Vol. 82, No. 9; p. 4358.

Ambasht, N.K *et. al.* (1971), *Education and Economic Condition and Employment Position of Eighteen Tribes*; NCERT; New Delhi.

—— (1970), *A Critical Study of Tribal Education*; S. Chand and Co.; New Delhi.

—— (1970), *Reducing Educational Wastage in Tribal Areas*; NCERT, New Delhi.

—— (1971), Policy of Tribal Education: A Suggestion; *Vanyajati*; Vol. 19, No.1, pp. 43-45.

—— (1993), Curriculum and Material for the Education of Tribal Children; Report of the National Workshop on Tribal Education; New Delhi.

Ansari, S.A. (1986), *Socio-economic Development in the Tribal Areas of Manipur*; D.K. Publishers, New Delhi.

Arches, W.G. (1984), *Tribal Law and Justice: A report on the Santhal. (3 Vols.)*; Concept publication; New Delhi.

Arensberg, Canrad. M (1961), "The Community as object and Sample; *Journal of American Anthropologists*; Vol. 63. No. 1961, pp. 263-64.

Arora, G.L. (1978), Relationship of Sex with Creativity, General Anxiety, Vocational Anxiety and Teaching Success; *Journal of Education and Psychology;* Vol. 36. No. 3; pp. 133-37.

Arora, R.K. (1981), An Investigation into The Problems of Students of Professional Course of Medicine, Law, Engineering and Education in Relation to Personality Factors; Unpublished Ph.D. Thesis in Education; A.M.U.; Aligarh.

Assam, Govt. of (1980), *Tribes of Assam Plains: A profile*; Directorate of Welfare; Gauhati.

Assam, Govt. of, *Schedules Caste and Scheduled Tribes (1961),* Vol. 4; Part 5(*a*), Manager of Publications; New Delhi.

Aswal, G.S. (1982), A Study of Student-Activitism as Related to Personality Factors and Socio-Economic Conditions; Unpublished Doctoral Thesis in Education; Garhwal University.

Austin, A.W. (1964), Socio-Economic Factors in Achievement and Aspirations of the Merit Scholars; *Personal Guidance Journal,* Vol. 42.

Ausubol, David, P. (1968), *Educational Psychology, A Cognitive View*; Holt. Rinehard and Winston, Inc; New York.

Azubuike, I. (1996), Relationship between self-concept of Lgbo children in Imo State of Nigria and their Academic Achievement, age, SES and Gender; *Dissertation Abstracts International*; Vol. 58; No. 3; p. 732(*a*).

Babbie, E.R. (1973), *Survey Research Methods*; Calif. Wardsworth Publishing Co, Belmont.

Balakrishna (1982), Effect of Socio-Cultural Deprivation on Some Cognitive and Non-Cognitive Abilities of Tribal Adolescents; Unpublished Ph.D. Thesis in Psychology; Magadh University.

Banerjee, B.G. (1984), On Development and Tribal Development; *Tribal Research Bulletin;* Vol 7; No. 1 pp. 9-11.

Banerjee, M. (1954), *Primitive Man in India*; India Publications; Ambala Cant.

Banton, Michael (1968), *International Encyclopedia of Social Sciences*; Vols. 1-6; Macmillan; New York.

Bapat, N.V. (1964), A Few Thaughts on Tribal Education; *Vanyajati* Vol. 12, No. 4 pp. 190-99.

—— (1968), Residential Schools in Tribal Areas, *Vanyajati;* Vol 16; No. 4, pp. 154-59.

—— (1971), Tribal Education for Employment and Material prosperity; *Vanyajati* Vol. 19, No. 1; pp. 5-7.

Bardoloi, B.N. *et. al.* (1987), *Tribes of Assam; Tribal Research Institute*, Gauhati.

Bareja, J.D. (1982), *New Horizons of North East*; Western Book Depot. Gauhati.

Barkataki, S. (1969), *Tribes of Assam*; National Book Trust; New Delhi.

Barla, A. (1965), Medium of Instructions for Tribal Students *Vanyajati;* Vol. 4; No. 11; pp. 33-35.

Baron, F. (1969), *Creative Person and Creative Process*; Holt Reinhart and Winston, Inc.; New York.

—— (1976), *Need for Order and Disorder in Arioti – Creativity The Magic Syntheses*; Basic Book Inc; New York.

Bastia, K.C. (1982), A Study of the National Adult Education Programme in the Tribal Region of Orissa State; Ph.D. Thesis in Education; M.S. University, CASE, Baroda.

Basu, A.R. (1985), *Tribal Development Programme and Administration in India*; National Book Organization; New Delhi.

Basu N.C. (1987), *Forests and Tribals*; Manisha Granthalaya; Calcutta.

Basu, M. (1963), Anthropology in Tribal Education; *Bulletin of the Cultural Research Institute;* Vol. 2; No. 1; pp. 22-27.

Bentley, J.C. (1966), Creativity and Academic Achievement, *Journal of Educational Research*; Vol. 59, pp. 269-72.

Bernstein, B. (1961), Social Structure, Language and Learning; *Educational Research*; Vol. 3; pp. 163-76.

Bhartiya Adimjati Sevak Sangha, (1960), Report: Conference for Tribes and Tribal Areas; *Journal of Bharatiya Adimjati Sevak Sangha.*; New Delhi.

Bhatia. H.R. (1984), *General Psychology*; Oxford and IBH Publishing Co.; New Delhi.

Bhattacharya, S.K. (1984), Social Stratification and the System of Education – A Study of Social Mobility in Three Generations in West Bengal; Unpublished Doctoral Thesis; Department of Sociology, University of Calcutta.

Bhowmick, K.L. *et. al.* (1986), *Tribal India: A profile in Indian Ethnology*, World Press, Calcutta.

Bhowmick. P.K. (1967), Ways To Educate The Tribals, *Adibasi*; Vol. 9, No. 1; pp. 29-39.

Bihari, L.R (1969), Wastage and Stagnation in Primary Education Among the Tribes; *Journal of Tribal Research and Training Institute*; Gujarat Vidyapeeth; Ahmedabad.

Biswas, N.B. (1999), *Education in North East India*; Shipra Publications; New Delhi.

Biswas, P.C. (1955), Anthropology and Tribal Education; *Vanyajati;* Vol. 3. No. 2; pp. 81-89.

Bogaert, M.V.D. *et. al.* (1973), Education and Self Employment among Tribals: A Case Study; *Social Action*; Vol. 23. No. 2; pp. 137-62.

Bopegamage, A. *et. al.* (1978), Educating Tribal Children: Extent of Westage and Stagnation in Schools; *Economic Times;* May 17th; p. 5.

Bose, A.B. (1970), Problems of Educational Development of Scheduled Tribes, *Man in India;* Vol. 50; No. 1; pp. 27-28.

Bose, J.K. (1980), *Glimpses of Tribal Life in North East India*; Institute of Social Research and Applied Anthropology; Calcutta.

Bose, N.K. (1966), Some suggestions on Tribal Education; *Folklore;* Vol. 7; No. 2; pp. 47-57.

Bose, P.K. (1982), *Social Strata Among the Tribes in Tribal Regions of Bengal*; Centre for Social Studies; Surat.

—— (1985), *Classes and Class Relations Among Tribals of Bengal*; Ajanta Publications; New Delhi.

Bose, S. (1963), Socio-Psychological Study of the Adolescent Tribal Children of West Bengal Himalayan Regions for the Purpose of National Integration in Relation To Co curricular Participation; Unpublished Doctoral Thesis in Education at Calcutta University; Calcutta.

Buch, M.B. ed. (1974), *A Survey of Research in Education, CASE*; M.S. University; Baroda.

—— ed. (1979), *Second Survey of Research in Education (1972-'78)*, Society for Educational Research and Development, Baroda.

—— ed. (1987), *Third Survey of Research in Education*, NCERT; New Delhi.

Buch, M.B. & Singh (1978), *Third All India Educational Survey*: Teachers; NCERT, New Delhi.

Burgess, R.G. (Ed.) (1984), *The Research Process in Educational Settings: Ten Case Studies;* Falmer Press, London.

Burgess, T. and Adams, E. (Eds.) (1980), *Outcomes of Education;* Macmillan, London.

Caldas, S.J. *et. al.* (1997), Effects of School Population, Socio-Economic Status on Individual Academic Achievement; *The Journal of Educational Research*; Vol. 90; No. 5; pp. 269-78.

Casey, K. (1990), Teachers as mother: Curriculum theorizing in the life histories of contemporary women teachers; *Cambridge Journal of Education*; Vol. 20, No. 3; pp. 301-20.

Catsambis, S. (1995), Gender, Race, Ethnicity and Education; *Psychological Abstracts*; Vol. 82; No. 10; pp. 48-58.

Cattel, R.B. *et. al.* (1970), *Handbook of 16 Personality factors*; IPAT, Champaign.

Census Handbook on Tribal Population, published by the Registrar General and Census Commissioner, Govt. of India, 1971 and 1961.

—— (1981).

—— (1991).

Census of India, *Final Population Totals (1992)*, paper 1 of 1992, Vol. 1; Manager of publications; New Delhi.

——, *Scheduled Castes and Scheduled Tribe Population' in Census of India*, 1993; Paper 1, Registrar General and Census Commissioner; India.

——, Special Tables for S.T.s' (1961) 'Vol. I. Part V-A (2), Manager of Publications; G.O.I. Press; New Delhi.

Census Reports: *On Scheduled Caste and Scheduled Tribe Population*: Series I of 1993 and all other back volumes; published by the Registrar General and Census Commission. Govt. of India (1993 & preceding years).

Chakraborty, H. (1984), Educational Dynamism in the Social Perspective of Purulia—A Typical Under-Developed District in West Bengal; Unpublished Doctoral Thesis in Education; University of Calcutta.

Chakraborty, M. *et. al.*(1983), Indian Tribes; Swaraswat Library; Calcutta.

Chalam, K.S, (1988), Education and Weaker Sections; Inter India publications; New Delhi.

Chand, J. (1985), A Comparative Study of Various Naga Tribal Pupils in Relation to Their Self Perception, Socio-Economic Status, Vocational and Educational Aspirations and Academic Achievement; Ph.D. in Education, NEHU; cit. in Buch, M.B. (Ed.); *Fourth Survey of Research in Education*; SERD; Baroda.

Chattopadhya, N.A. (1961), Psychological Study of Intelligence of Tribal and Non-Tribal Children of Tripura; D.Phil in Psychology; Calcutta University; cit. in Buch, M.B. (Ed.); *Second Survey of Research in Education*; SERD; Baroda.

Chattopadhyay, K.P. (1953), Tribal Education in *Man In India*; Vol. 33, No. 1; Church Road; Ranchi.

—— (1963), *Some Material for Social Education of Tribals in Eastern India*; Calcutta.

Chattopadhyay, S. (1946), *Report on the Santhals in Northern and Western Bengal*; Calcutta University Press; Calcutta.

—— (1973), *Racial Affinities of North East Indian Tribes*; Munshiram Manoharlal; Calcutta.

Chaudhuri, B. (ed.) (1983), *Tribal Development in India: Problems and Prospects*; Inter-India Publications; New Delhi.

Chaudhuri, Uma (1953), Need for Mental testing for formulation of Education Schemes among Tribal People; Paper on Conference; *Journal of Bharatiya Adimjati Sevak Sangh,* New Delhi, pp. 287-91.

Chaudhury, P., & Sinha, U.P. (1959), A Comparative Study of Concrete Intelligence of the Tribal and Non Tribal School Girls of Ranchi; The Bihar Tribal Research Institute; Ranchi.

Chauhan, S.S. (1989), A Survey of Causes of Educational Backwardness Among Tribal Women of Himachal Pradesh; UGC Research Project Report; H.P. University, Shimla.

Cherian, V.I. (1992), Parental Interest And Academic Achievement of Xhosa Children; *Psychological Abstracts*; Vol-79, No.6.

Chilukala, G.K. (1981), Social Attitude of Indian Academic Elit; Unpublished Ph.D. Thesis in Sociology; Osmania University.

Chitinis, S. (1974), First Survey in Social Sciences; ICSSR; New Delhi.

—— (1974), The Educational Problems of SC and ST College Students in Maharashtra; ICSSR Financed Project Report; TISS; Bombay.

—— (1979), The Indian Academic Profession – Crisis and Change and Altbach, P.G. (Ed) the Teaching Community; Macmillan and Co.; Bombay.

Chitinis, S. & Altbach, P.G. (Ed.) (1979), The Indian Academic Profession – Crisis and Change and the Teaching Community; Macmillan and Co.; Bombay.

Chitlangia, P.D. (1997), *The President of FTS, reported in the Asian Age*, Calcutta.

Chopra, R. (1993), *Report on the Status of Teachers in India*, NCERT, New Delhi.

Chopra, R.K. (1982), A Study of Organizational Climate of Schools in Relation to Job-satisfaction of Teachers and Students Achievement; Unpublished Ph.D. thesis in Education, Agra University.

—— (1993), Status of Teachers In India; Research Report on Teacher-Education; Financed by Educational Research and Innovation Committee (ERIC), NCERT, New Delhi.

Cole, B. (1986), The Black Educator: An endangered Species; *Journal of Negro Education;* Vol. 55, No. 3; pp. 326-34.

Collier-Thomas, B. (1982), The impact of Black Women in Education: A Historical Overview, *Journal of Negro Education;* Vol.-51; No. 3; pp. 173-79.

Colin, M. Turnbull (1983), *The Human Cycle*; Simon & Schuster; New York.

Cooley, Charles, H. (1899), 'Personal Competition', *Economic Studies*, Vol. IV, No. 2, pp. 78-86.

Dalton, Edward Tuite (1872), Descriptive Ethenology of Bengal; Govt. Printing Press, Calcutta.

Das Gupta, M. (1984), *Tribal Unrest*; *EPW*; Vol.-19; No. 11. pp. 449-51.

Das Gupta, N.K. (1959), Tribal Language and Education; *Man in India*; Vol. 39, No. 1; pp. 61-64.

—— (1963), Problems of Tribal Education and the Santhals; *Journal of Bharatiya Adimjati Sevak Sangha*; New Delhi.

Das, A.K. *et. al.* (1966), *Handbook on Scheduled Caste and Scheduled Tribes of West Bengal*; Tribal Welfare Department; Govt. of West Bengal; Calcutta.

Das, G. (1961), Tribal Education: Transition from orthodox education towards education for modernity, *Adabasi*; Vol.-9; No. 2; pp. 21-27.

Das, J.P. (1973), Cultural Deprivation and Cognitive Competence; *International Review of Research in Mental Retardation*; Vol. 6; Academic Press; New York.

Das, J.P. & Singha, P.S. (1975), Cast, Class and Cognitive Competence; *Indian Educational Review*; Vol. 10; pp. 1-8.

Das, N. (1969), Priorties for Tribal Education; *Adabasi*; Vol-10; No. 3&4; pp. 1-10.

Datta Roy, B. (1989), *Tribal Identity and Tension in North East India*; Omsons Publications; New Delhi.

David, G. (1964), *Teaching & Students: The Views of Negro and White Teachers*; cit. in Sociology of Education, Vol. 27.

Davis, G.A. (1966), Current Status of Research and Theory in Human Problem Solving; *Psychological Bulletine;* Vol. 66; No. 1; pp. 36-54.

Dececc, John. P. *et. al.* (1977), *The Psychology of Learning and Instruction*; Printice-Hall of India Pvt. Ltd.; New Delhi.

Decker, S. (1969), *An empty spoon*; Harper and Row; New York.

Dehbar, Sir. U.N. (1961), *Report of the Scheduled Areas and Scheduled Tribes Commission*, Vol. 1, Ministry of Home Affairs, New Delhi.

Dell, W.A. (1986), *The Tribes of the Bramhaputra Valley: A Contribution on their physical types and affinities*; Concept Publications; New Delhi.

Delors, Jacques (Ed.), (1996), *Report to UNESCO of International Commission on Education for the twenty-first Century*; UNESCO; Paris.

Dentler, R.A. *et. al.* (1964), Originality: Some Socio Personal determinants; Journal of Behavioural Science; Vol.-9; pp. 2-7.

Desai, B. & Patel. A. (1981), Ashram Schools of Gujarat: An Evaluative Study; Tribal Research and Training Center; Gujarat Vidyapeeth; Ahmedabad.

Desai, I.P. (1974), A Profile of Education Among the Scheduled Tribes in Gujarat, ICSSR; New Delhi.

Dhebar, D.N. (1962), Report of the Scheduled Areas and Scheduled Tribes Commission; Vol. I, Govt. of India Press, New Delhi.

Dhongade, U.D. (1986), A Critical Study of Non-Enrolment, Wastage and Stagnation During The First Two Years of Primary Education of Tribal Students in Maharashtra; Unpublished Ph.D. Thesis on Education; SERD; Baroda.

Doly, N.Y. (1971), *Isolation of Backward Community Students*; Janata Publishing Co., New Delhi.

Dube, S.C. (1988), *Tribal Education; Cit. in Antiquity to Modernity in Tribal India*; Bhupinder Singh (Ed.), Vol. II, Inter India Publications, New Delhi.

Dubey, S.M. (1974), Study of Scheduled Caste and Scheduled Tribe College Students in Assam – Project Report Financed by ICSSR, Department of Sociology; Dibrugarh University.

Dunningham, A.A. (1974), *A Black Woman's Experience: From School House to white House*; Philadelphia; Dorrance.

Dupre, B. (1986), Problems regarding the survival of future Black Teachers; Journals of Negro Education; Vol.-55; No. 2; pp. 55-66.

Durkheim, Emile (1965), *Elementary forms of Religious life*; Free Press; New York.

Dutta, B. (9184), The Tribal and the Non Tribal in the context of Assam Society and Culture; *Journal of N.E. India Council for Social Science Research*; Vol. V; No. 2; Shillong.

Dutta, M.L. (1983), Socio-Psychological Study of the Tribal High School Male Students of Himachal Pradesh With High Achievement Motivation; Ph.D. in Education; M.S. University; cit. in Buch, M.B. (Ed.); Fourth Survey of Research in Education, SERD; Baroda.

Dutta, M.N. (1956), *The Santhal: A Study in Cultural Change*; Manager of Publications; Govt. of India Press, Calcutta.

Ebel, R.L.(Ed.) (1969), *Encyclopedia of Educational Research*; The Macmillan Co.; London.

Edwards, A.L. (1957), *Techniques of Attitude Scale Construction*; Appleton-Century Crofts; Inc; New York.

Elwin, V. (1959), *A Philosophy for NEFA; Shillong*; North-East Frontier Agency; Shillong.

Elwin, Veriar (1954), A Philosophy for NEFA; North-Eastern Frontier Agency, Shillong.

—— (1955), *The Religion of an Indian Tribe*; Oxford University Press; Bombay.

—— (1957), *Ten Years of Progress in North-East Frontier Agency*; NEFA, Shillong.

—— (1960), *Report of the Committee on Special Multipurpose Tribal Blocks*, Ministry of Home Affairs, New Delhi.

—— (1965), *Democracy in NEFA*; Research Department; NEFA; Shillong.

Ethridge, S. (1979), Impact of the 1954 brown v. Topeka Board of Education decision on Black educators; *Negro Educational Review*, Vol. 30; No. (3-4), pp. 217-32.

Eysenck, H.J. *et. al.* (1972), *Encyclopedia of Psychology*; Search Press; London.

—— (1972), *Human topology*; Academic Press, New York.

Farooqui, J. (1975), Academic Elite and Social Structure; Unpublished Doctoral Dissertation in Sociology; A.M.U.; Aligarh.

Fatima, S.M.B. (1986), A Study of Achievement Related Motivations Among Tribal and Non-Tribal High School Students; Ph.D. Thesis in Psychology; Magash University; cit. in Buch, M.B. (Ed.); *Fourth Survey of Research in Education*; SERD; Baroda.

Feinberg, W. (1983), *Understanding Education: Towards a Reconstruction of Educational Enquiry*, Cambridge: Cambridge University Press.

Ferguson, L.W. (1939), The Requirements of an Adequate Attitude Scale; *Psychological Bulletine*, Vol.-36, pp. 665-73.

Festinger, L. *et. al.* (1970), *Research Methods in Behavioural Sciences*; Amerind Publishing Co. Pvt. Ltd; New Delhi.

Flanders, N. (1969), 'Teacher Effectiveness' in *Encyclopedia of Educational Research*; The Macmillan Co; London.

Foster, M. (1987), "*It's Cooking now*": An ethnographic study of a successful Black teacher in an Urban community College; Doctoral Dissertation, Harvard University.

—— (1989), *Recruiting Teachers of Colour: Problems, Programmes and Possibilities*; Arizona State University; Tempe.

—— (1990), The Politics of Race: Through African – American teacher's eye's; *Journal of Education*; Vol. 172, No. 3; pp. 123-41; New York.

—— (1991), Constancy, Change and Constraints in the Lives of Black Women teachers: Somethings change, most stay the same, *NWSA Journal*; Vol.-3, No. 2; pp. 233-61.

—— (1991), Just Go and Find a Way: Case Studies of the lives and practice of exemplary black high school teachers; *Equal Education*, Vol. II, pp. 273-309; AMS Press, New York.

—— (1994), Effective Black Teachers: A Literature Review In E.R. Hollins, et. al. (Ed.); *Teaching Diverse Populations; Formulating Knowledge Base*, pp. 225-41; State University of New York Press; Albany.

Fowler, H.W. and Fowler, F.G. (1995), *The Concise Oxford Dictionary*, OUP, New Delhi (rpt).

Francis, K. (1993), *Education and Development*; Discovery Publishing House, New Delhi.

Franklin, V.P. (1979), *The Education of Black Philadelphia: The Social and Educational History of a Minority Community*, 1900-'50, University of Pennsylvania Press, Philadelphia.

Freeman, F.S. (1965), *Theory and Practice of Psychological Testing*; Oxford IBH Publishing Co.; New Delhi.

Fuchs, S. (1973), *The Aboriginal Tribes of India*, Macmilan & Co.; New Delhi.

—— (1985), Tribes of India: A Struggle for Survival; Oxford University Press; New Delhi.

Gafoor, K.A. (1952), *The Social and Tribal Welfare in Hyderabad*; Social Service Department, Hyderabad.

Gakhar, S. (1975), Intellectual and Personality Correlates of Creativity: Ph.D. Thesis in Psychology, Punjab University; Chandigarh.

Gamst, F.C. and Edward Norbeck (1976), *Ideas of Culture: Sources and uses*; Holt Rinehart & Winston, New York.

Ganguly, J.B. (1970), *Tribal Students between Tradition and moderanity*; Educational Miscellany, Vol. 7; No. 1-2; pp. 61-69.

Garrett, H.E. (1962), *Statistics in Psychology and Education*; Allied Pacific Privet Ltd; Bombay.

Gayatonde, D.V. (1977), The Problems of Social Education in India; Ph.D. Thesis in Education; University of Poona.

George, E.L. (1975), Educational Problems of the Scheduled Caste and Scheduled Tribe College Students in Kerala; Project Report Financed by ICSSR and Conducted in the Department of Psychology; University of Kerala.

Gibbs, J.L. (1965), *Peoples of Africa*; Holt Rinehart and Winston, New York.

Gilbert, P. (1978), *Tribal India: A Systematic View of Primitive Man*; Rawat Publications; Jaipur.

Godson, I. (1988), *Teachers, Life histories and Studies of Curriculum and School: The making of Curriculum*; Flamer Press, Philadelphia.

Good, C.V. Ed. (1959), *Dictionary of Education*, McGraw Hill book Company, New York.

Gore, M.S. (1971), Education and Modernization; Cit. in the *Essays on Modernization of Under-developed Societies*, A., R. Desai (Ed.), Thacker Publication, Bombay; pp. 228-39 .

Goswami, P.C. (1972), *Socio-Economic Research in Tribal Areas*; Agro-Economic Research Centre, Net; Jorhat.

Goyal, J.C. (1980), A Study of Relationship Among Attitude, Job Satisfaction, Adjustment and Personal Interest of Teacher – Educators in India; Unpublished Ph.D. Thesis in Education; University of Delhi.

Goyal, J.C, & Chopra, R.K. (1984), A Comparative Study of Teacher profile in their Rural and *Urban Settings in Elementary School System*; Memo; N.C.E.R.T., New Delhi.

Goyal, R.P. (1974), *A Study of some personality correlates of Creativity in Secondary School Teachers under training*; Ph.D. Thesis in Education. Punjab University, Chandigarh.

Graham, P.A. (1987), *Black teachers: A drastically scarce Resource*; Delta Kappan; Vol. 68; No. 8; pp. 598-605.

Grigson, W.V. (1947), The Challenge of Backwardness: Some Notes and Papers on Tribal and Depressed Classes: Policy with Special Reference to Hyderabad State; Govt. Printing Press; Hyderabad.

Guha, B.S. (1935), *Racial Affinity of The People of India*, in Census of India, Vol. 1, Part III-A&B (Ethnographic notes), Manager of Publications, New Delhi.

Guilford, J.P. (1950), Creativity, *American Psychologist*; Vol. 5, pp. 444-54.

—— (1959), Traits of Creativity in M.M. Anderson (Ed.), Creativity and it's cultivation, Harber And Brothers, New York.

——, Creativity: Yesterday, Today and Tomorrow; *The Journal of Creative Behaviour*; Vol. 1; No. 1

—— (1959), Three faces of Intellect; *American Psychologist*; Vol. 14; pp. 469-79.

Gupta, M.D. (1978), A Study of the Status of Secondary School Teachers in Eastern U.P.; Unpublished Doctoral Thesis in Education, B.H.U..

Gupta, S.P. (1965), A Study of Adivasi Students in Ranchi District; the Bihar Tribal Research Institute; cit. in Buch, M.B. (Ed.); *Fourth Survey of Research in Education*; SERD; Baroda.

Haimendorf, C.V. (1982), *Tribes in India: The Struggle for Survival*; OUP; Delhi.

Hallowell, A.I. (1955), *Culture and Experience*; University of Pansylvania Press; Philadelphia.

Hammerton, J.A. (1984), *Tribes, Races and Cultures of India and Neighbouring Countries*; Mittal Publications, New Delhi.

Hans, Nicholas (1994), *Comparative Education*; Routledge and Kegan Paul Limited, London.

Harbinson and Mayers (1964), *Social Change and Education*, New York.

Harris, Marvin (1968), The Cultural Ecology of India; *Current Anthropology*; Vol. 7; pp. 51-66.

Haviland, W.A. (1990), *Cultural Anthropology*; the Dryden Press, Vermont.

Hembram, P.C. (N.A.), *Sari-Sarna*; Indian Publishers Distributors; New Delhi.

Henry, J. (1965), *Culture Against Man*; Vintage Books; New York.

Heredia, R.C. (1992), *Tribal Education for Community Development: A Study of Schooling in Talasari Mission Area*; Concept Publishing; New Delhi.

Hers Kovits, M.J. (1964), *Cultural Dynamics*; New York.

Hickman, *et. al.* (1995), High School Parent involvement: Relationships with Achievement Grade, Level, SES and Gender; *Psychological Abstracts*; Vol. 82, No. 12, pp. 571-78.

Hill, A (1980), *The Changing Black-Teacher and diminishing opportunities for Black Teachers*; Nor folk State University Press, Norfolk.

Hillway, Tyrus (1964), *Introduction to Research*; Houghton Mifflin Company, Boston.

Himendorf, C.V. (1948), *Tribes in India – The Struggle for Survival*; O.U.P.; New Delhi.

Hitt, W.D. *et. al.* (9165), The relation between Psychological characteristics and Creative behaviour; *Psychological Research*; Vol.-25. No. 2 pp. 233-40.

Hutton, J.H. (1986), *Census of India (1931), with Complete Survey of Tribal Life and System*; Vol. 1-3, Gain Publishing House, New Delhi.

Hymes, Dell (1964), *Language in Culture and Society*; Harper & Raw; New York.

ICSSR (1975), *Educational Problems of the SC and ST School and College Students in India*; ICSSR, New Delhi.

India, Govt. of (1961), *Ethnographic Study: Dimasa Kachari of Assam.*; Vol. I, Part V-B (4), Manager of Publications, New Delhi.

—— (1961), West Bengal and Sikkim: Special Tables, Scheduled Tribes' Vol. 16, Part 5(*a*), No. 2; Manager of Publications; New Delhi.

—— (1966), *Report of the Education Commission*, 1964-66. Ministry of Education and Culture, New Delhi.

—— (1971), '*Scheduled Tribes*' in Census of India; Series 20, Part 2 c (1) and 5 A, Controller of publications; New Delhi.

—— (1971), Education and National Development: Report of the Education Commission (*D.S. Kothari Commission Report*), 1964-'66, NCERT, New Delhi.

—— (1973), Service Rules for Govt. Servants; Gauhati.

—— (1975), 'Schedules Castes and Schedules Tribes; Series 1. Paper 1 of 1975; Manager of Publications; New Delhi.

—— (1980-85), *Report of the Working Group on Tribal Development during sixth plan*, Ministry of Home Affairs; New Delhi.

—— (1981), *Catalogue of Tribal Specimens*; in Census of India; Series 1, Occasional Paper No. 1 g 1981; Controller of publications, New Delhi.

—— (1981), *Primary Census Abstract of Scheduled Casts and Scheduled Tribes*', in Census of India, Series IV, paper 2 of 1982, Controller of publications; New Delhi.

—— (1981), *Primary Census Abstract*; Scheduled Tribes; Series 1, Part 2 B (3), Controller of publications; New Delhi.

—— (1982), Citations-National Awards for Teachers, Ministry of Human Resource Development. New Delhi.

—— (1982), *West Bengal: Final population Table*; Total Population, Scheduled Casts and Scheduled Tribe Population', in Census of India; 1981, Series 23, paper 1 of 1982; Director of Census operations; Calcutta.

—— (1983), *A Handbook of Educational and Allied Statistics*, Ministry of Education and Culture, New Delhi.

—— (1983), *Scale of Pay for School Teachers in India*; Ministry of Human Resource Development. 1982-83, New Delhi.

—— (1984), *Analysis of Budgeted Expenditure on Education*, 1981-'82 to 1983-'84; Ministry of Education and Culture New Delhi.

—— (1984), *Citations-National Awards for Teachers*, Ministry of Education and Culture New Delhi.

—— (1984), Selected Educational Statistics, 1982-'83; Ministry of Education and Culture, New Delhi.

—— (1985), *Challenge of Education—A Policy Perspective*; Ministry of Human Resource Development, New Delhi.

—— (1985), *Report of the National Commission on Teachers*; Ministry of Human Resource Development. New Delhi.

—— (1985-90), Report of the Working Group on Tribal Development During Seventh Plan, CSCST, New Delhi.

—— (1986), *National Policy on Education*, Ministry of Human Resource Development, New Delhi.

—— (1986), *Programme of Action*, Ministry of Human Resource Development. New Delhi.

—— (1987), Constitution of Indian Republic; Govt. of India Press, New Delhi (Rev. Ed.).

—— (1989), *Report of the Working Group on Development and Welfare of the Scheduled Tribes during Eight Five Year Plan*, Ministry of Welfare, New Delhi.

—— (1991), Catalogue of Tribal Specimens 'in Census of India, Series 1, Occasional paper No. 1 of 1991; Controller of Publications, New Delhi.

—— (1991), *Primary Census Abstract*; Scheduled Tribes, in Census of India, 1991, Series-1, Part 2B(3), Controller of Publications, 1993, New Delhi.

—— (1993), Education for All: The Indian Scene; MHRD, Department of Education, New Delhi.

—— (1993), Selected Educational Statistics, MHRD, Department of Planning, Monitoring and Statistics Division.

—— (1994), *Report of the Working Group on Development and Welfare of the Scheduled Tribes during Ninth Five Year Plan*, Ministry of Welfare, New Delhi.

—— (1997), *Selected Educational Statistics* (1995-1996), Ministry of Human Resource Development, Department of Education, Planning, Monitoring and Statistical Division, New Delhi.

—— (2002) Census Report, 2001, Manager of Publications, New Delhi.

—— (2002), *Selected Educational Statistics–2001*, MHRD, New Delhi.

——, *Report of the Planning Commission on the Development of Scheduled Tribes during Tenth Five Year Plan*, Ministry of Human Resource Development, New Delhi.

Irrine, J. (1988), An analysis of the Problem of the disappearing Black Educator; *Elementary School Journal*; Vol. 88; No. 5; pp. 503-13.

Jain, S.P. & Shah, J.M. (1974), Socio-Cultural Background and Educational Aspirations National Institute of Rural Development; Hyderabad.

Jaiswal, H.K. (1979), *Demographic Structure of Tribal Society*; Meenakshi Prakashan; Meerut.

Jarial, G.S. *et. al.* (1980), Creativity and it's Components as effected by intelligence, personality and their interaction; *Asian Journal of Psychology and Education*, Vol.-6, No. 21; pp. 26-32.

Jay, Edward, J. (1970), *A Tribal Village of Middle India*; Anthropological Survey of India; Calcutta.

Jha, S.K. (1975), An analysis of Certain dimensions of Creativity; Ph.D. Thesis in Education. M.S. University, Baroda.

Job, A.M. (1976), A Study of the Relationship Between Socio-Economic Status and Role–Perception of Secondary School Teachers in Poona District; Ph.D. Thesis Education, Poona University.

Jopling, Carol. F. (1971), *Art and Aesthetics in Primitive Societies: A Critical Anthropology*; Dutton, New York.

Joshi, N.D. (1981), Problems Faced by Some Certain Tribal Groups in Trivandrum District In Relation to Provision and Use of School Facilities; Deptt. of Education; Kerala University (U.G.C. sponsored).

—— (1985); Socio-Cultural and Educational Conditions of Adivasis in Kerala; Doctoral Thesis in Education; Kerala University.

Joshi, R.J. (1974), A study of Creativity and some personality traits of the intellectually gifted high school students; Ph.D. Thesis in Education; M.S. University Baroda.

Joshi, R.R. (1984), *Tribals: Islands of Deprivation*; National Book Trust; New Delhi.

Joshi, S.D. (1979), Educational Problems of the Scheduled Castes and Scheduled Tribes of Baroda District; Unpublished Ph.D. Thesis in Education; M.S. University; Baroda.

Kailash (1993), *Tribal Education and Occupation*; Nanak Publication, New Delhi; 1993.

Kalanek.C.B. (1996), Self esteem in relation to gender, SES, Ethnic cultural origin, family characteristics and academic achievement in Middle School Students; *Dissertation Abstracts International*, Vol. 57, No. 8, pp. 33-91.

Kamilla, B.B. (1985), An Evaluative Study of Harijan and Tribal High Schools in Orissa in Respect of Student-achievement; Unpublished Ph.D. Thesis in Education, Visva Bharati.

Kar, B.C. (1975), Pattern of Tribal Education: A Psychological Approach; *Journal of the University of Guwahati*, Vol. VIII; pp. 55-72; Guwahati.

Karlinger, F.N. (1978), *Foundations of Behavioural Research*; Holt, Rinehart and Winston, Inc.; New York.

Khathuria, P.R. (1982), Scholastic Achievement and Vocational Interests as related to prolonged Deprivation, Ph.D. Thesis in Psychology; M.S. University, Baroda.

King, J. (1991), *Black Student Alienation and Black teacher's emancipator Pedagogy*; A.M.S. Press, New York.

Kothari, Prof. D.S. (1971), *Education and National Development*, Report of the Education Commission—1964-'66, NCERT, New Delhi.

Kulashrestha, S.P. (1979), *Educational Psychology*; International Publishing House, Meerut, U.P.

Kulkarni, P.M. (1992), and Krishnamurthy, S.: Gender Inequality in Literature : Measurement and Pattern; *Social Change*; Vol. 22; No. 4; pp. 21-26.

Kumari, Kanta (1995), Political orientation of women students, *Bharatiya Siksha Sodh Patrika*, 14(1), pp. 11-23.

Kundu, C.L. (1966), Differential Personality Traits in Juvenile Offenders Belonging to Scheduled Tribe and Other Communities: Doctoral Thesis Department of Education; Rajasthan University.

—— (1976), *Educational Psychology*; Sterling Publishers Pvt. Ltd. New Delhi.

Kundu, M. (1990), *Cultural Anthropology and Tribal Education*; Amar Prakashan; New Delhi.

Ladson-Billings, G. (1991), Returning to the source: Implication for educating teachers of black students; *Equal Education*, Vol. II, pp. 227-44; AMS Press, New York.

Lakra, S. (1976), Impact of Education on the Tribals of Ranchi District; Unpublished Doctoral Thesis; Department of Education, Patna University.

Lal S.K. & U.R.Nahar (1978), *Higher Education: Scheduled Castes and Scheduled Tribes*; Jainsons, Jodhpur.

Lal, P. & B.K. Dasgupta (1979), *Lower Siang People: A study in Ecology and Society*: Anthropological Survey of India, Calcutta.

Latham, H.G. (1983), *Tribes and Races: A descriptive Ethnology of Asia, Africa and Europe*; Cultural Publishing House, New Delhi.

Law, Bimala, C. (1926), *Ancient Indian Tribes*; Sanskrit Book Depot, Lahore.

Lieton, G.K. *et. al.* (ed) (1989), *Women, Migrants and Tribals: Survival Strategies in Asia*; Monohar Publications, New Delhi.

Likart, R. (9132), A Technique for the Measurement of Attitudes, *Arch. Psychological*; No. 140.

Linton, Ralph (1936), *The Study of Man; Appleton-Century-Crofts*, Inc; pp. 113-19.

Mackenzie, A. (1884), *History of the Relations of the Government with the Hill Tribes of the North-East Frontier of Bengal*; Home Department Press; Calcutta.

Mackenzie, A. (1884; rpt 1979), *The North-East Frontier of India*; Mittal Publications, New Delhi.

Mackinnon. D.W. (1962), What makes a Person Creative; *Sturday Review*; Vol. 45, No. 6, pp. 15-17.

Madan, T.N. (1952), Education of Tribal India; *Eastern Anthropologist*; Vol. 5, No. 4; pp. 179-82.

Mahapatra, A.K. (1987), *Tribal Politics in West Bengal*; Suhrid Publications; Calcutta.

Mahapatra, P.C. (1987), *Economic Development of Tribal India*; Ashish Publications New Delhi.

Mair, L.P. (1961), *Studies in Applied Anthropology: University of London*, London.

Malinowski, B. (1954), *Magic, Science and Religion*, Anchor Books, Garden City, New York.

Mani, K.C. (1977), Education, Mobility and Social Origin of Teachers: A Sociological Study of Teacher's Community of Ballia and Rasra (U.P.); Unpublished Doctoral Dissertation in Sociology; Gorakhpur University.

Manu, R.S. (1984), Culture and Population: A Theoretical Perspective; *Man in India* Vol. 63, No. 4; pp. 370-538.

Markar, N.S. (1975), Survey of Teacher Education in the State of Maharastra; Ph.D. Thesis in Education; Bombay University.

Masavi, M. (1970), Wastage and Stagnation in Primary Education Amongst the Tribals of Gujarat; Tribal Research and Training Institute; Gujarat Vidyapeeth; Ahmedabad. (1971), SERD; Baroda.

—— (1976), Wastage and Stagnation in Primary Education in Tribal Areas; Tribal Research and Training Institute; Gujarat Vidyapeeth; Ahemedabad.

Maslow, A.H. (1962), *Towards a Psychology of Being*; Princeton N.J.D. Van; Nostrand.

May, R., The nature of Creativity; in *Creativity and it's Cultivation*, H.H. Underson (ed).; Harper, New York.

Mazumder, D.N. (1957), The Functioning of the School System in a Polyandrous Society in Jaunsar Bawar; *The Eastern Anthropologist*, Vol. 10; Nos. 3 and 4.

Mc. Dermott, P.A. (1995), Sex, Race, class and other Demographics as Explantions for children's Ability and Adjustment: A National Appraisal; *Psychological Abstracts*, Vol. 82, No. 7, pp. 33-65.

Mc. Donald, F.J. (1965), *Educational Psychology*, Wadsworth Publishing Co.; Selmont; California

Mc. Kinnon. D.W. (1961), *The Study of Creativity and Creativity in architects*; University of California.

Mishra, A. (1977), *Role of Education in Tribal Development*, Ministry of Home Affairs, New Delhi.

Mishra, G.: (1977), The Concept of Prolonged Deprivation and its Measurement; *Indian Journal of Behaviour*; Vol. I, No. 48.

Mishra, G. and Tripathi, L.B. (1977), The Concept of Prolonged Deprivation and its Measurement; *Indian Journal of Behaviour*, No. 1, Vol. N.A. pp. 48-60.

Mishra, S.N. (1987), *Dynamics of Tribal Politics in Orissa*; S.S. Publications, Bhubaneswar.

Mishra, S.S. (1975), A Cross-Cultural Study of Status and Vocational Aspiration Among Aborginal Tribes of Bastar; Concept Publications; New Delhi.

Modi, B.M. (1981), Influence of Education on Socio-Economic Status; Unpublished Ph.D. Thesis in Education; Gujarat University, cit. in Third Survey of Research in Education; Buch, M.B. (Ed.); NCERT; New Delhi.

Mohan, J. *et. al.* (1982), Socio-Economic Status, Personality, Academic Achievement and Personal Problems; *Indian Psychological Review*; Vol. 2; No. 2.

Mondal, P.K. (1977), Tradition and Modernity among the Santhals: A Micro Study; *Vanyajati*; Vol. 25, No. 4, pp. 25-26.

Monroe, S. (1988), *Goldman, P. Brothers: Black and Poor: A True Story of Courage and Survival*, Bullantine Books; New York.

Morgan, D.N. (1953), Creativity Today; *Journal of Aesthetic Art and Creation*, p. 12.

Mukherjee, C. (1962), *The Santhals*; (NA), Calcutta.

Murray, A. (1970), *Black experience And American Culture*, Vintage, New York.

Murrell, P. (1991), Cultural Politics in Teacher Education: What's Missing in the Preparation of Minority Teachers; in M. Foster (Ed.) *Readings in Equal Education*; Vol. II, pp. 205-25, AMS Press; New York.

—— (1991), *Cultural Polities in Teacher Education*; what's missing in the preparation of minority Teachers; investigations into schools and schooling; AMS Press; New York.

Mutatkar, R.K. (1973), *Education in Tribal Culture: A Caste Study*; Eastern Anthropologist, Vol. 26; No. 1

Muzumdar, D.N. (1944), *The Fortunes of Primitive Tribes*; Universal Publications; Lucknow.

N.C.E.R.T. (1967), *Tribal Education in India*; Report on the National Seminar on Tribal Education in India, New Delhi.

—— (1971), *Developmental Needs of the Tribal People*; NCERT; New Delhi.

—— (1981), *Adjustment Problems of Tribal Students in Residential Schools of Rajasthan Vidya Bhawan*, G.S. Teacher's College; Udaipur.

—— (1982), *Fourth All India Educational Survey*; N.C.E.R.T.; New Delhi.

Naidu, A.R. (1966), Informal Education among Tribals; *Vanyajati*, Vol. 14, No. 4, pp. 183-91.

—— (1966), Scholastic Backwardness in Tribal children; *Indian Education*, Vol. 5; No. 6, pp. 20-25.

—— (1967), Problems of migration of Some-educated tribal boys, *Indian Education*; Vol. 6. No. 3; pp. 28-36.

Naik, J.P. (1971), Education for Scheduled Tribes; *ICSSR Journal*, p. 40.

Naik, T.B. (1969), *Impact of Education on the Bible: Cultural Change in Tribal Life of M.P.*; Planning Commission; New Delhi.

—— (1975), *Scheduled Cast and Tribe High School and College Students in Madhya Pradesh*; ICSSR; New Delhi.

Nair, M.K. Sundaram,(1987), *Tribal Economy in Transition*; Inter-India Publications; New Delhi.

Nair, S.P. (1964), Tribal Education: The American Experience; Paper on 7th Conference of Tribes and Tribal (Scheduled) areas; *Journal of Bharatiya Adimjati Sevak Sangh*, New Delhi., pp. 70-73.

Nancy, Chodorow (1971), 'Being and Doing: A Cross-Cultural Examination of the socialization of Males and Females ", in *Woman in Sexist Society;* Vivian, G. & Barbara, K. Moran (Eds), Basic-Books, New York. p. 193.

Nandy. R. (1983), *North and North-Eastern Frontier Tribes of India*; Cultural Publishing House; New Delhi.

Narayan. S. (1988). *Movements, Development*, Police and Judiciary in Tribal World; Inter India Publications, New Delhi.

Narayan, S. (1988), *Tribe in Transition*; Inter India Publications; New Delhi.

Nash, G. (1988), Forging Freedom: The formation of Philadelphia's Black Community, Harvard University Press, Cambridge.

Nautiyal, K.C. & Sharma, Y.D., Equalization of Educational opportunities for Scheduled Castes and Scheduled Tribes; *National Council for Educational Research and Training*; New Delhi.

NASSDOC (1987), Scheduled Casts and Scheduled Tribes (bibliography), *ICSSR*, New Delhi.

Nayar, D.P. (1974), Education For Tribals; *Kurukshetra*; oct. 10th, pp. 38-40.

Negi, S.S. (1984), *North and North-Eastern Frontier Tribe in India*; Manash Publication, New Delhi.

—— (1988), *Tribal Welfare development and Administration*; D.K.; New Delhi.

Nehru, J. (1948), *The Tribal World* (Ref. N.A.).

NIEPA (1980), *Post Matric Scholarship Scheme for Scheduled Tribes: A Pilot Study*; New Delhi.

—— (1986), *An In-depth Analysis of Ashram School*; New Delhi.

—— (1990), *Education in Ashram Schools*, NIEPA–Occasional Papers; New Delhi.

Nuna, S.C. (Ed.) (1993), *Regional Disparities in Educational Development Among the Tribals*; South Asian Publication; New Delhi.

Oad, L.K. (1968), *Research Needs in Comparative Education*; (Eds). Shankar, U & Ahluwalia, S.P.; Kurukshetra University Books & Stationary; Kurukshetra.

Oliver, Douglas, Z. (1964), *Invitation to Anthropology*; Natural History Press; Garden City; New York.

Om Prakash, S. (1986), Cast and Politics in Indian Education; Unpublished Research Report; Department of Humanities and Social Sciences, IIT, Kanpur.

Oswalt, W.H. (1972), *Other Peoples, Other Customs: World Ethnography and it's History*; Holt, Rinehart and Winston, New York.

Padhy, K.S. & P.C. Satapathy (1989), *Tribal India*; Ashish Publishing House; New Delhi.

Pakrasi, K.B. (1956), Some Aspects of Tribal Education, *Vanyajati*, Vol. 4; No. 4; pp. 11127-133.

Pamecha, R. (1985), *Elit in Tribal Society*; Printwell Publication, Jaipur.

Panda, B. (1995), *Functions and Organization of Tribal Schools*; Anamika Publishers, New Delhi.

Panda, B.N. (1987), Personality, Adjustment, Mental Health and Acculturation Among Saora Tribe; Ph.D. Thesis in Education; Kurukshetra University, cit in Buch, M.B. (Ed.); *Fourth Survey of Research in Education*, SERD, Baroda.

Panda, S.C. (1983), An Empirical Study of Education of Tribals in Orissa; Unpublished Ph.D. Thesis on Education; Utkal University.

Pande, R. (Ed.) (1984), *Tribal Movements*; Shedhak; Jaipur.

Pandey, N.R.: Social Aspects of Academic Achievement and Aspiration of Scheduled Tribe Students; Ph.D. in Sociology; cit. in Buch, M.B. (Ed.) *Fourth Survey of Research in Education*, SERD, Baroda 1981.

Pandey, S. (1993), Education of SC and ST Girls in Orissa; *Social Change*; Vol. 23, No. 4; pp. 71-77.

Pareek, Udai, (1967), *Directory of Behavioural Science Research*; Macmillan & Co., New Delhi.

Park, R.E. & Burgess, E.V. (1921), *Introduction to the Science of Sociology*; University, Chicago Press, Chicago, pp. 708-14.

Park, R.E., 'The City', in the *American Journal of Sociology* Vol. XX.

Patel, M.L. (1972), *Agro-Economic Problems of Tribal India*; Progress Publications, Bhopal.

—— (1984), *Planning Strategy for Tribal Development*; Inter India Publications; New Delhi.

Patel, S. (1991), *Tribal Education in India: A Case Study*; Mittal Publications; New Delhi.

Patel, T. (1983), *Education Among Tribal Women*; Mittal Publication; New Delhi.

—— (1984), *Development of Education Among Tribal Women*; Mittal Publications; New Delhi.

Pati, R.N. & Jena B. (Eds.) (1989), *Tribal Development In India*, Ashish Publishing House. New Delhi.

Penniman, T.K. (1965), *A Hundred Years of Anthropology*, Duck worth, London.

Prashad, R. (1988), *A Study in Cultural Ecology and Tribal Dynamics*, D.K. Publication, New Delhi.

Prashad, S. (1971), Modern Education among the Tribals; *Man In India*, Vol. 57, No. 4; pp. 364-93.

Pratap, D.R. *et. al.* (1971), Study of Ashram Schools in Tribal Areas of Andhra Pradesh, Tribal Cultural Research and Training Institute; Hyderabad, cit. in Buch, M.B. (Ed.); *Third Survey of Research in Education*; SERD; Baroda.

—— *et. al.* (1973), Study of Aided Elementary Schools of Srikulam, Visakhapatnam, East Godavari and West Godavari District of Andhra Pradesh; Tribal Cultural Research and Training Institute; Hyderabad; cit. in Buch, M.B. (Ed.); *Third Survey of Research in Education*; SERD, Baroda.

Primary Census Abstracts for general population, Scheduled Casts and Scheduled Tribes, published by the Registrar General and Census Commissioner, Govt. of India 1991 and 1981.

Provenzo, E. (1988), Black and White Teachers: Patterns of Similarity and Difference Over Twenty Years; *Proceedings of the Meeting of the American Educational Research Association*; New Orleans.

Punalekar, S.P. & Ranadive, J. (1984), Tribal Education: An Inter State Study; *Journal of Center for Social Studies*, Surat.

Purna, S., Balda S. & Sangawan, S. (1993), Mutal Perception of Girls Status. *Prachi Journal of Psychocultural Dimensions*, 9(1), pp. 33-38.

Raghava Kumari, A.S. (1986), Social Attitude and Problems of SC and ST Girls in Secondary Schools; Deptt. of Education; Mysore University; Sponsored by NCERT; New Delhi.

Raghaviah, V. (1971), *Tribal Revolts Audhra Rashtra Adimjati Sevak Sangh*; Nellore.

Raina, M.K. (1968), A study of some Correlates of Creativity in Indian Students; Doctoral Dissertation in Psychology, University of Rajasthan; Jaipur.

—— (1969), *A Study of Sex difference in in Creativity in India; Journal of Creative Behaviour*; Vol. 3, No. 2; pp. 111-14.

Raina, V.K. (1981), A Factional Study of the Personalities, Attitudes to Teaching and Creativity of In-service and Student Teachers Belonging to Three Subject Areas; Ph.D. Thesis; Deptt. of Education and Psychology, M.S.U.; Baroda.

Rajora, S.C. (1987), *Social Structure and Tribal Elites*; Himanshu Publications; Udaipur.

Rana, B.S. (1989), *The People of Meghalaya*, Punthi Pustak; Calcutta.

Ranjana, K. & Radhakrishnan S. (1989), *Higher Education and Scheduled Tribe Youth: A Case Study of Chattishgarh*; Radiant Publications; New Delhi.

Rao, D.B. (Ed.) (1996), *Encyclopedia of Education for All: The World Conference*, Vol. 1, ABH Publishing Corporation, New Delhi.

Rath, R. (1972), Cognitive Growth and Classroom Learning of Deprived Children in the Primary Schools; Proceeding of the East-West Centre for Cross-Cultural Studies; Honolulu.

—— (1974), Teaching and Learning Problems of Disadvantaged Children; Presidential Address; Proceedings on *12th Annual Conference of the Indian Academy of Applied Psychology*; Utkal University; Bhubaneswar.

Rathnaiah, E.V. (1974), *Structural Constraints in Tribal Education: A Regional Study*; Ph.D. Soc; Andhra University; Cit. In Buch, M.B. (Ed.); Second Survey of Research in Education, SERD; Baroda.

—— (1977), *Structural Constraints in Tribal Education: A Regional Study*; Sterling Publishers; New Delhi.

Ravindranathan, M.N. (1983), *The Problem of Cultural Integration of the Tribals: Education as a chief instrument of change*; Education Quarterly, Vol. 35, No.4; pp. 20-24.

Ray, B.C. (Ed), (1989), *Tribals of Orissa: The Changing Socio-Economic Profile*; Gain Publishing House; New Delhi.

Raza, Moonis, *et. al.* (1985), *Tribal Literacy in India: The Regional Dimension*; NIEPA; New Delhi.

Report of the *Committee* on Special Multipurpose Tribal Blocks (*Elwin Committee*), Ministry of Home Affairs, New Delhi, 1960.

Report of the Education Commission (Teacher's Status, Part I, chapter I, III, IV and VI), 1964-65, published by the National Council for Educational Research and Training, 1966.

Report of the Scheduled Areas and Scheduled Tribes Commission (*Dhebar Commission*), Vol. I, 1960-'61.

Report of the Study Team on Social Welfare and Welfare of the Backward classes, *Renuka Roy Committee Report*, 1959.

Report of the Working Group on Tribal Development during Sixth Plan (1980-85), published by the Ministry of Home Affairs, Govt. of India.

Report of the Working Group on Tribal Development during Seventh Plan (1985-90), published by the Ministry of Home Affairs, Govt. of India.

Report of the Working Group on Development and Welfare of Scheduled Tribes during Eighth Five Year Plan; published by the Ministry of Welfare, Govt. of India, November 1989.

Report of the Working Group on Development and Welfare of the Scheduled Tribes, during Ninth Five Year Plan; published by the Ministry of Welfare, Government of India, 1995.

Report on the Status of Teachers in India, R.C. Chopra, Ed. published by NCERT, 1993.

Risley, H.H. (rpt, 1981), *The Tribes and Castes of Bengal*; Vol. I & II; Bengal Secretarial Press; Firma KLM.; Calcutta.

Rout, P.C. (1985), A Multidimensional Approach for Analysis of Trends, Perspectives and Educational Programmes in Tribal Education and Formulation of Action Strategies; Ph.D. Edu; Utkal University; Cit. in Buch, M.B. (Ed.); *Fourth Survey of Research in Education Baroda*, SERD.

Roy Burman, B.K. (1970), '*Demographic & Socio-Economic Profiles of the Hill Areas of NE India*', cit. in Census of India; 1961; Vol. I & II; Manager of Publications; New Delhi.

Roy Chowdaury, B.K. (1963), Comparative Study of the progress of Secondary Education among the Scheduled Castes and Scheduled Tribes of West Bengal; *Bulletin of the Cultural Research Institute*, Vol. 2, No.1; pp. 40-52.

—— (1964), *Factors regarding tribal Education in West Bengal*, *Bulletin of the Cultural Research Institute*, Vol. 3, No. 2, pp. 25-40.

—— (1972), Tribes of India, *Journal of Bharatiya Adimjati Sevak Sangh*; Vol. I & II; New Delhi.

Roy, Kanchan (Ed.) (1989), *Education and Health Problems in Tribal Development: A Study in National Integration*; Concept Publishing; New Delhi.

Roy, R. (1996), *Creativity in Relation to Tribal Teachers Towards Their Teaching Interest*, unpublished Master's Dissertation, Visva-Bharati.

—— (2005), A Study on Religious Status of Ethnic Teachers in East and North East India, *Journal of North East India Education Society,* X(1), pp. 1-15.

—— (2005), Society, Culture and Education, *Indian Science Cruiser*, 19(2), pp. 29-36.

—— *et. al.* (2004), Technology and Education for Human Resource Development in Asia and Pacific, Cit. in the *Post-conference Proceedings of International Conference on New Challenges in Technology Education for HRD in Asia and Pacific Region,* pp. 114-25.

—— *et. al.* (2004), Interface between Creativity and Education, Cit. in the *Proceedings of All India Seminar on Applying Creativity and Systems Thinking for Business Innovation*, pp. 67-72.

Roy, R., Paira, A. & Das, N. (2006), Participation of Tribes in Higher Education: The Gender Issue, *Perspectives in Education*, 22(3), pp. 147-54.

Roy, Renuka (1959), *Report of the Study Team on Social Welfare and Welfare of the Backward Classes*, Ministry of Home Affairs.

Roychowdhury, S.K.(1977), *Ethnographic Museum: A Tribal Profile; Scheduled Caset & Tribal Welfare Department*; Calcutta.

Sachchidananda (1957), Anthropology and Education; *Jagriti* Rachi.

—— (1967), Socio-Economic Aspects of Tribal Education, in Report of the National Seminar on Tribal Education in India, NCERT, New Delhi, pp. 99-105.

—— (1967), The Special Problems of Education of the Scheduled Tribes, *Vanjati.*

—— (1968), *The Tribal Village in Bihar: A Study in Unity and Extension*; Munshiram Monoharlal; New Delhi.

—— (1971), Socio-Economic Aspects of Tribal Education; In the Proceedings of the National Seminar on Tribal Education in India; NCERT; New Delhi; pp. 99-105.

—— (1974), Education among the Scheduled Caste and Scheduled Tribes in Bihar; ANS Institute of Social Studies; Patna (ICSSR Sponsored Project).

—— (1989), *Education and the Disadvantaged: A Study of Scheduled Castes & Scheduled Tribe;* Uppal Publications; New Delhi.

Sansanwal, D.N. (1979), Personality Difference Among High and Low-Creative & Jarial, G.S.: Teacher Trainees; Ph.D. Thesis in Education; Indore University.

Santra, B. (1985), Education of the Santhals: Identification of Educational Needs, Probabilities and Problems; Unpublished Ph.D. Thesis on Education, Visva-Bharati, Santiniketan.

Sarkar, R.M. (1986), *Adivasi Nritattya*, Modern Book Agency, Calcutta.

Shah, B. (1992), *Tribal Education Perspective and Prospects*, Nyaya Prakashan; Calcutta.

Shah, G.S. (1986), *Tribal Education in Gujarat*; Ajanta Publication; New Delhi.

Shah, K. (1982), Socio-Economic Background of Primary School Teachers and Job Satisfaction: A Sociological Study; Unpublished Doctoral Thesis in Sociology; Kashi Vidyapeeth.

Shah, V. and Patel, T. (1997), Who Goes To College? – A Study of Scheduled Caste and Tribe Post-matric Scholars in Gujarat; Department of Sociology, Gujarat University.

Shah, V.P. & Tara Pael (1985), *Social Contexts of Tribal Education*; Concept Publication, New Delhi.

Sharma, B.D. (1976), *Planning for Educational Development in Tribal Areas*; Ministry of Home Affairs; Govt. of India Press; New Delhi.

—— (1978), *Tribal Development*; Prachi Prakashan; New Delhi.

Sharma, G.D. (1983), A Study of Relationship Between Educational Level, Social Status, Attitude and Family Size of Middle-Aged Parents; Unpublished Ph.D. Thesis in Education, Himachal Pradesh University.

Sharma, K.R. (1991), *Education and Lifestyle of Tribal Students*; Concept Publication, New Delhi.

Sharma, R.N. & Bakshi, S. (1984), *Tribes and Tribal Development*; Uppal Publications; New Delhi.

Sharma, Thakur, G.C. (1997), Tribal Development and Anthropology: An Interface; cit. in *Communities in North East India*, (Ed.) Vikas Pub. New Delhi; A brief perusal over the available surveys of research also establish the fact.

Shyamlal (1987), *Education among Tribals*; Printwell Publication; New Delhi.

Siddler–Walker, E.V. (1993), Relationships between community and school; *Harvard Educational Review*; Vol. 63, No. 2; pp. 161-82.

Singh, A.K. (1980), Parental Support and Scholastic Achievement; *Social Change*, Vol. 13, No. 12, pp. 9-14.

—— (1980), Social Disadvantage and Academic Achievement, *Social Change*, Vol. 10, No. 12, pp. 15-18.

—— (1984), *Tribal Development in India*; Classical Publishing; New Delhi.

—— (1985), Education and Development in India: The God That Failed; *Social Change*; Vol. 15, No. 9; pp. 3-16.

—— (1988), Attitudes of Tribals and Non-tribals in South Bihar; *Social Change*, Vol. 18, No. 2, pp. 3-27.

Singh, A.K. & Jabbi, M.K. (Eds.) (1995), *Tribals in India: Development, Deprivation and Discontent*; Har Anand, New Delhi.

—— (Ed.) (1996), *Status of Tribals in India: Health, Education and Employment*; Har Anand Publications; New Delhi.

Singh, A.K. & Jayaswal, M. (1981), Correlates of Academic Achievement of Socially Disadvantaged Students; *Social Change*; Vol. II, No. 1, pp. 23-28.

Singh, A.K. & Ohri, R. (1983), Educational Status of Tribal Women in India; *Social Change*; Vol. 23; No. 4; pp. 66-70.

Singh, A.K. & Rajyalakshmi, C. (1993), Status of Tribal Women in India, *Social Change*, Vol. 23, No. 4, p. 4.

Singh, K. (1982), Problems in Measurement of Creative Thinking; *ISPT Journal of Education and Psychology*, Vol. VI, No. 2; pp. 22-25.

Singh, K.S. (1989), *Jawaharlal Nehru: Tribes and Tribal Policy: A Centennial Tribute*; Seagull Books on behalf of Anthropological Survey of India, Calcutta.

Singh, N.K. (1975), Educational Problems of the Scheduled Caste and Scheduled Tribe Students in Rajasthan; Department of Sociology; Rajasthan University.

Sinha, D. (1980), Some Cognitive and Motivational Concomitants of Poverty; *Social Change*; Vol. 10; pp. 3-8.

Srikant, L.M. (1953), *Report of the Commissioner for Scheduled Castes and Scheduled Tribes for the Year 1952*; Manager of Publication, GOI; New Delhi.

Srivastava, L.R.N. (1968), Plans and Programmes for Social Education for the Tribal People; *Bulletin of Cultural Research Institute*; Vol. 7; Nos. 1 and 2; pp. 39-50.

—— (1969), *Annotated bibliography on tribal Education in India*; New Delhi.

—— (1971), *Developmental Needs of Tribal People*; NCERT; New Delhi.

—— *et. al.* (1971), *An Integrated and Comparative Study of a Selected Tribal Community Living in Chotanagpur Areas*; NCERT; New Delhi.

Srivastava, P. (1986), A Socio-Psychological Study of Stagnation Among Tribal and Non-tribal Students of Class VIII; Unpublished Ph.D. Thesis on Education; Lucknow University; Lucknow.

Sterling, P. (1972), *The Real Teachers: 30 Inner-city School Teachers Talk honestly about who they are, how teach and why*; Random House Press, New York.

Strong, E.K., *Vocational Interests of man and woman*, p. 8.

Stubbings, J. Robert (1968), *A Comparison of the TTCT and Guilford's measures of Creative ability on Sex, Cognitive and Personality variables*; Ed.D. Thesis in Education; University of Virginia, U.S.A.: Dissertation Abstracts, Vol. 28, pt. 4, 1967-68; 28 (4)-4497A.

Sujatha, K. (1980), An Investigation into the Constraints on Education of the Nellor District Yanadis with a View to Suggest Some Strategies of NFE; Unpublished Doctoral Thesis in Education, Andhra University, A.P..

—— (1983), *An In-depth Study of Ashram Schools in Andhra Pradesh*; NIEPA; New Delhi.

—— (1987), *Education of the forgotten children of the Forests: A Case Study of Yenadi Tribal*; Konarak Publications; New Delhi.

—— (1987), Inequalities in Educational Development of Tribes: A Case Study of Andhra Pradesh; *Journal of Educational Planning and Administration*; Vol. I, No. 2; NIEPA; New Delhi.

—— (1993), *Evaluation of Single Teacher Schools in Tribal Areas in Andhra Pradesh*, NIEPA; New Delhi.

—— (1993), *Inter and Intra Tribal Disparities in Education*; South Asian Publishers; New Delhi.

—— (1993), Tribal Perception of Education; *Indian Journal of Adult Education*; Vol. 54; No. 1.

—— (1994), *Educational Development Among Tribes*; South Asian Publishers; New Delhi.

Talesra, Hemlata (1989), *Tribal Education: A Quest for Integration in the Regional Mainstream*; Himangshu Publications, Udaipur.

Taylor, C.W. (1959), *A Tentative Description of the Creative Individual*; University Press of Utah.

—— (1964), *Creativity Progress and Potential*; Mc Graw Hill; New York.

Taylor, C.W. & Baron John F. (1968), *Scientific Creativity: It's recognition and Development*; Wiley & Sons, New York.

Thakkar, A.V. (1941), *The Problems of the Aborigines in India*; Gokhale Institute; Poona.

Toppo, Sita (1979, 1983), *Dynamics of Educational Development in Tribal India*; Classical Publications; New Delhi.

Torrance, E.P. (1959), *Education and Creative Potential*; University of Minnesota Press; Minneapolis.

—— (1962), *Guiding Creative Talent*; Prentice-Hall, Inc.; New Jersey.

—— (1963), The question asking behaviour of highly creative basic business teachers identified by a paper and Pancil test; *Psychological Reports*; Vol. 17, pp. 81518.

—— (1969), Prediction of Adult Creative Achievement Among High School Seniors; *Gifted Child Quarterly*; Vol. 1113, pp. 71-81.

—— *et. al.* (1965), The question-asking behaviour of highly creative basic, business teachers identified by a paper and pencil test; *Psychological Report.* Vol. 17.

—— *et. al.* (1970), Verbal Originality and Teacher Behaviour: A predictive Validity Study; *Journal of Teacher Education*; Vol. 21; pp. 335-41.

Tripathi, L.B. (1975), Cognitive Activities as a Function of Prolonged Deprivation; *Psychological Studies*; Vol. 21; pp. 54-61.

UNESCO (1951), *Learning To be: The World of Education: Today and Tomorrow*; Sterling Publishers; New Delhi.

—— (1996), Report to UNESCO of the International Commission on Education for the twenty first century, UNESCO Publishing, France.

Vaikunthan, Y. (1980), Spread of Education and Social Change in Andhra (1880-1920); Unpublished Ph.D. Thesis in History; Osmania University.

Van Dalen, D.B. & Meyer, M.J. (1980), *Understanding Educational Research*; Mc Graw Hill Book Co.; Torento.

Varghese, N.V. (1994), *School Quality and Student Learning: A Study of Primary Schooling in Kerala*; p. 301 in DPEP: Base Line Assessment Study of Kerala; NIEPA; New Delhi.

Varma, M. (1965), *An Introduction to Educational and Psychological Research*, Asia Publishing House; New Delhi.

Vernon, P.E. (1967), *Personality test and Assessment*, Mc. Graw Hill, New York.

Vidyarthi, L.P. (Ed.) (1986), *Tribal Development and its Administration*; Concept Publication, New Delhi.

Vijaya Lakshmi, J. (1975), Academic Achievement in the State of Maharastra; Unpublished Ph.D. Thesis in Education; Bombay University.

Vyas, N.N. (1969), *The Backward Classes Hostels in Rajasthan: A Study in Socio-Cultural Aspects*; Tribal Research Institute and Training Center; Udaipur.

—— (1970), *The Dropouts in a Tribal Situation*; Tribal Research Institute and Training Center, Udaipur.

Vyas, N.N. & Chaudhury, N.D. (1976), The Dropouts in a Tribal Situation; Project Report Published by Tribal Research Institute and Training Center, Udaipur.

Vyas, N.N. & Mann, R.S. (eds.) (1980), *Indian Tribes in Transition*; Rawat Publishers; Jaipur.

Waghmare, B.K. *et. al.* (1988), *Teaching Tribals Through Gramsevak and Voluntary Agency*; Metropolitan Pub.; New Delhi.

Waghmare, S.K. *et. al.* (1988), Bridges of Tribal Upliftment; Metropolitan Pub., New Delhi.

Wallace, A.F.C. (1966), *Religion: An Anthropological View*; Random House; New York.

Wallas, G. (1926), *The Art of Thought*; Harcourt Brace, New York.

Werthimar, M. (1945), *Productive Thinking*, Harper & Co, New York.

Whitehead, A.N. (1962), *The Aims of Education and other Esseys*, Ger nest Benn Ltd. Great Britain, Mentor Book.

William Benton (Ed.) (1965), *Encyclopedia Britanica*, Vol. 10, University of Chicago Press, Chicago, p. 924.

Woods, P. (1977), *The Ethnography of the School;* Milton Keynes: Bucks Open University.

Woolfson, P. (1972), "Language, Thought and Culture", in *Language;* Clark, P.V. *et. al.* (Eds), St. Martin's, New York, p. 4.

Yadav, B. & Singh, W.G. (1985), Tribals: Myths and Reality; *Link (Suppl)*. Vol. 27; No. 26; pp. 29-33.

Yamamoto. K. (1963), Creative Writing and School Environment; *School and Society*; Vol. 91; pp. 307-08.

Zigrami, D. and Zigrami, P. (1980), A Personal view of the Stresses of being an Ethnographer, *Journal of Class Room Intervention*. Vol. 16, No. 1, pp. 19-24.

Znaniecki, Florian (1940), *The Social Role of the Man of Knowledge*; Columbia University Press, Columbia, pp. 13-19.

Index